LIKE A LOADED WEAPON

LIKE A LOADED WEAPON

The Rehnquist Court, Indian Rights,
and the Legal History of Racism in America

Robert A. Williams, Jr.

Indigenous Americas

University of Minnesota Press ▪ Minneapolis ▪ London

Published by the University of Minnesota Press
111 Third Avenue South, Suite 290
Minneapolis, MN 55401-2520
http://www.upress.umn.edu

Library of Congress Cataloging-in-Publication Data

Williams, Robert A., 1955–
    Like a loaded weapon : the Rehnquist court, Indian rights, and the
legal history of racism in America / Robert A. Williams, Jr.
        p.   cm. — (Indigenous Americas)
    Includes bibliographical references and index.
    ISBN 0-8166-4709-7 (hc : alk. paper) — ISBN 0-8166-4710-0 (pb :
alk. paper)
        1. Indians of North America—Civil rights—History.   2. Race
discrimination—Law and legislation—United States—History.
3. Racism—United States—History.   4. United States—Supreme
Court.   5. Rehnquist, William H., 1924–   I. Title.   II. Series.
    KF8210.C5W55 2005
    342.7308'72—dc22

                                                                    2005018328

Printed in the United States of America on acid-free paper

The University of Minnesota is an equal-opportunity educator and
employer.

12 11 10 09 08 07 06 05   10 9 8 7 6 5 4 3 2 1

For Vine

A military order, however unconstitutional, is not apt to last longer than the military emergency. Even during that period a succeeding commander may revoke it all. But once a judicial opinion rationalizes such an order to show that it conforms to the Constitution, or rather rationalizes the Constitution to show that the Constitution sanctions such an order, the Court for all time has validated the principle of racial discrimination. . . . The principle then lies about like a loaded weapon ready for the hand of any authority that can bring forward a plausible claim of an urgent need. Every repetition imbeds that principle more deeply in our law and thinking and expands it to new purposes. All who observe the work of courts are familiar with what Judge Cardozo described as "the tendency of a principle to expand itself to the limit of its logic."

—*Justice Robert Jackson, dissenting, in* Korematsu v. United States

Contents

Acknowledgments

M any friends, colleagues, and students generously helped me in writing this book. My wife, Joy Fischer Williams, deserves special thanks. I thank my close friend and colleague, Jim Anaya, for his patience and insight in helping me to shape and refine many of the ideas here. I also acknowledge my debt to Adam Carvell, Vince George, Megan McClurg, Sudha Peri, and Angela Poliquin for their invaluable research assistance. I am most grateful to the Open Society Institute, Soros Senior Justice Fellows Program, for its generous research support of this project. James Henderson and Joseph Singer commented on earlier drafts of this manuscript, and the Legal History Roundtable at Boston College Law School, where I delivered a talk based on this manuscript, was the source of many valuable comments as well. My dean at the University of Arizona James E. Rogers College of Law, Toni Massaro, has provided me with invaluable institutional support and encouragement, as have George Davis, provost, and Richard C. Powell, vice president for research, at the University of Arizona. I am greatly indebted to Jace Weaver and Robert Warrior, editors of the Indigenous Americas series for the University of Minnesota Press, for their encouragement and suggestions.

I benefited from many other types of support in writing this book. I thank especially the library staff at the University of Arizona James E. Rogers College of Law. I also thank Joni Coble, Sandy Davis, Davon May, and Leo Morales-Egizi, who helped me produce the manuscript for this book.

Introduction

There is a very telling *Far Side* cartoon by Gary Larson that I like to share with people whenever I'm asked to talk about the history of Indian rights in America. The cartoon depicts an Indian in buckskins and full feathered-headdress regalia standing next to a teepee, addressing members of his tribe. The dozen or so Indians he's speaking to are also dressed in buckskins. They're all sporting either feathers or braids in their long, black hair. The Indian standing in front of the group, obviously the leader of this tribe, is shown holding up a necklace made of a few tacky beads. In the cartoon bubble above his head, he proudly proclaims to his assembled little band, "To begin, I'd like to show you *this*! Isn't it a beaut'?" The caption below the cartoon simply reads, "New York 1626: Chief of the Manhattan Indians addresses his tribe for the last time."

A good number of folks always seem to think they get the joke in this cartoon right away. After their laughter and chuckles subside, I like to ask them why they think they get it. Typically, they say something like, "It's all about the Indians selling Manhattan to the Dutch for a bunch of worthless beads and trinkets." Some of them can even tell me exactly how much the Indians supposedly were paid by the Dutch for the sale of Manhattan. Even some of the people who thought they didn't get the cartoon at first now remember: "The Dutch paid the Indians twenty-four dollars for Manhattan" or "something like that." They're sure they could look it up, "somewhere on the 'net," they tell me.[1]

I'm not done with these people who think they get this joke about Indians. If you let them go on, they'll say that everybody knows that Indians usually got ripped off in their treaties with the white man. "Common knowledge," they'll say. "Come on, you're the one who's supposed to be the expert."

With undaunted courage, I press on. I want to know more about this core organizing belief that so many people seem to have about Indians and their worthless treaty deals. What types of iconic symbols and mythical metanarratives are evoked in their minds by the infamous story of the Indians selling Manhattan to the Dutch, of all people, for twenty-four dollars in lousy beads and trinkets? Why is it that so many people seem to believe that Indians had this relatively primitive, unsophisticated way of life that supposedly made them clueless as to the "real" value of what they were selling when they made treaties with the white man for their lands? No one can ever seem to remember exactly where or how they acquired this type of cultural metaknowledge about Indians. It's just one of those things a person somehow picks up along the way while growing up in America, or so I'm told. It's all part of our racial imagination.

Once I get people to confess their basic ideas about Indians, Indian lands, and stupid Indian treaty deals, it's relatively easy to deconstruct this cartoon for them. The reason they think they get it, I explain, is because of a commonly held, long-established negative racial stereotype about Indians in the American racial imagination. Most people in this country believe that Indians were a primitive people when the white man finally "discovered" them in the New World. That's why the tribes were totally clueless as to the real value of the real estate they gave up in their treaties. They were savages.

Though his readers may not be precisely aware of it, Larson is subversively playing upon this basic stereotype that he knows most people in America have about Indians, iconically represented by the apocryphal tale of the sale of Manhattan. If the Indians were too primitive and savage to appreciate the true value of their land, then why are they about to get rid of their chief for selling Manhattan for a bunch of lousy beads? Get it?

Larson's cartoon works precisely because it plays against this long-established racial stereotype of Indians as unsophisticated savages, making us re-imagine the Indians' actual reaction to news of the sale of Manhattan from a different, nonstereotyped perspective. The cartoon's somewhat jolting view of what happened to that Indian chief when he reported back the news to his tribe conflicts with our commonly held stereotypes of Indians as too uncivilized and ignorant to know what an idiot their chief was for selling Manhattan for twenty-four dollars. What makes the cartoon so funny to those people who think they get it is this rather confounding reversal of a commonly held racial stereotype. That disorienting shift in perspective makes us laugh, or at least chuckle, because we never really thought about Indians like that. Maybe they weren't so savage, ignorant, and uncivilized after all. Maybe they just had a stupid chief who made a bad deal for their land, which offers a whole new perspective on a very old story about a very old treaty. What a surprise this is to some people (and this element of surprise is what usually makes for a good joke, in Indian humor at least),[2] to discover that a cartoon can so easily manipulate their stereotypical images of Indian people.[3] Now they're not so sure if they really did get the joke in the cartoon, or if it got them instead.

Here's one way to tell if Larson's cartoon let your stereotypes get the best of you. Ask yourself this question: Can you say anything knowledgeable about any other Indian treaty, besides the treaty for Manhattan? Unfortunately, the apocryphal tale of the sale of Manhattan is the only Indian treaty story most folks seem to know anything about, and it's basically organized around a racial stereotype of Indians as being too stupid, savage, and backward to know the real value of their land.[4]

I know it makes some people uncomfortable, being confronted for the first time with their negative racial stereotypes of Indians. But the fact that so many people respond to this racialized image of Indians as uncivilized, easily duped savages—and the fact that there is not much to counter that pervasive, clichéd stereotype in their minds—is just one illustration of the continuing, organizing force of a long-established, well-known way of talking, thinking, and writing about Indians in the

American racial imagination. There is, in other words, a language of racism in America directed at Indians, and most of us, whether we are conscious of it or not, are very familiar with it.

What most people are not very familiar with are the scores of legal battles Indians have fought throughout American history to protect their rights to their lands and other important legal interests guaranteed in literally hundreds of treaties with the United States. Most people don't bother to familiarize themselves with the fact that Indians still regard these treaties and their ancient promises as solemn and perpetual pledges of peace and protection between two peoples, pledges that create a sacred relationship of trust. I tell them they can go look it up if they want.[5]

One of the most important lessons taught by Larson's cartoon is that there are innumerable points of subversive entry into a broad narrative terrain of negative stereotypes, apocryphal tales, and other well-known forms of racial imagery[6] in American history. This terrain of fact, fiction, and fable defines a tradition in our history; a textually rich, long-established narrative tradition in America's racial imagination that embraces not just Indians. We all know that other minority groups in our society have also been subjected to this ever-evolving narrative tradition of American racial profiling and to its use of a well-known language of race-based stereotypes and denigrating racial imagery.

We also know *what* this tradition of racial profiling is about. It's about the stigma of racial and cultural inferiority historically attached to certain groups of people in this country. We can even come to basic agreement on the precise groups of people, defined by their "races," who have been most negatively affected by the perpetuation of this tradition in American history.[7] But this doesn't necessarily mean that any of us personally endorses any part of this tradition. I'm not accusing any of my fellow Americans in general of being "racist" just because they chuckled at a *Far Side* cartoon that let them see their own clichéd stereotypes about Indians at work in their minds. I do, however, tell people that even if we ourselves make a conscious choice, or at least the effort, to refrain from doing anything that helps keep this tradition alive in our daily lives and interactions with others, such a choice doesn't mean that this familiar way of talking, thinking, and writing about certain minority groups in our history doesn't continue to affect the world we live in today. It does, in very subtle and sometimes very dangerous ways. The negative racial stereotypes, apocrypha, and other forms of racial imagery that we all know about are part of the history of racism in America. That history is an important part of our cultural memory and continues to define who we are and how we got that way as a people. As H. J. Ehrlich, the noted twentieth-century scholar on the social psychology of prejudice, has written:

> Stereotypes about ethnic groups appear as part of the social heritage of society. They are transmitted across generations as a component of the accumulated knowledge of society. They are as true as tradition, and as pervasive as folklore. No person can grow up in a society without having learned the stereotypes assigned to the major ethnic groups.[8]

The fact that so many people laugh, or at least chuckle, at Larson's cartoon while thinking that they get it illustrates that a long-established tradition of stereotyping Indians as savages is still a vital, subverting part of our national heritage. It's an indelible feature of the American racial imagination.[9]

The Long-Established Tradition of Negative Racial Profiling of Indians as Stereotypical Savages in the Supreme Court's Indian Rights Decisions

Given our cultural heritage as a settler-state nation of different peoples whose history has been defined, to a significant degree, by questions of race and racism, no one should be at all surprised to discover that a number of long-established and well-known languages of racism in America can be found reflected in many of the Supreme Court's most important decisions on minority rights under the Constitution and laws of the United States. Given the persistence and pervasiveness of negative racial stereotypes and hostile racist imagery in shaping our history, these languages have inevitably found their way into that part of our national heritage involving the written decisions of the Supreme Court. For the most part, after all, the justices were born and raised here in America and were exposed to these languages. They know what these languages are all about: These languages are about the use of negative stereotypes, racial images, and apocryphal tales to justify the stigma of inferiority attached to certain racially subordinated groups in our society. In fact, you can tell the justices know all about the language of racism historically directed against Indians in America simply by reading their opinions on Indian rights.

During the Marshall Court Era

In this book, I focus on a well-defined set of familiar racial images and stereotypes that can be found at work in numerous leading decisions of the Supreme Court on important questions of Indian rights in America. Indians, for example, are unembarrassedly referred to as "heathens" and as "fierce savages, whose occupation was war, and whose subsistence was drawn chiefly from the forest," by Chief Justice John Marshall in his 1823 opinion in *Johnson v. McIntosh,* one of the most important Indian rights cases ever handed down by the Supreme Court. Nor was this an isolated incident of legalized racial profiling by the man whom most historians and legal scholars revere as the greatest chief justice of all time.[10]

In the landmark opinions on Indian rights that John Marshall wrote for the Supreme Court in the early nineteenth century, Indians are routinely referred to as a racially inferior group of people who were living as savages at the time of the coming of the white man to America. The case of *Cherokee Nation v. Georgia,* for example, is another leading Supreme Court decision authored by Marshall. In that oft-cited, landmark case on Indian rights, Marshall described Indians as constituting a race of people who were "once numerous, powerful, and truly independent" but who had gradually sunk "beneath our superior policy, our arts and our arms." They sought redress for their legal grievances, Marshall explained, not by going to a court of law like white people do, but by appealing to the "tomahawk."[11] And in *Worcester v. Georgia,* one of the most cited, celebrated, and relied upon Supreme Court Indian law cases of all time, Marshall, writing for the Court, referred to Indians as a people who "had made small progress in agriculture or manufactures, and whose general employment was war, hunting, and fishing."[12]

It's not surprising to find that Indians lost more times than not, at a ratio in fact of 2 to 1, during this "heroic age of the Supreme Court" when the greatest chief justice of all time talked about them this way.[13] How would you as a lawyer like those odds, arguing for the rights of your Indian client before a justice of the Supreme Court who said the types of things Marshall said about Indians in his seminal opinions on Indian rights? You might feel that such a justice was highly prejudiced against Indians as a group and therefore probably biased against your client's rights and interests in the case. To avoid even the appearance of impropriety, such a justice ought to be recused in a case involving an Indian tribe.

Throughout the Nineteenth-Century Supreme Court's Decisions on Indian Rights

Unfortunately for tribes and their lawyers, the odds of encountering justices on the Supreme Court who have talked the same way about Indians that Marshall did have always been pretty high. Lots of Supreme Court justices have followed the precedent set by Marshall and have used this same type of colorful, oftentimes overwrought, occasionally even over-romanticized, but always thoroughly racist language of Indian savagery in their opinions on Indian rights.

The Supreme Court, in fact, used to routinely rely on this type of racist language in deciding important, precedent-setting cases on Indian rights.[14] Throughout the nineteenth century and even well into the twentieth century, the justices seemingly couldn't help themselves from talking about Indians as if they were hostile savages who deserved to disappear from the American cultural landscape. They talked this way about Indians, in fact, *even* in cases where Indians were directly involved as litigants pleading their rights before the Court. Whenever one of those old Supreme Court decisions set out an important precedent that defined Indian rights under the Constitution and laws of the United States, it seems that the justice writing the opinion couldn't help but go off on some crazy tangent, calling Indians these backward, ignorant, lawless, warlike, lazy, or drunken savages and claiming they were getting just what they deserved under our Constitution and laws.

No one should be surprised or upset about it. It's just the way Indian law was back then. You'll be reading a Supreme Court decision on Indian rights, and all of a sudden you think you've hit upon the Web site for one of those Ku Klux Klan or Aryan Nation hate groups. Out of nowhere, the Court's opinion will start saying gratuitous, hateful things: that Indians were separated from the white race "by the instincts of a free though savage life," that they had been conquered and were now governed by "superiors of a different race," that the white man's civilized rule of law was "opposed to the traditions of their history, to the habits of their lives, to the strongest prejudices of their savage nature," or that attempting to measure "the red man's revenge by the maxims of the white man's morality"[15] would offend basic norms of civilized justice and basically be a total waste of time. It's crazy, I know, even disturbing at times to encounter this type of legalized racist hate speech directed against Indians in a U.S. Supreme Court opinion, but it's there in just about all those old Indian rights cases. Some of the most hostile racial attitudes in nineteenth-century America toward Indians can be found in the Indian rights decisions of the Supreme Court.

For instance, one of the most important Indian rights decisions issued by the late-nineteenth-century Supreme Court is *United States v. Kagama*. *Kagama* uses this judicialized form of racist hate speech against Indians and their rights to justify the unilateral imposition of federal criminal law on tribes even though the Constitution, as the Court itself admits in the case, nowhere expressly delegates such a power to Congress. The justices of the *Kagama* Court nevertheless unanimously declared that under U.S. law, Indians were regarded legally as "wards of the nation." Because they were "dependent on the United States—dependent largely for their daily food; dependent for their political rights"—these "remnants of a race once powerful, now weak and diminished in numbers" were under the plenary authority of Congress. The United States could therefore impose "its laws on all the tribes" if it wanted to, regardless of whether Indians liked it or not,[16] and it really didn't matter what the actual text of the Constitution might have to say on the issue.

Despite its nineteenth-century racist language and antiquated notions of Indian racial and cultural inferiority, *Kagama* is still regarded as a leading precedent in the Supreme Court's Indian law. The case, decided in 1886, is unembarrassedly cited and relied upon, for instance, by the twenty-first-century justices of the Rehnquist Court as still a good authority on Indian rights in America today.[17]

Still Crazy after All These Years: The Maintenance of a White Racial Dictatorship in the Supreme Court's Post-*Brown*-Era Indian Rights Decisions

Of course, back in the nineteenth century when the justices of the Supreme Court were issuing opinions like *Johnson, Cherokee Nation,*

Worcester, and *Kagama*, America, racially speaking at least, was a much different type of place. It really was crazy back then, with things like slavery, lynchings, and forced military relocations of entire Indian nations, not to mention the horrible stuff that was done to the Chinese, Japanese, and Mexican people who came here in search of the American dream. There are some historians who look at America back then and say that it was basically a "racial dictatorship," with white people on top and all the colored ones on the bottom.[18]

Now for some folks, calling America a white racial dictatorship might be going too far. But as a general rule, white people in America used to do some pretty crazy things to people of color back in those days. And "those days" really weren't all that long ago. It wasn't until 1954, after all, the year Elvis Presley cut his first hit record and, at least according to some, changed everything about white America's racial imagination,[19] that the Supreme Court finally decided that blacks should be treated the same as whites under the Constitution of the United States in the landmark civil rights case *Brown v. Board of Education*.[20]

Most people seem to assume that because Elvis and *Brown* revolutionized America's racial imagination when it came to blacks, the story must have gotten better for all the other minority groups in America after that.[21] At least that's the lesson they've been taught to believe: Everything got better in America, racially speaking at least, after Elvis and *Brown*.[22]

For Indians, though, it really didn't get that much better, at least in terms of keeping all the hostile nineteenth-century racial stereotypes of Indian savagery out of the Supreme Court's opinions on Indian rights.[23] Every schoolchild in America learns that the justices decided the landmark civil rights case of *Brown v. Board of Education,* finally removing the long-established badge of legalized racial inferiority and recognizing black Americans' equal rights as citizens of the United States, in 1954. What most Americans don't know is that the Court issued one of the most racist Indian rights decisions of all time, *Tee-Hit-Ton v. United States,*[24] the very next year! The Court's 1955 *Tee-Hit-Ton* decision unembarrassedly embraced the same basic racist language of Indians as culturally and racially inferior wandering, ignorant savages that the justices of the nineteenth-century Supreme Court routinely used in their decisions on Indian rights.

"Every American schoolboy knows," Justice Stanley Reed declared for a six-person majority in *Tee-Hit-Ton,* "that the savage tribes of this continent were deprived of their ancestral ranges by force and that, even when the Indians ceded millions of acres by treaty in return for blankets, food and trinkets, it was not a sale but the conquerors' will that deprived them of their land."[25] In other words, in 1955, the year *after* the Supreme Court's landmark civil rights decision in *Brown,* a majority of the justices expressly relied on the same racist stereotype of Indians and their worthless treaty deals that the cartoonist Larson relied on in his *Far Side* cartoon. The difference was that Larson used this racial imagery as the basis of a subversively intended joke that plays on our stereotyped racial beliefs. There was nothing funny about the way the justices used this negative racial stereotype of Indian savagery in *Tee-Hit-Ton:* They turned it into a generalized interpretive principle for understanding the legal history of all the treaties ever negotiated by any Indian tribes with the United States. Based on their racial profiling of the Indians who brought the *Tee-Hit-Ton* case, the Court held that the indigenous tribes and other native groups of Alaska had no right to be compensated under the Fifth Amendment of the Constitution when the United States unilaterally took their lands away from them.

As *Tee-Hit-Ton* demonstrates, the legally sui generis nature of the language of racism used by the Supreme Court to decide Indian rights cases throughout American history was unaffected by the holding of *Brown.* *Brown*'s paradigm of equality of rights applied to black Americans was not applied by the Court to Indians. And the reason is plainly stated in *Tee-Hit-Ton:* Indians were savages at the coming of the white man to America, and their lands were taken by a superior civilization.

Even after the *Tee-Hit-Ton* case, decades following the great civil rights struggles of blacks and other minority groups for racial equality in America, we see Supreme Court justices who persist in relying upon and citing cases and legal precedents replete with hostile racist stereotypes of Indians as inferior savages with lesser rights than other Americans. As crazy as it may seem, the language of racism directed at Indians that was so popular with the justices in the nineteenth century is still being perpetuated by the Supreme Court in many of its most important decisions on Indian rights in the post-*Brown* era.

Take the case regarded by the Rehnquist Court as one of the most important Indian rights decisions of the twentieth century, *Oliphant v.*

Suquamish Indian Tribe.[26] Written by then associate justice William Rehnquist in 1978 (the year after Elvis died, by the way), *Oliphant* has been unwaveringly cited and adhered to by the justices as the leading precedent of the Court on the critical issue of tribal jurisdiction over nonmembers on the reservation.[27]

Oliphant holds that an Indian tribe lacks criminal jurisdiction over non-Indians committing crimes on its reservation, even if the crime was committed against the tribe's *own members*. Rehnquist's opinion cited and quoted more than a dozen nineteenth-century Supreme Court precedents, executive branch policy statements, and congressional legislative enactments and reports to justify the decision in *Oliphant*. Virtually every text Rehnquist uses from this period of white racial dictatorship in America consistently and unembarrassedly stereotypes Indians as lawless, uncivilized, unsophisticated, hostile, or warlike savages. As Rehnquist's opinion in *Oliphant* clearly demonstrates, these precedents show conclusively that in the nineteenth century Indians were uniformly regarded by the dominant society and by the justices of the Supreme Court as an inferior race and as therefore entitled to lesser rights than whites. And according to *Oliphant*, a case decided almost a quarter century after the landmark civil rights decision in *Brown v. Board of Education*, that's precisely the way the Court is going to keep on treating Indians and their rights in present-day America.

For example, at a very early point in his opinion in *Oliphant*, Rehnquist relies upon a rarely cited 1891 Supreme Court Indian law case, *In re Mayfield*.[28] Rehnquist not only resurrected this obscure nineteenth-century Indian law case as reliable precedent in his opinion, he actually used its blatantly racist nineteenth-century judicial language of Indian savagery and white supremacy to justify the Court's holding that Indians have always possessed diminished and inferior rights compared to the white population under United States law:

> In *In re Mayfield*, the Court noted that the policy of Congress had been to allow the inhabitants of the Indian country "such power of self-government as was thought to be consistent with the safety of the white population with which they may have come in contact, and to encourage them as far as possible in raising themselves to our standard of civilization."[29]

Based on this nineteenth-century racist stereotype of Indian cultural inferiority embedded in the reasoning of the *Mayfield* decision, Rehnquist's opinion in *Oliphant* held that the Court had no choice in 1978 but to deny Indian tribes this privileged form of self-governing power over non-Indians committing crimes upon tribal members on the reservation today: "[W]hile Congress never expressly forbade Indian tribes to impose criminal penalties on non-Indians, we now make express our implicit conclusion of nearly a century ago [in *In re Mayfield*] that Congress consistently believed this to be the necessary result of its repeated legislative actions."[30]

This is not the only instance in which Rehnquist cited and even directly quoted a nineteenth-century text containing overtly racist stereotypes of Indians in support of his twentieth-century holding in *Oliphant*. Throughout his opinion, Rehnquist perpetuates a nineteenth-century language of racism to justify the Court's holding in *Oliphant*. For instance, he quoted from an 1834 congressional report issued at the height of the genocidal Removal era of U.S. Indian policy[31] to support *Oliphant*'s general "principle" that Indians do not have criminal jurisdiction over non-Indians. This "principle," he writes,

> would have been obvious a century ago when most Indian tribes were characterized by a "want of fixed laws [and] of competent tribunals of justice." H.R. Rep. No. 474, 23d Cong., 1st Sess., at 18 (1834). It should be no less obvious today, even though present day Indian tribal courts embody dramatic advances over their historical antecedents.[32]

Throughout *Oliphant,* Rehnquist repeatedly cited and quoted from a large number of nineteenth-century texts that expressly displayed an overtly hostile, racist attitude toward Indians and Indian tribal culture. And *Oliphant* is simply one of many instances in which a Supreme Court justice, post-*Brown,* relied on a long-established tradition of negative racist stereotypes, apocrypha, and images of Indian savagery to justify the Court's decision in an important Indian rights case. *Oliphant* is simply part of a much larger legal history of racism directed at Indians, perpetuated by the racist nineteenth-century precedents and accompanying judicial language of Indian savagery found in leading decisions of the U.S. Supreme Court. The justices continue to uphold a form of legalized racial dictatorship dating from the nineteenth century and in doing so give legal sanction to a long-established language of racism directed against Indians in America.[33]

The Legal History of Racism against Indians in America as Perpetuated by the Supreme Court's Indian Rights Decisions

The continuing legal force of a long-established, deeply embedded, and widely dispersed language of racism directed at Indians can be found at work throughout the Supreme Court's Indian law decisions, beginning with the Marshall Court's foundational precedents on Indian rights laid down in the early nineteenth century and continuing in the Rehnquist Court's leading Indian rights decisions of the twenty-first century.

The racist precedents and language of Indian savagery used and relied upon by the justices throughout this ongoing historical period of legalized racial dictatorship have most often worked, this book argues, to justify the denial to Indians of important rights of property, self-government, and cultural survival. In other words, take away the long-established legal tradition of stereotyping Indians as savages, and there is usually no other stated justification to be found for the way that Indians are treated by the justices. Indians get treated legally by our "present day"[34] justices just as Indians were treated by the justices in the nineteenth century: as savages whose rights are defined according to a European colonial-era legal doctrine of white racial superiority over the entire North American continent.[35]

I do not pretend to explain in this book all the reasons why the justices of the Supreme Court have persisted in perpetuating this racist legal mythology in their Indian law opinions. I do try to explain what I think is at least one of the major reasons why the justices can continue to sanction and legalize such outmoded racial beliefs about Indians and get away with it. The legal history of racism against Indians as perpetuated by the justices of the Supreme Court demonstrates, in a compelling and undeniable fashion, the pervasive and continuing subversive power of certain well-known ways of talking, thinking, and writing about Indians.[36] As evidenced by their own stated opinions on Indian rights, a long legacy of hostile, romanticized, and incongruously imagined stereotypes of Indians as incommensurable savages continues to shape the way the justices view and understand the legal history, and therefore the legal rights, of Indian tribes.

The Indian law decisions of the justices, from the seminal opinions issued by the Marshall Court in the early nineteenth century to the latest pronouncements on Indian rights handed down by the twenty-first-century justices of the Rehnquist Court, demonstrate an unquestioning judicial adherence to a long-established racial mythology of Indians as lawless, uncivilized savages. Indians, according to this judicially sanctioned racial perspective, were too primitive, warlike, and backward to be "amalgamated" into the superior white settler-state society that had conquered them and colonized their lands.[37] And according to the justices of the Rehnquist Court, this historically established fact of Indian tribalism's backwardness and incommensurability has continuing legal meaning and controlling significance in the Supreme Court's Indian law.

I believe that one of the major reasons why the justices have been able to continue to perpetuate this long-established tradition of racial profiling of Indians with little expression of surprise, much less embarrassment, by most Americans is that most Americans themselves continue to believe, "deep down," in this deeply entrenched national mythology of Indian savagery, epitomized, for example, by the tale of the Indians selling Manhattan for twenty-four dollars. Most Americans, including the present-day justices of the Supreme Court, are simply unable to think about Indians and Indian rights without calling upon and invoking in their own minds such long-established stereotypes, images, and apocryphal tales of Indian tribalism as an inferior and fatefully doomed way of life in comparison to the superior European-derived civilization that colonized and conquered America. It's that unthinking, unconscious, and unreflective state of mind and belief embedded in the American racial imagination, I argue in this book, that determines and defines what most Americans care to think about Indians and Indian rights (if they care to think at all about such things). That uncritical, stereotypical way of thinking about Indians, I also argue, is certainly one reason why most Americans aren't very much discomforted by what the justices of the Rehnquist Court, for example, do to those rights in their Indian law decisions.[38]

Aside from Indians and their lawyers, most Americans generally express little concern or notice, and virtually no discomfort at all, when the Rehnquist Court issues an important legal opinion that stigmatizes Indians as being too backward to enjoy the same rights to property or self-government, for example, as do non-Indians. No headlines scream out from our nation's leading newspapers, "Rehnquist Court Holds That Indians Have Inferior Rights to Self-Government Because They Once Were Savages" or "Court Continues Its Racist Old Ways in Indian Law," even though these are precisely the types of things the Rehnquist Court is in fact doing in many of its present-day Indian rights decisions. The Court's continuing reliance on long-established stereotypes of tribal Indians stands, quite literally, on the far side of most contemporary Americans' concerns. Most of us still respond to Indians, if at all, by reference to a well-known set of persistent racial beliefs that have been perpetuated in America since the earliest days of the European colonial era (see chapter 3). There is nothing, therefore, for most Americans to get too upset or even surprised about when the Supreme Court relies on legal precedents that embrace the same stereotypical beliefs. If anything, the twenty-first-century Rehnquist Court's opinions have now given a renewed form of legal sanction to those beliefs, reinforcing and revivifying their enduring hold on the racial imagination of the vast majority of the American public.[39]

Getting "Practical": The Hard Trail of Confronting the Justices with Their Racial Profiling Techniques in Indian Rights Cases

My hope in writing this book is to challenge the marginalization of Indian rights concerns in America today by first bringing to the fore and then confronting the racist judicial precedents and language of Indian savagery that the Supreme Court has insistently relied upon and perpetuated ever since the early nineteenth century to justify its Indian law decisions. So that no one misconstrues precisely what it is I am trying to do, let me address three key points about the set of arguments I make in this book and also about my discourse-based approach to critiquing and combating the Court's legalized racial profiling.

First, I am *not* arguing for a theoretical approach to protecting Indian rights that suggests to Indian people that they would be better off "ignoring the Supreme Court."[40] I do not believe that the Court is a hopelessly racist institution that is incapable of fairly adjudicating cases involving the basic human rights to property, self-government, and cultural survival possessed by Indian tribes as indigenous peoples. I would never attempt to stereotype the justices in that way (see the conclusion to this book).

Nor does the discourse-based approach to reforming Indian rights that I argue for in this book mean to suggest that Indians should focus their primary legal energies on nondomestic legal and political forums, such as the international human rights system. As a "practical matter,"[41] having worked for Indian clients and Indian rights in both the domestic courts of the United States and within the international human rights system, I have no illusions about the intractability of the deeply entrenched racist attitudes and stereotypes that surround the discourses of indigenous peoples' rights in both of these forums.[42]

I'm also aware that the U.S. Supreme Court will not soon surrender its interpretive privilege as prime arbiter of Indian rights in this country, no matter what the international human rights system has to say about indigenous peoples and their treatment under U.S. law. The Court simply *cannot* be ignored by Indian rights advocates. It's the proverbial eight-hundred-pound gorilla that blocks the way of every legal struggle aimed at protecting Indian rights in the United States today. And as every international human rights lawyer knows, you certainly can't ignore the Supreme Court if you want to use the international human rights system's adjudicatory processes to protect Indian rights. Domestic remedies normally have to be exhausted first to even get a hearing in that system.[43]

I believe that Indian rights lawyers and scholars must engage these entrenched racist attitudes and stereotypes "on all fronts by whatever means necessary."[44] In theory *and* as a practical matter, I recognize that the Supreme Court is one of the most important of those fronts. What I do urge is adoption of a strategy of direct confrontation that challenges the continuing use of racial stereotypes, racial profiling techniques, and spurious racist imagery and apocrypha in thinking and talking about Indian rights by the Court, by the U.S. Congress, by the international human rights system, and even by Joe Six-Pack down at the local bar.[45]

My argument on the need for this type of confrontational strategy that focuses on identifying and bringing to the fore the nineteenth-century racist judicial language of Indian savagery used by the present-day Court in its major Indian rights decisions does entail one axiom of belief and Native knowledge: Indian rights will never be justly protected by any legal system or any civil society that continues to talk about Indians as if they are uncivilized, unsophisticated, and lawless savages.

The first step on the hard trail of decolonizing the present-day U.S. Supreme Court's Indian law is changing the way the justices themselves talk about Indians in their decisions on Indian rights.[46]

Let me also say at the outset that I know this will not be an easy task. As one of the justices recently conceded, the Court is a reactive institution; "real change comes principally from attitudinal shifts in the population at large. Rare indeed is the legal victory—in court or legislature—that is not a careful byproduct of an emerging social consensus."[47] Although I sense a subtle but demonstrable attitudinal shift in the society at large that does seem to signal an emerging consensus that the use of any racial stereotype depicting Indians as savages is inappropriate in present-day U.S. society, I also recognize that there is a lot of work that needs to be done to make this slowly crystallizing consensus palpable to the justices on the Court.

It's a hard trail that lies ahead. The salutary effects of the growing number of high schools and colleges that have abandoned the use of stereotyped Indian mascots and insignia,[48] for instance, are instantaneously diminished in a singularly reinforcing jolt to the American public's racial imagination by a single, widely reported decision, issued by a federal district court judge sitting in Washington, D.C., reversing the U.S. Patent and Trademark Office Appeals Board's 1999 ruling that the Washington "Redskins" trademark is racially disparaging to Indians, and must therefore be canceled.[49] The less stereotyped and less demeaning way that schoolchildren in America are taught about Indian culture and history today as opposed to just a generation ago[50] is instantaneously overwhelmed by a simple click of the mouse and the mass-marketing cultural force of "Kaya," the American Girl Indian doll, who "draws strength from her family, the legends her elders tell her, and the bold warrior woman who is her hero."[51] While there are signs of a general shift in the way we talk about Indians in this society, such countersigns as these tell us that we're not there yet. The hard trail that must be traveled as a society in ridding ourselves of these types of degrading and diminishing stereotypical images of Indian savagery, iconic primitiveness, and alien otherness has only just begun.

The Indian law opinions of the justices of the Rehnquist Court show that they are as conflicted, confused, and disabled as the rest of us when it comes to recognizing that a racist nineteenth-century language of Indian savagery continues to shape the way we think about Indians.

The Rehnquist Court's twenty-first-century Indian rights decisions, as I show in this book, continue to use the same legalized racial profiling techniques that the Supreme Court justices regularly relied on in the nineteenth century (see chapters 4 and 5).

I hope that one of the lessons to be taught by this book is that before we can confront the justices with the way they talk about Indians and Indian rights in their opinions, we need to confront our own bad habits of stereotyping and imagining Indians as savages. We must make the conscious effort to change the way we talk and think about Indians, to refrain from using a language of white racial superiority that traces back to the European colonial era's war for America. Once we do that, through a strategy of "intention, attention, and effort," we ourselves help to validate and confirm that emerging social consensus.[52] We become advocates for a twenty-first-century reformulation of the American racial imagination that rejects the Supreme Court's use of a nineteenth-century racist language to decide important questions of Indian peoples' most basic human rights.

We can all participate in making this reformulated vision of racial justice more palpable to the justices of the U.S. Supreme Court by engaging in any number of subversive and even overt practices. A law clerk to one of the justices, for instance, can leave this book lying around next to the watercooler at work. Lawyers representing tribes before the Court can point out in their briefs and also during oral argument that opposing counsels' precedents and case citations routinely refer to Indians in these negative, stereotyped terms and ask the justices to make them stop.

Law professors can get together and write a huge legal treatise showing the justices why Indian law needs to be purged of the negative racial stereotypes and images that support so many of the Court's leading precedents. Journalists and maybe even the Fox News Channel might be persuaded to give fair and balanced coverage to an important emerging question in the American legal academy and Indian bar: Should the Supreme Court be relying at all upon cases from an era of white racial dictatorship in deciding Indian rights cases in the twenty-first century?

Congress, lobbied by Indian tribes to reject the archaic stereotypes and images, can pass legislation overturning or at least modifying what Indians and their advocates regard as the Rehnquist Court's most racist and dangerous decisions on Indian rights in America.[53]

And, of course, the justices themselves (at least five of them) can come to the realization that they are relying on and perpetuating outmoded nineteenth-century racist precedents and legal language. They can walk away from that watercooler and decide that even without a societal consensus condemning such archaic, racist language, they can find better, less-stereotyped ways, more consistent with the Constitution's egalitarian spirit and values, to decide Indian rights cases. They can decide not to rely on a nineteenth-century racial perspective that views tribal Indians as inferior, conquered peoples. They can take the first step on that long, hard trail by recognizing that Indians should have their fundamental human rights to property, self-government, and cultural survival protected by the Supreme Court without resort to a racist stereotype of Indians as savages.

"A Winning Courtroom Strategy"

My argument on the need to confront the justices of the Supreme Court with their continuing reliance upon racist nineteenth-century precedents and language in their Indian law opinions requires me to address another oft-made characterization about the discourse-based approach I urge in this book. I know there are sincere, committed, well-intentioned, and very experienced Indian rights advocates who think they get the crux of my argument about how to go about protecting Indian rights in this country, and then dismiss it as not being very "practical." It won't "translate," they say, "into a winning courtroom strategy." They simply don't believe that the Supreme Court is ever going to abandon the approach it's been using since the early nineteenth century, "and make its decision on some independent standard" borrowed, say, from the emerging norms of the international human rights system respecting indigenous peoples and their rights.[54] In their view, given the "actual state of things"[55] in the present-day United States, it is a waste of time to even think seriously about adopting such a strategy that seeks to confront the Court with its racist approach to deciding Indian rights cases.

A major problem with this type of dismissive characterization is that it ignores a number of important lessons that can be learned from a more general study of the legal history of racism in the United States and of the Court's role in helping perpetuate it. Indian rights advocates and scholars are simply wrong as an empirical matter of history in holding to an overly parochial and pessimistic professional worldview that the Court is incapable of a major racial paradigm shift when it comes to the way it approaches, talks about, and decides minority rights cases. To the contrary, the legal history of racism in America teaches us that the most successful minority rights advocates of the twentieth century recognized that the real waste of time was trying to get a nineteenth-century racist legal doctrine to do a better job of protecting minority rights. It is useful to recall Thurgood Marshall's response to those many sincere, well-intentioned, and experienced legal advocates who told him, when he was legal counsel for the National Association for the Advancement of Colored People (NAACP), that it was impractical to expect the Supreme Court to abandon the nineteenth-century constitutional law doctrine of "separate but equal" enshrined in *Plessy v. Ferguson*.[56] Asking the Supreme Court to overturn *Plessy*, Marshall steadfastly believed, was indeed a winning courtroom strategy.[57]

Indians, their lawyers, and that segment of the American legal academy that teaches and writes about their rights have a lot to learn from the history of the racial paradigm shift represented by *Brown*, from Marshall's heroic example as the most successful minority rights advocate of the twentieth century to argue before the Supreme Court, and from the many other human rights stories of resistance, struggle, and triumph in America. These stories are the most important parts of the more general story of the legal history of racism in America and the Supreme Court's role in perpetuating it. The history of the civil rights movement for blacks, for example, quite clearly teaches us that one does not successfully advocate for a historically oppressed minority group's rights by writing legal briefs or legal treatises showing the justices how to get the racist principles and doctrines of the past to work better in protecting minority rights in the present-day United States.

I believe that one of the most important lessons taught by *Brown* and its legacy is that the justices must be continuously confronted with the pernicious, persistent, and continuing effects of a long-established language of racism in America.[58] As the Supreme Court itself recognized in rejecting the "separate but equal" legal discourse of *Plessy* in *Brown*, the practical, real-world impact of such a language is far greater when it "has the sanction of law." As the Court recited in *Brown*, such language affects "hearts and minds, in a way unlikely ever to be undone."[59] Removing this form of legal sanction by repudiating the precedents that perpetuate racist language in the Supreme Court's Indian law opinions is a first critical step that must be taken on the long hard trail of bringing about a major racial paradigm shift in the way the Supreme Court approaches its job of protecting the basic human rights of Indians in America. Any approach that ignores this step, I believe, is ultimately going to be the real waste of time.

My focus on the important lessons that can be learned from landmark civil rights cases like *Brown* concerning the need for a less parochial, more intensively engaged approach to the study of the legal history of racism in America requires me to address what I fear will be another form of mischaracterization of my argument. In urging a strategy for protecting Indian rights that confronts the Supreme Court with its use of and reliance upon such precedents, I am *not* advocating an approach that is focused purely on revealing the use of racist language and its harmful effects and then waiting for a resulting, inevitable transformation in the justices' racial attitudes. I am not, in other words, being insufficiently attentive to Derrick Bell's famously stated "interest convergence dilemma," which holds that minority rights are only recognized by the dominant society when that society perceives that it is in its own best interest to do so.[60] In fact, I view a discourse-based approach to protecting Indian rights as being preparatory and partial but nonetheless integral to the much harder task of discovering those points of convergence that might exist between the interests of the dominant society and Indian tribes in protecting important Indian rights.

I therefore take it as axiomatic that "a winning courtroom strategy" for protecting Indian rights in this country cannot be organized around a set of legal precedents and accompanying legal discourse that views Indians as lawless savages and interprets their rights accordingly. Before rejecting out of hand this axiom that the precedents and language the justices use in discussing minority rights are vitally important to the way the Court ultimately identifies and defines those rights, I ask Indian rights lawyers and scholars to consider carefully the following question: Is it really possible to believe that the Court would have written *Brown* the way it did if it had not first explicitly decided to reject the "language in *Plessy v. Ferguson*"[61] that gave precedential legal force, validity, and sanction to the negative racial stereotypes and images historically directed at blacks by the dominant white society? As an empirical fact of history, affirmed by *Brown,* both the precedents and the language the justices use in talking about a particular minority group's rights will unavoidably shape the subsequent content of the rights that the Court defines according to those precedents and their accompanying language.

This is not to say that simply changing the way Supreme Court justices talk about Indians and their rights will dramatically and instantly change or transform long-established legal doctrines and precedents in the field of Indian law. Having been well-schooled by Professor Bell himself when I was a young, affirmative-action-oriented law student at Harvard and he was developing and testing his seminal materialist thesis upon those of us who were fortunate enough to have him teach us about race and racism in American law,[62] I have always regarded myself as a long-practicing and ardently committed racial realist when it comes to the task of protecting Indian rights.[63] I recognize that civil rights advances seem to come about only when it's in the perceived self-interests of the dominant majority society to recognize minority rights. I certainly do not want to be accused of making the jejune mistake of believing, in the words of Richard Delgado, that "minority misery is unnatural and certain to be corrected once pointed out to those in power."[64] I know, indeed, that we are not saved simply because the Court has changed the way it talks about a particular minority group in its opinions on that group's rights.

I know as well that as a basic strategic principle, showing the non-Indian majority, in society and on the Court, that it's in the broader public interest to protect Indian rights will materially improve Indian rights lawyers' chances of winning their cases.[65]

But before that type of racial realist showing according to the prescriptions of Bell's interest convergence paradigm is even attempted, the lessons of *Brown* strongly suggest that the long-established racial stereotypes and imagery in the Court's decisions and precedents must be first exposed and then attacked. Otherwise, the persistence of a language of racism in American society and in the Court's case law will make discovering such a community of interests, material or otherwise, between a particular minority group and the dominant society virtually impossible. It's incredibly hard, if not impossible, in other words, for any society to recognize the rights of a group of people that the law says can be treated like the "n" word. Similarly, the approach I'm advocating for protecting Indian rights holds that we are not likely to build progressive coalitions or envision a likely convergence of interests, hearts, or minds with a group of people that the Court says can still be legally treated like uncivilized, lawless savages.

My "Singularity Thesis" for Protecting Indian Rights in America

So that there are no misconceptions, let me therefore briefly put forward at the outset of this study what I call my "singularity thesis" for protecting Indian rights under U.S. law and show how it relates to Bell's interest convergence dilemma.[66] My thesis on the singularly problematic nature of protecting Indian rights in America builds on the work of the noted Indian law scholar and advocate for Indian rights Charles Wilkinson. As Wilkinson has keenly observed, "Indian issues veer away from other questions of race." Indian rights, in other words, are much different from the types of minority rights that were and remain at the center of the continuing struggle for racial equality represented by cases like *Brown:* "The most cherished civil rights of Indian people are not based on equality of treatment under the Constitution and the general civil rights laws."[67] Ultimately, what Indians are seeking from the Court is something much different. They are arguing for a right to a degree of "measured separatism," that is, the right to govern their reservation homelands and those who enter them by their own laws, customs, and traditions, even when these might be incommensurable with the dominant society's values and ways of doing things.[68]

This seemingly balkanizing, separatist aspiration for a measured degree of indigenous self-determination and cultural sovereignty thus situates most Indian rights questions upon difficult and very "unfamiliar intellectual terrain" for most of the American public.[69] My singularity thesis on Indian rights, as supported by Wilkinson's foundational critical insight on the divisive nature of Indian aspirations for a right to a degree of "measured separatism" in America, is that the unique types of autochthonous rights that tribal Indians want protected under U.S. law (and by the international human rights system, for that matter) are inherently problematic for the dominant non-Indian society and its judges in a way that the more general types of minority individual rights at the center of the struggle for racial equality represented by *Brown* were not. It's much harder, in other words, to secure recognition and protection for highly novel forms of Indian group rights to self-determination and cultural sovereignty in American society than for the far more familiar types of individualized rights that most other minority groups want protected.[70]

My singularity thesis for protecting Indian tribal rights recognizes, as a matter of both strategy and tactics, the inherent difficulty of convincing the American public that it is in its material interests, no matter how broadly defined, to recognize a measured right of Indian tribes to rule themselves on their reservation homelands by their own laws, customs, and traditions, particularly when that right appears to interfere with or threaten the dominant society's interests or values. It also recognizes that advocating for Indian rights to self-determination and cultural sovereignty requires addressing what I take to be the sincere and legitimate concerns of the Court, Congress, and Joe Six-Pack about the theoretical incommensurability and the real-world material consequences of recognizing, let us say, that Indian tribal courts can exercise criminal and civil jurisdiction over non-Indians on the reservation without affording them the precise protections of the Constitution's Bill of Rights.

Once we recognize the singularly problematic nature of Indian rights claims, we also come to realize the importance, as a preparatory matter, of the language that the American public and the justices themselves use in talking about Indians and their asserted rights to a degree of "measured separatism" under the Constitution and laws of the United States. If we continue to let the Court talk about Indians as if they are uncivilized and unsophisticated savages and use racist precedents that define their rights accordingly, we are not likely to make much headway in developing a winning courtroom strategy that convinces the justices that it is in the American public's interests to recognize an admittedly highly problematic and exclusive set of Indian rights to a degree of measured separatism in this country. In other words, the Supreme Court will not take Indian rights seriously if the justices are not first confronted with the continuing force of negative racial stereotypes and hostile racist imagery that have been directed at Indians throughout the legal history of racism in America, "down to the present day."[71] Eliminating this long-established language of Indian racial inferiority in America, as sanctioned and perpetuated by the justices' very own opinions on Indian rights, is the first step on the long, hard trail of decolonizing the Supreme Court's Indian law.[72]

Part I

Discovering a Language of Racism in America

> I remember one incident within the airport that showed me how Malcolm X never lost his racial perspective. Waiting for my baggage, we witnessed a touching family reunion scene as part of which several cherubic little children romped and played, exclaiming in another language. "By tomorrow night, they'll know how to say their first English word—n[——]r," observed Malcolm X.
>
> —ALEX HALEY, "EPILOGUE," THE AUTOBIOGRAPHY OF MALCOLM X

Malcolm X's inspired flight of racial imagination, as reported by his amanuensis, Alex Haley, that the "n" word would be the first bit of English a new immigrant child would learn upon arriving in this country remains, even today, a trenchant and disturbing insight into the workings of a language of racism in America.[1] Malcolm X knew that at that particular moment in American society, there existed a specific, inescapably encountered, and well-known way of talking about people like him. He understood, from experience, thought, and reflection, that there is a language of racism in this country organized around the "n" word and all that it stands for as part of our history and cultural heritage. And everyone in America learns how to speak it.

1

"Look, Mom, a Baby Maid!"
The Languages of Racism

The language of racism directed against blacks in America, as perceived by Malcolm X at the airport, exposes us to a wide variety of associated epithets, slurs, stereotypes, and other forms of racist imagery that haunt our society. All these words and terms are basically about the same thing and perform the same function in American life: They all perpetuate and reinscribe the basic racist mythology of "Negro" racial inferiority signified by the "n" word. And from Malcolm X's perspective, everyone in America, even the most recently arrived immigrant child, soon learns how to speak the language of racism organized around that hatefully stigmatizing word.[1]

Even if most Americans now consciously choose *not* to speak this long-established language, which Malcolm X identified in his speeches, writings, and life's work, we can still discover its continuing cultural force and multiple meanings at work in our society. It still seems to be the case that just about everybody in America still knows the language of racism organized around the "n" word. As Malcolm X realized, the "n" word and the language of racism generated by it will always provide us with a provocative and disturbing set of insights into who we are as a people in America and how we got that way.

Where Do You Find the Languages of Racism in America?
In the Music of the Younger Generation

There are of course a multiplicity of complex usages and cultural group appropriations of the language of racism organized around the "n" word in America. And they continue to proliferate throughout our contemporary society in ways that are surprising or even jolting. Black rap and hip-hop artists, for example, have created entirely new genres of music and poetical expression organized around the "n" word. Many people who cannot even name a contemporary rap or hip-hop artist can probably figure out what the members of one of the early influential rap groups, N.W.A., were trying to say about themselves in the strident, poetic, musical language organized around the complexities of the "n" word: They were using the "n" word in a trenchant and disturbing counterlanguage of racism, "straight outta Compton."[2]

A recent copyright case involving Marshall Mathers, the white rap artist professionally known as Eminem, shows us that rap's musical language of racism can be a highly volatile commodity; its counter-appropriations of the "n" word and related epithets and slurs are capable of igniting a host of complex responses and resentments in the American racial imagination. Mathers's record company, Shady Records, brought a suit for copyright infringement against *Source* magazine, a publication devoted to rap and hip-hop. *Source* had come into possession of a tape of two rap songs supposedly recorded by Mathers "as a youth, before the onset of his commercial fame and success, which use crude racist invective to denigrate black women." The magazine "loudly publicized" its discovery of Mathers's language of racism against black women by making "the sounds and texts of allegedly racist recordings available to its public in their entirety on its website." *Source* claimed that these "youthful recordings proved its point about Mathers's exploitative relation to black people and black culture."[3]

Before commencing his suit against *Source* for copyright infringement, Mathers apologized for what he called "youthful indiscretions occasioned by romantic disappointment."[4] In an opinion dismissing the counterclaims *Source* filed against Mathers in the suit, the federal district court had this to say about the bitter legal contest over commercial rights to Mathers's misogynistic counter-appropriation of rap's African American–derived counterlanguage of racism:

> Mathers is the most prominent of the handful of white hip-hop artists who have been artistically or commercially successful. Like other white musicians who have been successful in musical genres or forms pioneered by Africans or African-Americans, from Benny Goodman to Elvis Presley to Paul Simon, Mathers has been accused of exploiting black culture; he in turn has asserted his respect for his black role models and peers, and has maintained that he comes by his hip-hop success honestly, as a young man from a poor urban background who has long been associated with African-American friends, neighbors and mentors. Source's principals have been vocal critics of Mathers, and have derided his claims to hip-hop authenticity.[5]

As Eminem's legal battles attest, such culturally imbricated, musically syncopated, and psycho-sexually charged usages of the "n" word and related racial stereotypes provide fascinating insight into the multifaceted history of racism and white racial dictatorship in America.[6] While it may be true (and for the better) that the more enlightened segments of white society seem to have largely abandoned overt use or reliance upon such racist language, the historical and cultural legacy of the "n" word continues to be felt strongly as a negative, dividing force. In racial discrimination cases brought under our civil rights laws, in the contentious debates surrounding hate speech codes on our college campuses, and in countless other conflicted arenas in public life, including the contemporary music of an alienated youth culture in our society, the continuing power and force of this way of talking about black Americans suggests the continuing relevance of the lesson taught by Malcolm X: No one in America escapes the divisive legacy of the "n" word or the power of the language of racism organized around it.[7]

In a Book about Negrophobia

"Well that was then, this is now," my students like to say when I tell them about this Malcolm X guy at the airport. They don't use the "n" word—they just hear it all the time on the radio or downloaded onto their MP3 players—so they don't think they're racists. They may not be quite sure about what the "X" in "Malcolm X" stands for, but they can easily understand what Eminem is all about. In any event, they don't believe they have anything to be too disturbed about generally when it comes to their own personal beliefs about black people in America. They know what the Benetton ads full of multiracial, college-age, cultural trendsetters are telling them: It's not cool to be racist. It's not even a good business model. But, as I try to show my students, according to some researchers, it doesn't matter if their so-called multi-culti-generation uses the "n" word or not. The word still shapes the way they think about blacks. In other words, they might all be racists and not even know it!

Most Americans who aren't black resist the idea that they might still be somewhat racist in the way they think about black folks.[8] They don't believe that as Americans they inevitably share in what Charles Lawrence has called "a common historical and cultural heritage in which racism has played and still plays a dominant role." They don't buy the claim that whether they like it or not, this racist history and heritage is reflected in a cultural belief system that is literally saturated with derogatory stereotypes and racist imagery about blacks. They especially reject the notion that to the extent that this racialized cultural belief system has influenced all of us, as Lawrence explains, "we are all racists."[9]

That such a "cultural belief system" really exists as a knowable, empirically demonstrable, commodifiable reality has to be proved to most people in America. Besides rap, where else do we find evidence that our racial perspective on the world is shaped by long-established negative racial stereotypes and imagery associated with certain minority groups, whether we know it or not?

Jody Armour, in his thought-provoking book *Negrophobia and Reasonable Racism*,[10] examines the continuing force of the language of racism in the contemporary United States in his study on race and the American criminal justice system. Citing considerable evidence from social science research and studies conducted during the post-*Brown* era, Armour seeks to show that even if we personally reject the outmoded stereotypes and ways of talking about blacks organized historically around the "n" word, we continue to be influenced by them. To that extent, Armour argues, we might all be racists, at least in some degree, whether we are willing to admit to it or not.

For instance, most of us are familiar with the pervasive stereotype that black male youths, particularly in the urban core ghetto areas of our nation's large cities, are "prone to violence."[11] Continually reinforced, reinterpreted, and renewed by our mass media and cultural industries, the racial mythology of the violent, malevolent young black man is deeply embedded into our collective cultural psyche and national racial unconscious. This pervasive stereotype harkens back to the antebellum days of slavery, to the psycho-sexual fears of violent slave revolts led by "strapping," "unruly" young "bucks" on the plantation, and to the conspiratorial racial fantasies of the apocryphal end of white civilization, an end that would be engendered by diabolically insidious, unregulated race-mixing between white women and Negro men. The terrified belief in the violent proclivities of resentful black male youths and in what they would do if they were to get a white person alone in a dark alley is simply the contemporary sociopathic manifestation of the force that this long-established stereotype continues to have upon white America's racial imagination.

I use the word "sociopathic" to describe these hostile acts of racial imagination quite deliberately. We all know, "deep down,"[12] where the stereotype of blacks being "prone to violence" comes from: It comes from our history as a nation that violently enslaved black people as human chattels—property, in other words, protected under the Founders' Constitution.[13] Even if we don't overtly subscribe to the myth that black males are prone to violence against whites, it is simply too much a part of our history and cultural heritage as a former slaveholding society to be avoided or dismissed. We all know where this form of "Negrophobia," to use Armour's term, comes from, even if we consciously choose not to succumb or subscribe to it. And, as Armour's book seeks to show, the language of racism generated by this form of Negrophobia is reflected throughout the way our criminal justice system deals with black male youths.

At Work in a Young Child's Mind

The languages of racism at work in our society can be discovered in many places besides the rap music of a younger generation and our contemporary criminal justice system. Beginning with the landmark decision in *Brown v. Board of Education*,[14] a large body of research has been generated, cited, debated, and challenged that seeks to prove the continuing existence of racism in America. This research shows that these long-established stereotypes and images continue to circulate and to have force in our society.[15] The tragedy, as this research shows, is that no matter how anachronistic these stereotypes are thought to be or how discredited they are societally, they insinuate themselves into our minds and collective psyches very early. The traits that we somehow come to believe belong to certain groups are absorbed into our brains at a very young age. Long before a child possesses the cognitive ability to decide whether this way of talking and thinking about others is rational or personally acceptable, these stereotypes have become nearly ineradicable features of that child's view of the world and of certain others in it.[16] Through this type of absorptive, insidious process, these stereotypes become embedded as essential truths, lying deep within the recesses of the developing child's racial imagination. Phyllis Katz cites a compelling research example of the perniciousness and deeply entrenched, precocious nature of the stereotyping process at work in a young child's mind. She tells of a three-year-old white child who, seeing a black infant for the first time, said to her mother, "Look Mom, a baby maid."[17]

On the Subway with Bernard Goetz

Besides being embarrassing in certain types of social situations, negative racial stereotypes can produce some downright sociopathic consequences. To borrow a term from Patricia Williams, they can be "spirit-murdering." They are dehumanizing and harmful and can have highly destructive and insidious effects upon all of us as we grow up, mature, and attempt to form our own independent, unbiased beliefs about different groups of people in our society.[18] They can lead us to adopt subtle and even not so subtle racist attitudes, forms of reasoning and behavior directed against people whom we don't really know, whom we may never have even met before. As the Supreme Court itself recognized in *Brown,* a language of racism can generate a feeling of racial inferiority that affects a young child's view of the world "in a way unlikely ever to be undone."

Harmful, spirit-murdering forms of racial prejudice emerge, revivify themselves, and then reemerge out of the stereotypes and images that help form derogatory personal beliefs about certain others. According to researchers in numerous studies, these beliefs lead to actions and behaviors that reflect endorsement or acceptance of the stereotypes and imagery encountered over a person's lifetime. These "stereotype-congruent responses" can then themselves become the basis for socially divisive and even highly sociopathic and destructive patterns of thinking and acting.[19]

In other words, the racist stereotypes and imagery that we all carry around in our heads can make some of us do the craziest things. Take, for instance, the case of Bernhard Goetz, "the subway vigilante,"[20] who brought a loaded gun onto a subway car in New York City in 1984. Goetz, who was white, believed that the subways were full of violence-prone blacks and that he had the right as a law-abiding white citizen to defend himself, with deadly force if necessary. So one day while riding the subway, he shot four black youths, one of them in the back, after they demanded five dollars from him. And considering what he was eventually convicted of, you'd have to say he got away with it. The jury basically decided that his stereotypes of violent, malevolent young black males made him do it.[21]

A person doesn't have to possess the highly charged racial sensibilities of a Malcolm X to see that Goetz's actions, which he justified at his trial as having been taken in self-defense, were triggered by a volatile and dangerous set of negative racial stereotypes that he was carrying around in his head along with the gun in his jacket. In Goetz's case, the racial mythology of violence-prone black youths functioned in his mind quite literally like a loaded weapon. His hostile stereotypes about certain kinds of black people provided him with all the mental ammunition he needed to justify the use of deadly force against a group of people he didn't even know on a crowded subway train.[22]

Fortunately for our society, particularly for those of us who sometimes have to rely on mass transit, few of us are motivated by our negative racial stereotypes to the degree that we feel the need to take the same kind of violent, sociopathic action that the subway vigilante did. But if we grew up just about anywhere in America, we have all been exposed, from our earliest childhood on, to innumerable negative racial stereotypes and to the racist attitudes and beliefs they reflect and reinforce. They are powerful, motivating, and still-vital forces in our individual and collective lives, and they affect every one of us in many diverse, aversive, and insidious ways. As Americans, all of us have been exposed to various forms of what Armour calls "Negrophobia," even if we think we aren't really racist or prejudiced toward blacks in our own daily lives.

A Test for Negrophobia

It is important at this point to acknowledge that the hostile stereotypes we're talking about are not easy to change or to eradicate from our individual or collective cultural consciousness. Once they've insinuated themselves into our thought processes, they tend to stay there for a long time, whether we realize it or not. For one thing, as has already been mentioned, the stereotypes are constantly being reinforced in our racial imaginations through the mass media and other socializing agents. This is one reason why a change in our beliefs doesn't necessarily translate to getting rid of our habitual responses to well-learned stereotypes.[23] We are constantly being stimulated to respond to the stereotypes and racist imagery we carry around in our heads. Contemporary rap and hip-hop artists, for example, rely on this stimulus to provoke a predictable type of mental and emotional response. They incessantly repeat the "n" word in their songs or call themselves "N.W.A." or maintain that they come by their use of rap's language of racism "honestly," having "long been associated with African-American friends, neighbors and mentors."

It's not hard to understand, therefore, how these habitual, unthinking responses to a racial stereotype can continue in an individual long after that person has tried to renounce the racist attitudes reflected by the stereotype. Racist beliefs, perspectives, and stereotypes find their ways into our racial imaginations at such an early age that our unconscious, uncontrolled responses to them can be likened to something done without much conscious thought, almost like a kind of bad habit; "an action that has been done many times and has become automatic."[24] From this perspective, our automatic response to a negative racial stereotype can be seen as a kind of *very* bad habit that persists even though we might have long ago renounced any type of racial prejudice in our life. In other words, we may not be prejudiced, but that doesn't mean we aren't at least somewhat habitually racist in terms of the types of stereotypes that are lurking inside of our head, like a loaded weapon, primed and ready to go off at any moment. We may not even be aware of carrying the stereotype around until we experience something that triggers a stereotype-congruent response. We laugh at the *Far Side* cartoon because we think we get it, or we fire the gun in that subway car because we are subway vigilantes who think we know what those violence-prone individuals are about to do. From this perspective we are not just trapped in our minds by the history of racism and the violent legacy of white racial dictatorship in America. We are unavoidably condemned to repeat that history simply by living in a society with a stereotype-ridden, self-perpetuating, all-pervasive, habit-forming racialized cultural belief system. We may all be sociopathic racial profilers, subway vigilantes even, to one degree or another, and not even know it.

This realization that we may be almost hopelessly trapped in these bad habits of thought and action may seem rather depressing. It also seems contrary to what most of us have been taught to believe about our capacity as individuals to escape and transcend deeply entrenched social conventions and attitudes. That is why, most researchers tell us, attacking this type of hostile racist attitude is a particularly daunting challenge. As Peggy Davis has written, "it is difficult to change an attitude that is unacknowledged."[25]

So for all you empiricists out there who say, "Show me I'm a racial profiler and don't know it," here's a quick self-test I've designed and administered to my Indian law students to help them see whether they have been unconsciously influenced by racist stereotypes perpetuated against black people. This test is designed to show whether you have been afflicted with one of the more pervasive and widespread forms of Negrophobia without even knowing it.

Imagine for a moment what your reaction might be if you encountered a young black male on a lonely urban street late at night. Imagine that he's wearing a black stocking cap, gold chains and big jewelry, really dark sunglasses in the middle of the night, and he's making funny signs with his fingers. You know the type: He looks just like a violence-prone, malevolent black male youth to you.

Now imagine that this very threatening black-looking individual walks directly up to you and asks for change for a dollar to call a cab so he can get home. What would your reaction be: (1) To help him gladly by pulling out your wallet and giving him a dollar, in fact, make it two?

(2) To pull out your wallet, give him the whole damn thing, and run screaming down the street? (3) To wish you'd gotten off that street long before some violence-prone black guy ever got that close to you? (4) To try to be very alert in this type of situation?

Now ask yourself what your reaction would be if an elderly white woman came up to you in the exact same situation. Would your answer be anything like 2 or 3? Of course not. What about 4? What would you try to be "alert" to in this situation? A little old white lady walking up to you on the street? What in the world could she do to you? She probably wants you to protect her from that violence-prone black male youth coming up the block toward both of you at this very instant.

If you are at all like most of my students, the answers you honestly give to these two questions should help you see that you are probably suffering, even if just a little bit, from a pervasive and persistent form of Negrophobia. Like the subway vigilante and just about everyone else in America, you've been exposed to the language of racism and the negative stereotypes and images of blacks that have existed in this country since the days of slavery, lynchings, and Jim Crow. That language and those stereotypes belong to all of us as part of our history and cultural heritage. You come by your *Negrophobia,* in other words, "honestly."

Don't take my diagnosis of your Negrophobia too badly. If indeed you are suffering from this widespread affliction, you can take comfort in the fact that just about everybody in America seems to suffer from what most people feel is, to use Armour's term, "reasonable racism" toward black male youths.[26] Even the Reverend Jesse Jackson once admitted to being infected by this pervasive form of Negrophobia. The stereotype of the violent black youth, he once confessed, haunted the streets and back alleyways of his own American-born and -bred racial imagination.[27] If Jesse Jackson suffers from this affliction, then certainly you can't be blamed for having it too. Everybody in America has Negrophobia in one form or another.

It may be true today that people of goodwill of every color, race, and creed in a Benetton-imagined, multicultural, fetishized, Mall-of-America racial fantasy world can all agree that the familiar negative racial stereotypes and racist attitudes of the past are outmoded, irrelevant, and even gauche approaches to the complex problems of race relations in the United States today. This does not mean, however, that the history, culture, and legacy of racism, discrimination, and prejudice they have helped to engender and reinforce in our past will ever completely vanish from our society in the future. No matter how outdated these antiquated, embarrassing racial stereotypes might be, they retain a pervasive and persistent present-day influence on our culture, on our daily lives, and on the way we perceive others in our world. They are still a vital part of our national heritage.

A recognition of our own lingering Negrophobic attitudes is a first step toward understanding the intense, interconnected relationships among long-established traditions of negative racial stereotyping, the racist belief systems they reflect, and the persistent patterns of racial discrimination they might well still be capable of generating, perpetuating, and entrenching. This recognition should in turn help us realize the possibility that blacks, as a racial minority, probably encounter and contend with these same types of complex racial relationships every day. Many black Americans, in fact, say that they do confront them every day as part of the constructed and deconstructed reality of their lives.[28] Not only is being stereotyped embarrassing, they say, it can actually work to murder the spirit: Just imagine how it would feel if a little white child looked down into the baby carriage you were pushing and shouted out for all the world to hear, "Look Mom, a baby maid."

Seen an Arab at an Airport Lately?

It doesn't take a lot of effort to find that there are some still-very-powerful, widely dispersed languages of racism at work in America today and that blacks aren't the only minority group who are subjected to negative, spirit-murdering stereotypes. Just as there is a language of negative stereotypes, images, and tales about blacks, for instance, so too are there specifically identifiable and uniquely inflected languages of racism focused upon other discrete racial minority groups in America.

In our twenty-first-century, post-9/11 world, airports signify a place in the American racial imagination where stereotypes and images of certain people are more closely observed than ever before in our history as a nation. We find ourselves tested by our stereotypes and images of alien others in the world in ways that we as a society and as individuals never wanted to imagine were possible before.

Imagine for one moment seeing a solitary young man of Middle Eastern ancestry—an "Arab," if you prefer—at an airport. Make sure to put a beard on him, definitely give him an "accent," and put some sandals on him too. Now imagine your own reactions if this "Arab-looking" guy hanging around at the airport started boarding the same plane as you. Wouldn't you be literally *terrorized* by the thought of getting on that flight with someone who looks like he might be an Islamic terrorist suicide bomber?

It's unfortunate but true that the very idea of seeing an "Arab" at an airport these days can evoke this type of negative racial stereotype in the minds of many Americans. Because of the undeniable way the world has changed for the worse post-9/11, we may even feel that our reaction to the idea of an Arab at an airport is very "reasonable," just as Negrophobia is reasonable for most people who walk alone on city streets late at night. For whatever reasons, we've developed a very bad case of Islamophobia as part of our contemporary American racial imagination.

We can take some comfort in the fact that it's not really all our fault. We've been conditioned by society and the world as we know it to act in this hostile, aversive way toward people who happen to look like Arabs, particularly at an airport. We've been exposed to one of the longest-established traditions of negative racial stereotyping in the West, represented in the virulent language of racism that emerges out of a millennium of violent encounters and cultural conflict with the Arab-speaking world. Going all the way back to the Crusades of the Middle Ages, the organizing fear of the "Arab" as an irrational, murdering other has driven the West's colonial imagination totally crazy at times.[29] For all its seeming potency and contemporary urgency, the racial mythology of the Arab as conspiring terrorist assassin, as suicidal religious zealot, as lawless infidel blinded by fanatical hatred and resentment toward the West and all for which it stands, possesses an ancient genealogy, one that still resonates deeply as part of the cultural heritage and history of the Western colonial imagination. In the West's millennium-long, violent confrontation with the Islamic world, the followers of the Prophet Muhammad have been tirelessly stereotyped as infidels, as alien, impenetrable, irrational, religious fanatics.[30]

For all its contemporary urgency, it is not too difficult to recognize that the fearful racial fantasy of the Arab as Islamic terrorist bomber as it exists today in America's post-9/11 racial imagination perpetuates, reinforces, and feeds off the West's thousand-year history of fundamental, irreconcilable conflict with Islam in the East. The long-established stereotype of the Arab as Islamic terrorist assassin, a stereotype regenerated and reenergized by the horrible events of 9/11, draws a good deal of its raw emotional power from the continuing potency and force of the narrative and literary traditions of what Edward Said famously labeled "Orientalism"[31] in the present-day Western colonial imagination. The Reverend Jerry Falwell felt he had to apologize for calling the Prophet Muhammad, the founder of Islam, a "terrorist," but he was really only apologizing for engaging in the same bad habit that most Americans seem to have fallen into whenever they go to the airport, without being polite or particularly smart enough to keep his Islamophobia to himself.[32]

Conclusion

One lesson that we learn from our own reactions to the idea of encountering an Arab at an airport, and from our other discoveries about the pervasiveness of certain languages of racism in America, is that in a globalized world and society, we are always being subjected to new or rehabilitated versions of long-established negative racial stereotypes and imagery that are integral and organizing parts of our history and cultural heritage. In these historically and culturally charged tellings and retellings, the old languages and stereotypes are allowed to evolve, mutate, and sometimes even lie dormant until suitably retranslated and revived for renewed circulation in a more contemporary idiom, say for example, at the airport, on the radio, walking through the park, in the confessions of a black civil rights leader, in the babbling idiocies of a fundamentalist TV evangelist or, as is discussed in the next chapter, in a number of leading minority rights decisions of the U.S. Supreme Court.[33]

2

The Supreme Court and
the Legal History of Racism in America

The Founders Made Him Do It: The Language of Racism Perpetuated
by Chief Justice Taney in the Infamous *Dred Scott* Decision

Given the pervasiveness and force of certain long-established languages of racism in our history, no one should be too surprised to discover their use in many of the Supreme Court's most important decisions on minority rights.[1] The problem comes when the Court as an institution perpetuates and sanctions a language of racism and its precepts of racial inferiority against a particular group as a constitutive part of the Court's authoritative precedent.[2] By issuing a landmark decision using this type of language, the Court gives racism an authoritative, binding legal meaning in our legal system. The perceived inferiority of that group in our society has been given the sanction of law in the legal history of racism in America.

One of the most notoriously reviled examples of the Court's giving legal sanction to a language of racism is found in Chief Justice Roger Taney's "infamous"[3] 1856 majority opinion for the Court in *Dred Scott v. Sanford*. The *Dred Scott* decision denied all rights of federal citizenship to "negroes of the African race" under the Constitution and laws of the United States. Taney based his majority opinion on his stated belief that blacks had been regarded by the Founding Fathers as "a subordinate and inferior class of beings, who had been subjugated by the dominant race." They were simply "not intended" by the Founders, he wrote, to be included "under the word 'citizens' in the Constitution." Because of this interpretation of the Founding Fathers' original intent regarding "negroes," Taney's opinion for the Court held that Dred Scott, as a "negro," "can therefore claim none of the rights and privileges which that instrument provides for and secures to citizens of the United States."[4]

Most Americans today would readily agree that *Dred Scott* was an "infamous" decision, perhaps the most disgracefully racist opinion ever issued by the Supreme Court. The Court's holding that a "negro" could not become "a member of the political community formed and brought into existence by the Constitution of the United States"[5] is generally regarded by historians as having accelerated the United States along the disastrous path that ultimately led the country into Civil War.[6]

As a legal precedent, the *Dred Scott* decision has suffered a harsh fate. Overturned in effect by a bloody civil war and a victorious Union's constitutional amendment process, Supreme Court justices never cite it as an authority anymore except as a prime example of a very *bad* precedent.[7] *Dred Scott,* most Americans would agree, perpetuated a hostile form of racist reasoning, imagery, and apocrypha and a way of talking about blacks that is outmoded, unenlightened, and unreflective of the way that Americans, particularly Americans who are justices of the Supreme Court, ought to be talking about any group of people in the United States today.

Interestingly enough, Taney's opinion for the Court in *Dred Scott* gives the impression that Taney himself felt very much the same way at the time he handed down his decision in 1856. The Founders' anachronistic eighteenth-century views on "the African race," Taney explained in *Dred Scott,* made him do it. "It is difficult at this day to realize the state of public opinion in relation to that unfortunate race, which prevailed in the civilized and enlightened portions of the world at the time of the Declaration of Independence, and when the Constitution of the United States was framed and adopted," Taney wrote. But the Court nonetheless recognized the fact that African slaves had been regarded by the Founders as possessing "no rights or privileges but such as those who held the power and the Government might choose to grant them." As the chief justice described the plight of the African race "at that time":

> They had for more than a century before been regarded as beings of an inferior order, and altogether unfit to associate with the white race, either in social or political relations; and so far inferior, that they had no rights which the white man was bound to respect; and that the negro might justly and lawfully be reduced to slavery for his benefit.[8]

Given the prevalence of such hostile racial attitudes in America during the Founding era, it would have been impossible for the Court, at least according to Taney's nineteenth-century antebellum form of racial reasoning in *Dred Scott,* to hold that the Founders could have intended that the descendants of African slaves might ever be entitled to the rights of citizenship. In other words, Taney believed that the Supreme Court was required to hold that the descendants of African slaves had no rights or status as citizens in 1856 because of the continuing legal force of the Founders' antiquated eighteenth-century racial perspective and overt use of a supposedly discredited language of racism in talking and thinking about the rights of the "negro." As Taney himself explained:

> He was bought and sold, and treated as an ordinary article of merchandise and traffic, whenever a profit could be made by it. This opinion was at that time fixed and universal in the civilized portion of the white race. It was regarded as an axiom in morals as well as politics, which no one thought of disputing, or supposed to be opened to dispute; and men in every grade and position in society daily and habitually acted upon it in their private pursuits, as well as in matters of public concern, without for a moment doubting the correctness of this opinion.[9]

The Court's decision in *Dred Scott* teaches us an important lesson: A legal opinion issued by a particular justice can always declare that a language of racism and accompanying negative stereotypes are all an "unfortunate" part of an irrational, outmoded, and rejected legacy of a less-enlightened era. Fortunately, as the "enlightened" beings the justices' life tenure suggests they are, the justices themselves don't speak or think like that anymore, or so they tell us in their opinions.[10] But as

Taney's opinion in *Dred Scott* illustrates, such self-congratulatory acts of judicial self-absolution do not necessarily deter the Court from per-petuating the legal force of long-established traditions of racial stereo-typing. In fact, if a majority of the justices believe that the Founders themselves "habitually acted upon" the racial perspective and beliefs re-flected in that supposedly outdated language of racism, the Court really, they say, has no choice in the matter. When it comes to figuring out a particular group's rights under the Constitution and laws of the United States, sometimes, unfortunately, they will tell us, the Court has to rule as the Founders would have wanted. They will usually say all this with great subtlety and even compassion and sometimes even sincere regret, but ultimately what they are telling us is that *the Founders made them do it*. In such cases, as we have explained (see chapter 1), following the Founder's hostile exclusionary intent can be regarded as a kind of very bad habit that the justices have from time to time displayed in the Supreme Court's leading decisions on minority rights.

People of Violence: The Jurispathic Function of a Language of Racism When Used by the Justices of the Supreme Court

One of the twentieth century's most influential legal scholars, Robert Cover, writing on the inseparable relation between law and the nar-ratives "that locate and give it meaning," stressed the importance of a cultural process that he called "jurisgenesis"—the creation of legal meaning. The act of jurisgenesis, Cover explained, always takes place "through an essentially cultural medium":

> For every constitution there is an epic, for each decalogue a scripture.
> Once understood in the context of the narratives that give it meaning,
> law becomes not merely a system of rules, but a world in which we live.[11]

Cover's point is that the creation of legal meaning is a collective, social enterprise. Many groups in a society, bound by ties of religion, fellowship, or ideological commitment, will from time to time, or even more constantly, engage in the jurisgenerative process.

As Cover points out, there are many types of dynamic, law-creating jurisgenerative communities at work in a society such as ours. The state—of which the justices of the Supreme Court are a very important, constituent part under the U.S. system of government—obviously influences this jurisgenerative process of law creation. The justices in fact hold tremendous power over this process by exercising the state's privilege of selecting and enforcing one particular narrative, one singular interpretation, as the law of the land. But neither the state nor its justices can claim an exclusive monopoly over the process of creating legal meaning through creative group acts of jurisgenesis. Some groups will declare themselves outside the law and deny the monopolizing efforts of the state and the Court over the control of all forms of legal meaning. Some groups, in fact, will defy the state and the justices and engage in their own creative, law-making acts of jurisgenesis.

In our society, it is ultimately the justices of the Supreme Court, as Cover explains, who are recognized by the state as exercising its principal claim to authoritative interpretation and final jurisgenerative authority. It is the justices who are backed by the ultimate willingness of the United States to use violence to enforce the Supreme Court's view of what the law of the land is and will be against any outlaw group or its individual members. This is why, Cover charges, judges in general and the justices of the Supreme Court most especially "are people of violence. Because of the violence they command, judges characteristically do not create law, but kill it." Cover labels this killing of non-state-centered law the justices' "jurispathic" function: "Confronting the luxuriant growth of a hundred legal traditions, they assert that *this one* is law and destroy or try to destroy the rest."[12]

In exercising their destructive jurispathic function in our legal system, the justices of the Court, through their "implicit claim to authoritative interpretation," can and often do play a critical role in sanctioning and perpetuating racism against certain groups. The stereotypes or images that the Court has thus legitimated and expanded can now be used to legally justify a rights-denying, jurispathic form of racism against those groups. As Cover explains this jurispathic function, "[a] community's acquiescence in or accommodation to the judge's interpretation reinforces the hermeneutic process offered by the judge and extends, in one way or another, its social range."[13] In other words, the justices have the legal authority in our society to tell people that it's not only reasonable to act in a racially discriminatory and hostile way, it's perfectly legal as well.

One of the important lessons taught by a case like *Dred Scott* is that when the justices rely on a tradition of negative stereotyping in decisions interpreting a particular group's rights in America, their decision creates a lawful precedent giving legal meaning and sanction to that language of racism and perpetuates it in a particularly forceful way, jurispathically. In denying validity to any competing legal tradition or way of talking about that group's rights, the Supreme Court commits the violence of the state to enforcing its jurispathic powers of authoritative interpretation over that minority group and its own jurisgenerative aspirations. The justices' *legalization of racism* against that group, by virtue of the Court's interpretive authority, in effect, becomes both reasonable and lawful under the Constitution and laws of the United States. And so long as the rest of the society accepts, acquiesces in, or simply accommodates itself to the language of racism used by the Court to justify its decision, there is no reason to expect that the justices themselves will feel the least bit discomforted in repeating and reinforcing such a language. A tradition of negative racial stereotyping then takes on a life of its own, functioning jurispathically, like a loaded weapon aimed at destroying the rights of any minority group targeted by a judicially validated language of racism.

"Like a Loaded Weapon": The Language of Racism Used in the Supreme Court's *Korematsu* Decision

Dred Scott teaches us never to underestimate the rights-destroying, jurispathic power of a long-established language of racism once validated and perpetuated by a decision of the Supreme Court. The pernicious effects of the Court's use of such a language can unleash incredibly destructive forces in a society like ours, with its deeply entrenched history of racial hostility and overt discrimination. The sanction of law given to such a language in the Court's opinion, as the *Dred Scott* decision shows, can become a rallying point for justifying the perpetuation of an ever-expanding and infamously regarded form of white racial dictatorship.

There is a second important aspect to the rights-destroying jurispathic power possessed by the stereotypes perpetuated by Supreme Court decisions. The destructive force generated by a language of racism that has been embedded in a binding precedent in the law can influence and even control future decisions of the Court. Once the Court has perpetuated a tradition of stereotyping in a decision on a particular group's rights, this single judicial act of racial profiling can take on a life of its own. The Court's sanctioning of a language of racism can be infinitely magnified by the insidious, metastasizing force of the doctrine of stare decisis—that is, the doctrine, accepted by our courts, that like cases should be decided alike.[14]

Stare decisis, by its very nature, represents a persistent danger for the protection of minority rights in our legal system, threatening to expand the original principle of racial discrimination justified by a particular legal precedent to new purposes and applications. Even without possessing a hostile intent toward any particular minority group, a judge who feels bound to enforce prior precedents because of the doctrine of stare decisis can perpetuate, in the most subtle of fashions, a system of racial inequality. Even a judge who is personally committed to think about and decide cases in a "color-blind" way can reinforce the stigma of racial inferiority attached to members of certain groups simply by relying on prior precedents seemingly on point.[15] The insistence on continuing fidelity to past judicial precedents, in fact, can be seen at work again and again as a highly destructive force in the history of the Supreme Court's legalization of racism against certain minority groups in the United States.

The destructive force of a legalized principle of racial discrimination working in combination with stare decisis is powerfully illustrated by the Court's notorious 1944 *Korematsu v. United States* decision. The six-person majority opinion in *Korematsu,* written by Justice Hugo Black, upheld the constitutionality of the forced exclusion and military imprisonment of "all alien Japanese and persons of Japanese ancestry" from the entire West Coast area during World War II.[16] By a 1942 statute, passed within months of the Japanese surprise attack on Pearl Harbor, Congress had given the military broad wartime powers to deal with, in the Court's words, the "menace to the national defense and safety" represented by the resident Japanese population in the western United States.[17] The military interpreted these powers as giving them the authority to establish and administer internment camps for those of Japanese ancestry in America while the war continued.

The military orders upheld by the Court in *Korematsu* under the war powers clauses of the Constitution were quite broad, covering "all of California, Washington, Oregon, Idaho, Montana, Nevada, and Utah, and the southern portion of Arizona."[18] But, as Black's majority opinion in *Korematsu* explained, the Court had already upheld a curfew order imposed on all those of Japanese ancestry on the West Coast under this same 1942 act in *Hirabayashi v. United States.*[19] Given the legal precedent established by that prior decision, the Court majority felt bound under the principle of stare decisis to uphold the exclusion orders involved in *Korematsu:*

> Here, as in the *Hirabayashi* case, we cannot reject as unfounded the judgment of the military authorities and of Congress that there were disloyal members of that population, whose number and strength could not be precisely and quickly ascertained. We cannot say that the war-making branches of the Government did not have ground for believing that in a critical hour such persons could not readily be isolated and separately dealt with, and constituted a menace to the national defense and safety, which demanded that prompt and adequate measures be taken to guard against it.[20]

Korematsu's holding that under the Constitution the U.S. government was permitted to single out members of certain minority groups so that they could be "isolated and separately dealt with" by the military generated three strongly voiced and vigorous dissents. Each of the dissenters, Justices Owen Roberts, Frank Murphy, and Robert H. Jackson, wrote separately in explaining his profound disagreement with his colleagues in the majority.

Roberts's methodical dissenting opinion, appearing first among the trilogy of dissents, attacked the underlying logic of the two military exclusion orders "given sanction by the Act of Congress." These orders formed the basis of Fred Korematsu's arrest and conviction for remaining in a "military area" from which persons of Japanese ancestry had been excluded, yet as Roberts's dissent remarked, "The earlier of those orders made him a criminal if he left the zone in which he resided; the later made him a criminal if he did not leave." Summing up the sum and substance of Korematsu's truly Kafkaesque inside/outside dilemma, Roberts's dissent made the following procedural due process argument against the constitutionality of the conflicting military orders:

> I had supposed that if a citizen was constrained by two laws, or two orders having the force of law, and obedience to one would violate the other, to punish him for violation of either would deny him due

process of law. And I had supposed that under these circumstances a conviction for violating one of the orders cannot stand.[21]

At this point in his dissent, Roberts was ready to tell everyone exactly what he thought of the military's conflicting orders in this case: "The two conflicting orders, one which commanded him to stay and the other which commanded him to go, were nothing but a cleverly devised trap to accomplish the real purpose of the military authority, which was to lock him up in a concentration camp."[22]

Playing the Nazi card against the U.S. military commanders charged with maintaining homeland security for the entire West Coast of the United States wasn't enough for Roberts. After accusing the government of acting basically like the fascists the country was then fighting in World War II, he got personal and attacked the justices in the majority for their casuistic complicity and lack of judicial backbone in dealing with the real issues involved in *Korematsu:* "Why should we set up a fragmentary and artificial situation instead of addressing ourselves to the actualities of the case?"[23]

As if perfectly on cue, Justice Murphy's following dissent picked up precisely where Justice Roberts had left off, with the disturbing "actualities of the case." Murphy specifically addressed what he called the "utterly revolting" form of racism that had led to the military orders in *Korematsu.* As he stated in his dissent:

This exclusion of "all persons of Japanese ancestry, both alien and non-alien," from the Pacific Coast area on a plea of military necessity in the absence of martial law ought not to be approved. Such exclusion goes over "the very brink of Constitutional power" and falls into the ugly abyss of racism.[24]

Murphy's dissenting opinion sought to demonstrate that the exclusion "of all persons with Japanese blood in their veins" rested solely upon the racist assumption "that all persons of Japanese ancestry may have a dangerous tendency to commit sabotage and espionage and to aid our Japanese enemy in other ways." Viewing the flimsy evidence relied on by the military authorities, however, Murphy found it difficult to believe that reason, logic, or experience could be marshaled in support of such an assumption or of applying it to the entire Japanese population in the western United States:

That this forced exclusion was the result in good measure of this erroneous assumption of racial guilt rather than bona fide military necessity is evidenced by the Commanding General's Final Report on the evacuation from the Pacific Coast area. In it he refers to all individuals of Japanese descent as "subversive," as belonging to "an enemy race" whose "racial strains are undiluted," and as constituting "over 112,000 potential enemies . . . at large today" along the Pacific Coast.[25]

Murphy charged that the Commanding General's Final Report, authored by Lt. Gen. John L. DeWitt, rested "mainly upon questionable racial and sociological grounds not ordinarily within the realm of expert military judgment." The general's report described the Japanese as "a large, unassimilated, tightly knit racial group, bound to an enemy nation by strong ties of race, culture, custom and religion." They were given to "emperor worshiping ceremonies" and clung tenaciously to their "dual citizenship." Japanese language schools and allegedly pro-Japanese organizations were also cited by the general, Murphy tells us, as compelling evidence of possible "group disloyalty"[26] instead of simply the things Japanese people might be expected to do as part of their everyday, legally segregated lives in pre–World War II American society.

Murphy's dissent also cited General DeWitt's 1943 testimony, given in San Francisco before the House Naval Affairs Subcommittee to Investigate Congested Areas, as further evidence of his hopelessly bigoted attitude toward those of Japanese ancestry:

I don't want any of them [persons of Japanese ancestry] here. They are a dangerous element. There is no way to determine their loyalty. The west coast contains too many vital installations essential to the defense of the country to allow any Japanese on this coast. . . . The danger of the Japanese was, and is now—if they are permitted to come back—espionage and sabotage. It makes no difference whether he is an American citizen, he is still a Japanese. American citizenship does not necessarily determine loyalty. . . . But we must worry about the Japanese all the time until he is wiped off the map. Sabotage and espionage will make problems as long as he is allowed in this area.[27]

As Murphy noted, however, the general's views could not be said to represent a calm or detached scholarly reflection on the socioeconomic and geographic realities of the Japanese situation in the United States. Several academic studies cited by Murphy supported the more likely sociological hypothesis that failure of the Japanese to assimilate in the United States was "largely the result of certain social customs and laws of the American general public" that blatantly discriminated against those of Japanese ancestry. There had been, in other words, a long-established tradition of racial discrimination and hostile negative stereotyping directed against those of Japanese ancestry in the United States,[28] sanctioned by the laws and customs of the dominant white society in America.

Murphy also closely examined the sociological evidence regarding the general's assertion that "many of these individuals deliberately resided 'adjacent to strategic points,' thus enabling them 'to carry into execution a tremendous program of sabotage on a mass scale should any considerable number of them have been inclined to do so.'" As Murphy explained, the general's limited view of the situation on the West Coast ignored the fact that the main geographic patterns of Japanese population settlement had been "fixed many years ago":[29]

> Limited occupational outlets and social pressures encouraged their
> concentration near their initial points of entry on the Pacific Coast.
> That these points may now be near certain strategic military and
> industrial areas is no proof of a diabolical purpose on the part of
> Japanese Americans.[30]

In other words, it was the long-established practice of racial discrimination by the majority society against those of Japanese ancestry, and not the presumed inherent subversiveness of the Japanese, that better explained the contemporary settlement patterns of people of Japanese ancestry on the West Coast. The general's overtly expressed racial hostility to the Japanese, reflected in his repeated and persistent use of negative racial stereotypes and racist imagery to justify his opinions and actions, obscured, for him at least, the larger social realities of the constrained and demarcated lives lived by people of Japanese ancestry in the United States. The cultural and ethnic geography and settlement patterns of the West Coast reflected the powerful social forces of racism and a well-established tradition of hostile negative racial stereotyping directed against those of Japanese ancestry by the dominant society in this country. Where the Japanese lived, in other words, had nothing to do with Japanese disloyalty to the nation. Rather, it had to do with racism, prejudice, and the deficient performance over the years of the American legal system, the Supreme Court in particular, in protecting the rights of Japanese people under the Constitution and laws of the United States.[31]

As if to provide final, definitive evidence of the "utterly revolting" racial prejudice, bigotry, and animus evidenced by the general, Murphy pointed to DeWitt's "amazing" statement to Congress "that as of February 14, 1942, the very fact that no sabotage has taken place to date is a disturbing and confirming indication that such action will be taken." As Murphy noted, "apparently in the minds of the military leaders, there was no way that the Japanese Americans could escape the suspicion of sabotage."[32]

Murphy's dissent concluded with a stirring condemnation of the government's bogus justifications for the exclusion orders upheld by the *Korematsu* majority. They amounted, in his opinion, to little more than "an accumulation of much of the misinformation, half-truths and insinuations that for years have been directed against Japanese Americans by people with racial and economic prejudices—the same people who have been among the foremost advocates of the evacuation." And as Roberts had done in his dissent (see above), Murphy, too, played the Nazi card in concluding his rejection of the legalized principle of racial discrimination upheld by the majority in *Korematsu*. The U.S. government, he said, was using the same type of racist reasoning to support the abhorrent and despicable treatment of a minority group "that was being used by the dictatorial tyrannies which this nation is now pledged to destroy." For the Court itself to give constitutional sanction to this pernicious form of negative racial stereotyping, wrote Murphy, "is to adopt one of the cruelest of the rationales used by our enemies to destroy the dignity of the individual and to encourage and open the door to discriminatory actions against other minority groups in the passions of tomorrow." He therefore strongly dissented from what he called "this legalization of racism," represented by the military exclusion orders applying to all those of Japanese ancestry on the West Coast. "Racial discrimination in any form and in any degree has no justifiable part whatever in our democratic way of life. It is unattractive in any setting but it is utterly revolting among a free people who have embraced the principles set forth in the Constitution of the United States."[33]

With Roberts having destroyed the underlying constitutional logic of the government's case on procedural due process grounds and Murphy having revealed the "utterly revolting" and unconstitutional racist reasoning and stereotypes that the military had used to justify the exclusion orders, Justice Jackson focused his oft-quoted dissenting opinion, the final one of the trio of dissents to the majority's decision in *Korematsu,* upon the larger set of constitutional values that were threatened by the Court's holding in the case.[34] In a legal system that followed the principle of stare decisis, the majority's decision in *Korematsu,* in Jackson's opinion, set a very bad precedent.

The military order justifying Korematsu's exclusion and detention, Jackson explained, no matter how unconstitutional, was unlikely to last longer than the military emergency prompting it. "But once a judicial opinion rationalizes such an order to show that it conforms to the Constitution, or rather rationalizes the Constitution to show that the Constitution sanctions such an order," he wrote, "the Court for all time has validated the principle of racial discrimination." And that act of judicial validation, he warned, held very dangerous consequences for minority rights under the Constitution and laws of the United States. For the principle validated in that opinion now "lies about like a loaded weapon ready for the hand of any authority that can bring forward a plausible claim of an urgent need. Every repetition imbeds that principle more deeply in our law and thinking and expands it to new purposes."[35]

Jackson wasn't done yet. Reminding his brethren in the majority of Judge Benjamin Cardozo's trenchant observation on the nature of the judicial process and "the tendency of a principle to expand itself to the limit of its logic,"[36] Jackson described what happens when the Supreme Court reviews and approves a principle of racial discrimination as the doctrine of the Constitution: "There it has a generative power of its own, and all that it creates will be in its own image."[37]

Given its numerous intersections with issues of minority rights in a time of war, protection of homeland and national security, and the scope of the war-making powers assigned to the Congress and the executive branch under the Constitution, the Supreme Court's decision in *Korematsu* represents a singularly intense moment of cultural reflection and jurisprudential self-consciousness.[38] Like the *Dred Scott* decision, *Korematsu* focuses our critical attention on the dangerous jurispathic force of a language of racism in American history, most especially when that language is perpetuated and reinforced in a Supreme Court decision on minority rights. Because of the doctrine of stare decisis, that rights-destroying precedent, as Jackson reminds us in dissent, "lies about like a loaded weapon ready for the hand of any authority that can bring forward a plausible claim of an urgent need."

Part II

"Signs Taken for Wonders":
The Nineteenth-Century Supreme Court
and Indian Rights

> Anund pointed to the name of Jesus, and asked, "Who is that?" "That is God! He gave us this book."—"Where did you obtain it?" "An Angel from heaven gave it to us, at Hurdwar fair."—"An Angel?" "Yes, to us he was God's Angel: but he was a man, a learned Pundit."
>
> —HOMI K. BHABHA, "SIGNS TAKEN FOR WONDERS"

As Michael Omi and Howard Winant have written, "For most of its existence both as a European colony and as an independent nation, the U.S. was a *racial dictatorship*." Omi and Winant define this racial dictatorship as a coercive form of racial rule by whites who sought to legally eliminate all nonwhites from the sphere of political and civil society in the United States. The presumed racial inferiority and incompatibility of these nonwhite "others" disqualified them from full and equal participation in the superior form of civilization established for the enjoyment of the white race by the Constitution and laws of the United States.[1]

Supreme Court decisions like *Dred Scott* and *Korematsu* show us two distinct forms of this uniquely American-style, constitutionally sanctioned white racial dictatorship. Taken together, these two well-known examples of the Court's jurispathic perpetuation of long-established stereotypes can teach us a number of important lessons about the pernicious, insidious effects of such deeply entrenched racist attitudes on our legal system. These lessons extend well beyond the particular historical confines of these two decisions. They apply with equal force to and are highly relevant in understanding the legal history of racism and the forms of white racial dictatorship that have been sanctioned by the justices of the Supreme Court. They teach us the basic principle that a language of racism validated and sanctioned by the justices possesses an organizing and continuing generative power of its own. That the justices have such jurispathic, rights-destroying power and sovereignty explains why, whenever the dominant society in the United States has sought to subjugate or suppress a particular minority group, the Court has inevitably been called on to play the critical legitimating role of legalizing the principle of racial discrimination necessary to achieve such goals. For the justices alone wield the final jurispathic authority to uphold and then perpetuate a language of racism as binding precedent in our legal system, backed by the violence of the state.

Of course, other minority groups in this country besides blacks and people of Japanese ancestry have been denied their basic human rights by the Supreme Court's reliance on a legally sanctioned language of racism to uphold various forms of racial discrimination in the United States. Throughout the nineteenth century, the Court perpetuated a long-established language of racism in America, a language of Indian savagery, in its decisions upholding the dominant white society's racial dictatorship over Indian tribes.

3

"The Savage as the Wolf": The Founders' Language of Indian Savagery

A long-established language of racism that speaks of the American Indian as an uncivilized, lawless, and warlike savage[1] can be found at work throughout the leading Indian law decisions of the nineteenth-century U.S. Supreme Court. This judicial language of Indian savagery traces its origins and descent in the Western colonial imagination to ancient Greek and Roman myths of warlike, barbarian tribes and biblical accounts of wild men cursed by God. Renaissance-era travel narratives built upon this language of primitive human savagery to describe the newly "discovered" lands and "strange," alien peoples of the New World, called "Indians" by Europeans. Enlightenment-era philosophical constructions of the "state of nature," postulated by such theorists as Hugo Grotius, Thomas Hobbes, and John Locke, used the American Indian as the paradigm example of humanity in its pure, unadulterated savage state. The sociological theorizations on the "four stages" of human society (primitive, pastoral, agricultural, and commercial) proposed by the baron de Montesquieu and Adam Smith codified, as a constitutive part of the Western colonial imagination, this widely disseminated belief in the Indian's essential savage identity.

The ready identification of the Indian as incommensurable other resolved a number of acute problems for the West's religious traditions, which uniformly preached the unity of all humankind, and for its project of colonization of the New World, which required a justification for its conquests of other peoples' lands. As Omi and Winant explain, conquest of the American Indian "was the first—and given the dramatic nature, perhaps the greatest—racial formation project":

> [T]he "discovery signaled a break from the previous proto-racial awareness by which Europeans contemplated its "Others" in a relatively disorganized fashion. In other words, the "conquest of America" was not simply an epochal historical event—however unparalleled in its importance. It was also the advent of a consolidated social structure of exploitation, appropriation, domination. Its representation first in religious terms, but soon enough in scientific and political ones, initiated modern racial awareness.[2]

In inaugurating this unique form of European racial consciousness, the idea of the Indian as incommensurable, savage other helped constitute a new, imperial structure, organized around the struggle between civilization and barbarism in the Western colonial imagination.[3]

The significance of the "conquest of America" therefore extends far beyond the racial metes and bounds of the Western Hemisphere. The language of Indian savagery generated out of that colonial encounter defined the racial precepts of the Western colonial imagination, with savage peoples like the American Indian at the bottom of the stages of civilization and colonizing Christian Europeans at the top. As the trajectory of European imperialism ranged beyond the Americas to Africa, Asia, and the rest of the world, the paradigm example of savage humanity provided by the American Indian became one of the West's most valuable instruments of empire.[4]

The language of Indian savagery helped organize the West's will to empire on a global scale, and its deep imprints on the American racial imagination are even more profound. Every generation of Americans, from the Jamestown colony down to the present day, has been taught to speak a language of racism and racial identity that emerges directly out of the conquest of Indians in America. The violence of this vividly drawn language, with its images of the Indian as hostile, uncivilized savage, appears early on in the American racial imagination. The "savage tribes of Indians" are central antagonists in the racial imagination of European colonists throughout the early colonial histories of the seventeenth century. The repressed psycho-sexual dimensions of the idea of the Indian as a savage form of hybrid humanity are soon displayed; the widely popular captivity narratives of the late eighteenth century are among the first best sellers in the secular literature of America.[5]

The vanquished, vanishing, doomed Indian savage is a stock character in nineteenth-century American literary classics, dime novels, and Wild West shows.[6] Such romanticized discourses on the Indian's savage identity typically lament the loss of a paradigm example of humanity ennobled by a life lived closer to the state of nature. The broad dissemination of the "noble savage" as a countertheme to the dominant image of the Indian testifies to the plasticity of the language of Indian savagery in helping to constitute not only the Indian's immutable savage fate but white America's justificatory discourses of manifest destiny and national identity as well.[7]

In the twentieth century the language of Indian savagery in America is appropriated by a mass-market media culture and made digestible for large-scale commercial exploitation and consumption. Long-established stereotypes and apocryphal tales of Indian chiefs and young maidens have come to define what Indians look and act like. The racial fantasy of the Indian as uncivilized savage implacably opposed to the inevitable advance of the white man and his superior form of civilization becomes an obligatory element of an entire, clichéd genre, the Hollywood western.[8] By the closing decades of the century, a movie like Kevin Costner's *Dances with Wolves* could successfully market itself as a romanticized, film-version meditation on the cross-cultural ironies generated by the conflicted idea of the Indian as "uncivilized" yet possibly ennobled savage.[9]

Although the language of Indian savagery can be adapted for innumerable purposes, it works most effectively in affirming a singular set of racial precepts and beliefs. The Indian was supposedly living as a paradigm example of savage humanity when the conquest of America began. As such, as measured by European values, they were an uncivilized, radically different, inferior race of others. At the core of their otherness was their lack of cultural sophistication and refinement. They lived as hunters and gatherers in a primitive, savage lifestyle. They were lawless, rude, and ignorant of the benefits of civilization.

The language of Indian savagery could be evocatively manipulated to cast any of these essential savage character traits as noble virtues of primitive simplicity. But savagery itself possessed no ultimate redeeming value for the Indian. The Indian's supposed lack of sophisticated laws and formal institutions ultimately doomed his race in the competition with a superior civilization that was possessed of these essential features. Unable to organize a society for effective warfare or competition on Europe's imperial, global scale and incapable of producing those surpluses and commodities that an agricultural society generates through the security of laws and private property, Indian tribes, for good or bad, like all savage groups of humans recorded throughout history, were destined to be conquered by a superior, civilized race that cultivated the soil and engaged in highly sophisticated networks of commercial exchange, social intercourse, and imperial competition. The language of Indian savagery, whatever other purposes it might serve as part of the American racial imagination, ultimately confirmed the essential inferiority of Indians as conquered peoples and the racial and cultural superiority of the European-derived society that conquered them.

As the *Far Side* cartoon demonstrates, this language and the racial iconography of Indians it includes still circulates with varying degrees of intensity and vigor throughout our contemporary culture. Think of all the negative stereotypical images you yourself have encountered depicting Indians as ignorant, lazy, drunken, bloodthirsty, or lawless savages, a paradigm example of a race of hopelessly backward, uncivilized, unsophisticated peoples living in a primitive past, wandering over the plains and through the forests, living a life of meager subsistence and inescapably and irredeemably fated to eventual extinction.

Next, think of all the ways you yourself may have admiringly appropriated images, stereotypes, and tropes from this language. On the playground as a young boy, did you choose to play the cowboy or the Indian? As a young girl, did you dress up for Halloween as an Indian princess? Have you ever thought about buying your daughter one of those expensive American Girl Indian dolls, "Kaya" (see the introduction, note 51), in full buckskin regalia?

These long-established stereotyped roles and their ritualized construction of racialized and commodified ethnic identities are an inescapable and pervasive part of the metastasizing, conglomerating mass-media, market culture that just about every child in America, including those who grow up to become Supreme Court justices, gets exposed to at a very early age.[10] Even today, most children think they "know" what an Indian "looks like." "Real" Indians, they will readily report, have "red" skin, wear loincloth and buckskins, live in teepees, chase deer in the forest, roam the plains hunting buffalo, put feathers in their hair, and say neat things children can mimic, like "Ugh" and "How." That they possess all this "knowledge" about Indians teaches the same basic lesson illustrated by the story of the little white child seeing a "baby maid" for the first time (see chapter 1, in the section "At Work in a Young Child's Mind"). The way our own children talk and think about other different types of people in their world can teach us quite a lot about the continuing force of a long-established language of racism in our own world.

Language of Indian Savagery Proficiency Test

Even if you don't have any children of your own, you don't need an interpreter to figure out how the language of Indian savagery still speaks meaningfully to you in your own life. Let me present a short version of a test I've developed that measures your proficiency in the language of racism that has been specifically directed at American Indians. This test will help you determine how well you speak the language of Indian savagery and also whether you know of any other way to talk about Indians without resorting to well-known stereotypes, apocryphal tales, or demeaning racial imagery.

> *Question 1(a).* Write the names of five famous dead Indian chiefs who fought wars against the United States during the eighteenth or nineteenth centuries. You have one minute to answer this question.
>
> *Question 1(b).* Write the names of five Indians, famous or not, who are alive today. They can be your friends, former or present students, or people you simply know or just work with at the office. You get credit for this question if you can name any elected leader of a modern-day Indian tribe in the United States, a famous entertainer, a movie star—it doesn't matter who it is, you get credit for this question for just coming up with the names of five Indians who didn't kill white people in the eighteenth or nineteenth centuries

and who are alive today and acting just like white people do. You have one minute to answer this question.

Question 2(a). Write the names of five Indian tribes you're familiar with from Hollywood movies and TV westerns. You have two minutes to answer this question.

Question 2(b). Write the names of five Indian tribes living on reservations in the United States today that you did not name in Question 2(a). Take as long as you want to answer this question. Hint: Begin by trying to think of tribes with really big casinos.

Question 3(a). Write the names of five collegiate or professional sports teams that use Indian mascots or images of Indians on their uniforms or equipment. If you are male, take one minute to answer this question. If you are female, take as much time as you want.

Question 3(b). Write the names of five famous Indian athletes, alive or dead, besides Jim Thorpe. If you are male *or* female, don't waste your time on this question. You probably won't be able to come up with any other names. I've been giving this test for a while, and hardly anyone ever comes up with another famous Indian athlete, alive or dead, besides Jim Thorpe.

I think you get the point of my mini-test. It's designed to measure your level of proficiency in speaking and understanding a language of racism that has been directed at Indians in America ever since the colonial era. The test also helps gauge whether, aside from a certain set of familiar and clichéd racial stereotypes, you know anything much else at all about any present-day Indians in America. In other words, can you say anything meaningful about Indians in present-day America without relying on this language and these stereotypes?

Most present-day Americans have been trained, conditioned, and habituated since early childhood to think of Indian people for the most part as stereotypical savages, a race of people with no present or future role defined for themselves in the contemporary American racial imagination. Americans, children and adults, have played with, dressed up according to, and been entertained by the idea of the Indian as a radically different type of backward-looking and ultimately inferior humanity that has nothing to do with the way Indians live in the United States today. The organizing racial imagery of the Indian as savage constitutes such an integral part of our historical and cultural heritage that it crowds out all other ways of thinking and talking about Indians. It's been taught in our schools, appears throughout our national literature, and is still popular with the various forms of popular media and entertainment that help shape our contemporary, globalized culture. In the sense that the American racial imagination begins its processes of formation in its colonial encounter with the American Indian, the idea of the Indian as incommensurable savage ultimately serves to affirm an alien, radically fabricated form of otherness opposed to Western civilization. In more ways than we are likely to realize, therefore, we all probably suffer from some deep-seated form of Indianophobia.

Indian Rights and the "S-Word" in America's Founding History and Culture: "The Savage as the Wolf"

Indianophobia, as generated by the language of Indian savagery in American history, is an important part of who we are as a people in America. It's one of the original, founding forms of racism and racial hostility cultivated by Europeans in the New World, and it constitutes a primal, driving force in defining how we became who we are as a people today.

An overtly racist, hostile, and violent language of Indian savagery can be found in the first official U.S. legal document promulgated by the Founding Fathers, the Declaration of Independence. Among other misdeeds, that founding text of American liberty charged the king of Great Britain with having "excited domestic insurrections amongst us" and endeavoring "to bring on the inhabitants of our frontiers the merciless Indian Savages, whose known rule of warfare, is an undistinguished destruction of all ages, sexes and conditions."

The racist, organizing iconography of the Indian as irreconcilable and inassimilable savage other continued after the Revolution as one of the core organizing beliefs inspiring the Founders' vision of America's growth and potentiality as a new form of expansionary white racial dictatorship in the world.[11] We see this hostile racial belief system reflected throughout the first pronouncements on Indian policy generated by the Founding Fathers after the Revolutionary War.

On September 7, 1783, just four days after the signing of the definitive peace treaty in Paris ending the war with Great Britain, George Washington, commander-in-chief, at the specific request of the Continental Congress, delivered what turned out to be the basic blueprint for the Founding Fathers' first Indian policy for the United States. That blueprint is contained in Washington's carefully considered set of recommendations "relative to Indian Affairs" in the "Western Country." Notably, Washington's entire plan for dealing with the tribes of the Western Country was organized around the basic idea that the Indians on the frontier were bestial, war-loving savages and should be dealt with accordingly as a matter of U.S. policy.[12] They should be kept apart from the civilized population of the United States, behind a boundary line drawn to facilitate the gradual and planned colonial expansion on the country's western frontier.

In the imperial-minded fantasy world of the Founding Fathers, the "Western Country" signified the vast and fertile territory in North America between the eastern mountain ranges and the Mississippi River. Acquired under the Treaty of Paris from Great Britain as a hard-earned prize of the Revolutionary War, this valuable transmontane piece of real estate had long been identified by the Founders as the site where the westward territorial expansion of their new nation would begin. A potent and insistent signifier of desire and discipline in the Founders' colonial imagination,[13] the Western Country would be the place where a white-settler, agrarian nation would begin the conquest of the vast landed frontiers of North America.[14]

It was that virgin land upon which, to borrow Henry Nash Smith's famous phrase, a "fee simple empire" of liberty and virtue would flourish in North America.[15] A major problem of policy that confronted the Founders' plans for colonizing this intended empire with white yeoman farmers, however, was that the Western Country was presently claimed and occupied by large numbers of hostile Indian tribes. Most of these tribes on the western frontiers of the United States had either openly or covertly sided with Great Britain in the Revolutionary War.[16]

There were those in Congress and elsewhere throughout the new nation who were arguing for an aggressive, violent, militarily enforced policy of outright seizure of the lands in the Western Country claimed by these hostile tribes. The Indians who had turned against the rebelling colonies, under this view, had committed the most horrible atrocities and acts of treachery during the Revolution. They should therefore be treated as already-conquered enemies along with Great Britain, their ally and protector, and made to retreat northward to Canada along with those loyal to the British Crown. The tribes' lands would then be considered forfeited to the United States as a lawfully declared prize of war.

As commander-in-chief, Washington knew the practical realities of the situation on the frontier. Committing to this type of aggressive Indian policy would require an expensive military campaign against the hostile tribes of the Western Country. Washington, a veteran Indian fighter himself, did not look with favor on the prospect of savage warfare with Indian tribes on their own wilderness terrain, a war to be waged by a new nation that had just concluded a long and expensive war for independence from Great Britain.[17] His recommendations strongly opposed adopting any type of confrontational military approach with the tribes in the Western Country at that time.

He countered the bellicose argument for treating the tribes as conquered, vanquished enemies by laying out a carefully reasoned set of principles for dealing with Indians through the tried-and-tested tools of colonial governmentality[18] that had been used by the British Crown prior to the Revolution. Washington believed that ultimately, the best way to get the Indians to abandon the Western Country to make way for white civilization was to adopt a policy of negotiating, through diplomacy and treaties, for the peaceful surrender, cession, or sale of tribally claimed lands.

This type of peaceful treaty policy, Washington urged, would avoid "a great deal of Bloodshed" with the still-hostile tribes on the nation's western frontiers. As a first step in pursuing this policy, he recommended that the Congress should establish a "boundary line between them and us." As for any claims the tribes might continue to insist upon making to the lands on the U.S. side, that is, the easterly side, of this proposed boundary line, Washington advised that "compensation should be made them for their claims within it." In reiterating the reasoning behind his recommended policy of peaceful acquisition of these Indian-claimed lands, Washington drew upon an evocative simile that was part of a well-known language of racism in America that was spoken by all the leading members of the founding generation:

I repeat it again, that policy and economy point very strongly to
the expediency of being upon good terms with the Indians, and the
propriety of purchasing their land in preference to attempting to drive
them by force of arms out of their country; which as we have already
experienced is like driving the Wild Beasts of the Forest which will
return as soon as the pursuit is at an end and fall perhaps on those that
are left there; when the gradual extension of our settlements will as
certainly cause the Savage as the Wolf to retire; both being beasts of
prey though they differ in shape.[19]

Washington, it is worth pointing out, had no significant rival or peer
among the leading members of the founding generation when it came to
his depth and breadth of experience as an Indian fighter. He had been
fighting tribes on the Anglo-American colonial frontier since the earliest
days of the French and Indian War.[20] He was therefore speaking with a
great deal of well-recognized authority and expertise in expounding
upon his Indian policy paradigm of "the Savage as the Wolf." Assessing
the ultimate costs and benefits of attempting to pursue a policy of military conquest of the tribes of the Western Country, Washington sound-
ed an ominous warning note to Congress, a warning organized around
the horrifying image of the Indian's well-known savage methods of
warfare to intensify the persuasive force of his arguments: "In a word,
there is nothing to be obtained by an Indian war but the soil they live
on and this can be had by purchase at less expense, and without that
bloodshed, and those distresses which helpless women and children are
made partakers of in all kinds of disputes with them."[21]

Washington's recommendations to pursue a policy paradigm of peaceful purchase of Indian lands in the Western Country were, as was most
always the case with the general, eminently pragmatic and grounded
firmly upon his extensive military experience. His preferred policy approach to the tribes was based upon considerations of "expediency"
and "economy" and was organized in its entirety around the singular
terrorizing notion that the Indians of the Western Country who held
and fiercely defended this great and fertile region as their homeland
were uncivilized, merciless, war-loving savages. As such innately hostile, bestialized creatures, their methods of warfare inevitably entailed
the most horrid forms of atrocities and endless cycles of revenge and
bloodshed that experience taught should be avoided if at all possible.

Particularly given the policy goal of pursuing peaceful and orderly white settlement of the frontier, Washington argued that avoiding war with hostile Indian tribes was the best course for Congress to adopt. To continue a war with savage Indians in order to acquire full control of the territory they occupied made little economic or military sense in the commander-in-chief's view. Once driven from the country the Indians would return, as experience consistently demonstrated, as soon as the force that had expelled them left the region. This was their irredeemable savage nature, and nothing that the Founders could do would ever alter that invariable, antagonistic response by the tribes on the nation's western frontiers. Therefore, the huge costs of a military campaign in the Indian's own country, which would have to include the permanent garrisoning of an armed force to patrol and protect the frontier settlers who moved onto the lands seized from the tribes, far exceeded any possible return on investment.

It was far more expedient and economical, according to Washington's "Savage as the Wolf" Indian policy paradigm, to allow the tribes to remain peacefully within the limits of the United States, to convince them to voluntarily cede their territories by solemn treaties, and to establish a boundary line by those agreements. The United States should continue to regulate the trade with the Indians but should keep them on the other side of that line, until the forces of civilization achieved the Indians' certain extinction as a doomed race of savages. Pursuing this type of Indian-boundary-line policy would allow for the occupation of a significant area between what white Americans now inhabited to the east of the line and what the Indians might be allowed to keep on the far frontiers west of the line.

And, as Washington confidently assured his fellow Founders, even this remote frontier area retained by the tribes of the Western Country would eventually be brought under the complete control of the United States and cleared of all Indian claims. As the inevitable approach of white agricultural settlements advanced upon the frontier and the game that the Indians relied upon for their subsistence disappeared, according to Washington's Indian policy paradigm, they would eventually yield to the fated destiny of all backward races confronted by a superior form of civilization. They would vanish as a distinct race of peoples, and the lands that the United States then owned free and clear of all Indian claims would be available for white settlement.[22]

All of the Founders were familiar with the language of Indian savagery used by Washington to support his arguments on Indian policy for the United States. They all believed firmly in the organizing racial mythology of the Indians' essential, irreconcilably savage identity that inspired Washington's policy paradigm of "the Savage as the Wolf" for the Western Country. They were all highly conversant with the discourse of colonial governmentality generated by this racial fantasy, a discourse that regarded the Indian as inferior and justly fated to be driven off the lands of the United States. The belief in the Indian's racial inferiority was a form of knowledge and power confirmed by nearly two centuries of Anglo-American colonizing experiences and conflicts with the tribes of the Atlantic seaboard. Those tribes had all retreated, had been absorbed, or had disappeared entirely in their hostile confrontations with the agricultural civilization brought to the New World from Europe.[23] This form of knowledge and the system of colonial governmentality over a savage race of peoples it dictated sought to conserve colonial power as it most efficiently and economically organized its directive forces upon the Indian-held frontier. Thus, although the United States in theory held the right of conquest under the ancient laws of war to take the Western Country from the Indian tribes, by force of arms if it so desired, experience, "expediency," and a sound understanding of the Indians' irremediably savage nature and doomed fate dictated a better-reasoned and far more practical policy. Seeking the peaceful surrender and purchase of tribal land claims through treaty negotiations was the best means for dealing with the savage race of peoples on the western frontier.

Washington's tactical recommendations to pursue a policy of peaceful purchase and acquisition of Indian land claims on the frontiers of white settlement were immediately endorsed and adopted, virtually without modification, by the Continental Congress as the best and most effective means for achieving the goal of civilizing of the Western Country. The organizing paradigm of "the Savage as the Wolf" became the governing template for the Founders' first Indian policy, engendering a national mythos of white frontier conquest and racial dictatorship that was manifestly predestined to be imposed upon the entire continent of North America.

Two weeks after the commander-in-chief outlined his views on Indian policy, Congress issued a proclamation forbidding and voiding all white settlement on Indian-claimed lands on the western frontier. In effect, Congress had fully committed the United States to implementing the Indian-white boundary line recommended by Washington's "Savage as the Wolf" policy paradigm. A Congressional Committee Report, adopting virtually all of Washington's major recommendations, in some of its crucial passages nearly verbatim, was sent to the full Congress in mid-October 1783. By the winter of that year, tribes on the western frontier were being informed of the U.S. government's new policy of racial apartheid. The United States had the right to treat them as conquered nations, but if the Indians agreed to sign treaties voluntarily surrendering their lands according to a boundary line dictated by the Great White Father, then, as the Revolutionary War hero General Philip Schuyler explained to one group of Indians during treaty negotiations initiated under this policy, Congress was "willing to forget the injuries and give peace."[24]

This Founding-era system of colonial governmentality administered over the hostile Indian tribes upon the frontier borders of the United States was subsequently enacted into laws and implemented by a series of Indian treaties. As ratified by Congress, the treaties negotiated under this policy sought to establish and demarcate the racial boundary line proposed by Washington's paradigmatic principle of "the Savage as the Wolf." The Founding Fathers' first Indian policy was formally incorporated into the Constitution of 1787 by the simple expedient of vesting in Congress exclusive power over all "commerce with . . . the Indian tribes."[25] This broad grant of power, of course, comprehended the all-important, exclusive sovereign capacity of buying and selling all the lands held by the Indian tribes. Washington's founding vision of a white racial dictatorship imposed upon the entire continent of North America with "expediency" and "economy" had now become established as the law of the land. According to the original intent of the Founders' first Indian policy, "the Savage as the Wolf" would inevitably be made to disappear from the civilized territory of the United States.

4

Indian Rights and the Marshall Court

The Founders' organizing vision of a white racial dictatorship imposed over Indian tribes by the United States, so evocatively signified by George Washington's Indian policy paradigm of "the Savage as the Wolf," reflected the continuing force of a long-established language of racism in America. The stereotypes of the Indian tribes on the frontiers of white settlement as uncivilized, war-loving, and irreconcilably savage enemies had been used by colonizing Europeans since their first encounters with the native peoples of the New World.

The Indian policy metaphor of "the Savage as the Wolf" was therefore no sudden inspiration of the Founders' racial vision of America as a white Anglo-Saxon, fee-simple empire of liberty.[1] Emerging out of the most ancient and widely disseminated stories of origin and myth appropriated by the Western colonial imagination, the idea of the Indian as hostile savage was received and perpetuated by the Founders through a diverse and influential set of sources, texts, and narrative traditions.[2] This archive of incommensurable and alienated forms of human otherness reinforced the notion that the American Indian was a paradigm example of uncivilized savage humanity. The organizing significance to the Founders of this colonial-era racial fantasy about the Indian's irredeemable nature cannot be overstated.[3] As Roy Harvey Pearce wrote in his classic study on the idea of the Indian as savage in America, the Indian became the symbol "for all that over which civilization must triumph" in the Founders' colonial imagination.[4] Denied the right to exist as "truly other, something capable of being not merely an imperfect state of oneself,"[5] the Indian's doomed fate was inextricably tied to white America's ascendant destiny on the continent. The rise of a superior form of civilization would necessarily entail the destruction of the savage race.

The organizing power of the idea of the Indian as incommensurable savage inspired a new art of imperial government administered by the West's first modern settler-state society, the United States of America. Directed to the task of extinguishing the Indian's radically constructed otherness, the Founders' first Indian policy was the inaugural step in defining a white racial identity for the United States as a nation.[6] The legacy of white racial superiority over Indian tribes that constitutes such a vital, defining part of our nation's history and cultural heritage begins with the Founders' will to empire and the Founding-era vision of eliminating "the Savage as the Wolf" from the territory of the United States.

Given that this language of Indian savagery is so deeply embedded in the history and culture of the colonial era and given that it played such an important role in organizing the Founders' first Indian policy and in defining a national identity for the United States following the Revolutionary War, it is not surprising to find it being used by the justices of the Supreme Court when they were first asked to address important questions of Indian rights during the early decades of the nineteenth century. Steadfast beliefs in white superiority and Indian savagery can in fact be identified as central organizing principles in the Court's first set of landmark decisions on Indian rights. In three seminal opinions for the Court, *Johnson v. McIntosh* (1823), *Cherokee Nation v. Georgia* (1831), and *Worcester v. Georgia* (1832),[7] Chief Justice John Marshall, a member of the founding generation himself, developed a legal model of Indian rights that relied upon the same basic language that the Founders had used in defining the first U.S. Indian policy. As used in Marshall's model of Indian rights under U.S. law, this language served to justify the legal imposition of the white racial dictatorship over the tribes that had been envisioned as the ultimately intended goal of the Founders' inaugural Indian policy paradigm of treating "the Savage as the Wolf."

Amazingly, unlike with the decisions in *Dred Scott* and *Plessy v. Ferguson,* the justices of the Supreme Court continue to cite this trio of archaic, racist judicial precedents from the early nineteenth century in their present-day opinions on vitally important questions of Indian rights to property, self government, and cultural survival. The model of inferior and diminished Indian rights under the Constitution and laws of the United States laid out in these three seminal cases continues to define the Court's approach to all questions of Indian tribal rights. The justices, in fact, routinely cite and quote from these cases, despite Marshall's blatantly obvious perpetuation of a stereotype-ridden and overtly hostile and demeaning language of racism (see chapter 3).

Clearly one reason why *Johnson, Cherokee Nation,* and *Worcester* are still being dutifully followed by the present-day Supreme Court is because these three seminal opinions of the Marshall model were written by the person whom generations of American law students have been taught to regard as the greatest chief justice of all time. Generations of U.S. lawyers, in turn, have treated these three opinions by Marshall as if they were sacred texts, with oracular status when it comes to thinking and talking about Indians and their rights. They have been taught to believe that when used and interpreted correctly, the principles and doctrines derived from these foundational cases can work reliably and steadily enough to protect Indian rights in a legal system constructed upon a Founding-era vision of white racial supremacy and dictatorship intended to be established over the entire continent of North America. Firm in this belief, and stressing the importance of stare decisis, they keep telling us, in their legal briefs, treatises, and law review articles, that the Supreme Court must continue to abide by the correct interpretation of the legal principles laid out in the Marshall Model of Indian Rights. In this sense, to borrow from the postcolonial theorist Homi K. Bhabha, these three opinions by Marshall, which initiated this revered early-nineteenth-century judicial model of diminished Indian rights in the Supreme Court's Indian law, function as "signs taken for wonders."[8]

In his essay "Signs Taken for Wonders," Bhabha identifies a crucial, organizing scene "in the cultural writings of English colonialism." It is a scene that repeats itself, he says, insistently after the early nineteenth century, "and through that repetition, so triumphantly *inaugurates* a literature of empire." It is the scene, he writes, "played out in the wild and wordless wastes of colonial India, Africa, the Caribbean, of the sudden, fortuitous discovery of the English book."[9]

According to Bhabha, "like all myths of origin," the discovery of the English book is "memorable for its balance between epiphany and enunciation." Its discovery, he writes, is "at once a moment of originality and authority." But Bhabha also identifies in this great, revelatory discovery of the English book "a process of displacement that, paradoxically, makes the presence of the book wondrous to the extent to which it is repeated, translated, misread, displaced." The English book stands as emblem and insignia of colonial authority. A "signifier of colonial desire and discipline," the discovery of the English book becomes, as Bhabha describes it, an inaugural force in the cultural organization of the West's will to empire over non-Western peoples—evidence of "signs taken for wonders."[10]

In many ways, the Marshall Model of Indian Rights plays much the same kind of inaugural and paradoxical organizing role in the Supreme Court's Indian law as Bhabha's wondrous "English book" plays in the cultural writings of English colonialism. Its insistent use by the Supreme Court as a foundational source of the precedents and principles for deciding virtually all questions of Indian rights under U.S. law indeed identifies the Marshall model as a "moment of originality and authority," seeking to assimilate the Indian's radically conceived alterity within the complex schema of constitutional principles and legal values promoted by a self-identified superior form of civilization and its enlightened system of colonial governmentality. But this judicial act of authoritative interpretation of Indian rights also represents a highly problematic process of displacement and ambivalence as well. The Marshall model's organizing paradigm of Indian savagery and incommensurability triumphantly inaugurates an authoritative legal discourse of empire and judicially sanctioned white racial dictatorship in which Indians, so long as they remain in their backward state of civilization, are recognized as perpetually opposed colonial subjects possessing a hybrid form of inferior and diminished rights under U.S. law.[11] In this sense, the Supreme Court's "Indian law" always functions ambivalently in its limiting and unappealable pronouncements on Indian rights, as, simultaneously, a form of *anti*-Indian law. In carrying out its perpetually unresolved mission in the Supreme Court's Indian rights decisions, the Marshall model, "like all myths of origin,"[12] insistently repeats that moment of tension when the irreducible legal significance and ambiguous legal meanings of the Indian's essential savage nature as colonized subject are revealed and announced in Marshall's three oracular Indian law opinions.

The sacred, mythical, mystical nature of these three nineteenth-century opinions reveals itself in the fact that *Johnson, Cherokee Nation,* and *Worcester* have been traditionally referred to by legal scholars and historians of the Supreme Court's Indian law as the "Marshall Trilogy."[13] The revered, pundit-like status of the ghost of John Marshall is even more forcefully reflected in the fact that virtually every Indian rights decision of the Supreme Court contains at least one and often numerous citations to the cases of the Marshall Trilogy. Even today, in the twenty-first century, the Supreme Court insistently and unembarrassedly cites these early-nineteenth-century texts as authoritative precedents in defining Indian rights; faithfully repeated and adhered to despite their racist judicial language of Indian savagery, they function as signs taken for wonders in the Supreme Court's Indian law decisions (see chapters 10 and 11).

Johnson v. McIntosh

The Supreme Court's unanimous decision in *Johnson v. McIntosh,* written by Marshall in 1823, is, without question, the most important Indian rights opinion ever issued by any court of law in the United States. Its signal importance in the Supreme Court's Indian law derives from the fact that *Johnson* incorporated the European colonial era's "doctrine of discovery" as the originating source of Indian rights under U.S. law.[14] In a case in which Indians weren't even represented (the legal controversy in *Johnson* was between two non-Indian parties fighting over legal title to the same piece of land, a parcel that had once been occupied by Indians), *Johnson* held that European "discovery" of Indian-occupied land in the New World, in Chief Justice Marshall's oft-cited words, gave title "to the government by whose subjects, or by whose authority, it was made, against all other European governments, which title might be consummated by possession."[15]

According to the carefully scripted legal history lesson that begins

Marshall's opinion, the principle of white racial superiority asserted by the doctrine of discovery and validated by the Supreme Court in *Johnson* was part of the colonial-era European Law of Nations. The two-step process—discover and consummate by possession—legalized by the discovery doctrine was relied upon by all the colonizing, "great nations of Europe," Marshall tells us, to justify their claims to superior rights over all the lands held by the Indian tribes of the New World:

> On the discovery of this immense continent, the great nations of
> Europe were eager to appropriate to themselves so much of it as they
> could respectively acquire. Its vast extent offered an ample field to the
> ambition and enterprise of all.

The fact that there were Indians already living upon these newly discovered lands didn't matter much as far as the first European discoverer's superior rights under the discovery doctrine were concerned. As Marshall explained, the "character and religion" of the New World's inhabitants "afforded an apology for considering them as a people over whom the superior genius of Europe might claim an ascendancy."[16] Indian tribes, in other words, were presumptively regarded under the discovery doctrine and European colonial-era conceptions of international law as an inferior race of peoples who could be lawfully conquered and colonized. Conquest, in fact, perfected the superior title of the European nation that had acquired the rights of discovery to the lands occupied by Indians under the doctrine.

According to the colonial-era model of Indian rights that Marshall begins to adumbrate in *Johnson,* the doctrine of discovery provided a much-needed organizing legal principle of colonial governmentality for Europeans to regulate and apportion their conquests and claims to "ascendancy" over the Indians of the New World. The European colonial powers, in Marshall's felicitous words, "were all in pursuit of nearly the same object," that is, control and empire over the lands of non-European peoples deemed inferior by Europeans. It therefore became "necessary in order to avoid conflicting settlements, and consequent war with each other, to establish a principle, which all should acknowledge as the law by which the right of acquisition, which they all asserted, should be regulated as between themselves." That "principle" of white racial superiority under European international law, as Marshall noted, was embodied in the doctrine of discovery. The doctrine of discovery assigned the exclusive legal rights to conquer and colonize the Indian tribes of North America to the first European nation that had happened to "discover" and then effectively occupy their lands.[17]

Like all the other European colonizing nation-states, as Marshall explained, the United States, as successor to Great Britain's imperial interests under the European Law of Nations, recognized this foundational principle of white racial superiority and applied it to the entire North American continent. The United States had incorporated the doctrine of discovery as the original legal source of its exclusive colonial authority over Indian tribes and the lands they occupied:

> The United States, then, have unequivocally acceded to that great and broad rule by which its civilized inhabitants now hold this country. They hold, and assert in themselves, the title by which it was acquired. They maintain, as all others have maintained, that discovery gave an exclusive right to extinguish the Indian title of occupancy, either by purchase or by conquest.[18]

Two highly distinctive elements of Chief Justice Marshall's model of Indian rights can be seen clearly emerging out of his opinion for the Court in *Johnson*. First is the overarching principle of European racial and cultural superiority over the Indians of the New World. Because of their savage "character and religion," Indians were regarded as inferior peoples with lesser rights to land and territorial sovereignty under the European Law of Nations. They therefore could be lawfully conquered and colonized by any European-derived nation that desired to undertake the effort.[19] Second, the doctrine of discovery functioned under the European Law of Nations as part of a transnational legal discourse, considered authoritative, for regulating the claims of European racial superiority over the Indian tribes of the New World. According to the Marshall Model of Indian Rights, under this principle of white racial superiority, the rights of conquest and colonization belonging to Great Britain as first European discoverer of the tribes of North America and the lands they occupied had devolved to the United States when it won the Revolutionary War. Under the doctrine of discovery, the United States possessed the "exclusive right to extinguish the Indian title of occupancy, either by purchase or by conquest."[20]

A third distinctive element of the Marshall Model of Indian Rights also can be seen at work throughout the text of *Johnson*. Marshall uses the same stereotypes and imagery of Indian savagery to validate the denial of Indian rights in *Johnson* that the Founders had used to construct their exclusionary Indian policy paradigm following the Revolutionary War.

The Court's discussion of Indian rights in the case, in fact, expressly reprises and relies upon this familiar language of Indian savagery that the Founders had originally appropriated as part of their system of colonial governmentality. Marshall uses this language of racism in *Johnson* to justify and excuse the principle of European white supremacy that had been asserted by invading Europeans under the doctrine of discovery:

> But the tribes of Indians inhabiting this country were fierce savages, whose occupation was war, and whose subsistence was drawn chiefly from the forest. To leave them in possession of their country, was to leave the country a wilderness; to govern them as a distinct people, was impossible, because they were as brave and as high spirited as they were fierce, and were ready to repel by arms every attempt on their independence.[21]

At another point in his opinion, Marshall again uses this language of Indian savagery and implacability to assert that the "character and habits of the people whose rights have been wrested from them" provided "some excuse, if not justification," for the legal principles adopted by Europeans:[22]

> What was the inevitable consequence of this state of things? The Europeans were under the necessity either of abandoning the country, and relinquishing their pompous claims to it, or of enforcing those claims by the sword, and by the adoption of principles adapted to the condition of a people with whom it was impossible to mix, and who could not be governed as a distinct society, or of remaining in their neighbourhood, and exposing themselves and their families to the perpetual hazard of being massacred.[23]

The chief justice even resurrected the once-inspiring Revolutionary-era refrains of Washington's "Savage as the Wolf" Indian policy paradigm in describing the inevitable process of white dispossession of Indian land that had characterized the history of European colonization of the New World:

Frequent and bloody wars, in which the whites were not always the aggressors, unavoidably ensued. European policy, numbers, and skill, prevailed. As the white population advanced, that of the Indians necessarily receded. The country in the immediate neighbourhood of agriculturists became unfit for them. The game fled into thicker and more unbroken forests, and the Indians followed. The soil, to which the crown originally claimed title, being no longer occupied by its ancient inhabitants, was parceled out according to the will of the sovereign power, and taken possession of by persons who claimed immediately from the crown, or mediately, through its grantees or deputies.[24]

Besides its judicial appropriation and rearticulation of the organizing racist belief held by the Founders—that savage Indian tribes could be lawfully conquered and colonized by European-derived peoples— the Marshall Model of Indian Rights as elaborated in *Johnson* put forward one further distinctive element, one that comes to assume a critical role in many of the Supreme Court's most important future Indian law decisions. This fourth element seeks to explain and defend the Supreme Court's passive institutional role in enforcing and perpetuating the Founders' racist vision of Indian rights under U.S. law. Very much as Chief Justice Roger Taney would in his *Dred Scott* opinion (see chapter 2, "The Founders Made Him Do It"), Marshall went to great pains in *Johnson* to explain why the Court shouldn't be blamed for sanctioning this racial dictatorship. Though admittedly "opposed to natural right, and to the usages of civilized nations," the doctrine of discovery, Marshall declared in *Johnson,* was "indispensable to that system under which the country has been settled."[25] In other words, it was the "system" of colonial governmentality adopted by Europeans in the New World and unequivocally acceded to by the Founders that required the Court to rule the way it did in *Johnson v. McIntosh.* As Marshall explained, the principle of racial discrimination contained in the discovery doctrine had been "adapted to the actual condition of the two people" and "may, perhaps, be supported by reason and certainly cannot be rejected by Courts of justice."[26]

The European Law of Nations' discovery doctrine and the system of colonial governmentality perpetuated under it reflected the distilled legal experience of more than two centuries of racial warfare and ethnic-cleansing campaigns brought by Europeans against the Indian tribes of

America. In *Johnson*, the doctrine was appropriated by the Court to give legal sanction to the privileges of aggression and racial superiority asserted by Europeans in the New World. The Supreme Court, according to Marshall, was a creature and instrument of the system established under the doctrine of discovery and the European Law of Nations. The Court was therefore powerless to resist the doctrine's continuing force in interpreting Indian rights under U.S. law. As Marshall himself famously declared in *Johnson*, "Conquest gives a title which the courts of the conqueror cannot deny."[27]

As measured by today's racial sensibilities, *Johnson v. McIntosh* has to be considered one of the most thoroughly racist, nonegalitarian, undemocratic, and stereotype-infused decisions ever issued by the Supreme Court. It elevates a European colonial-era fantasy of white racial supremacy and dictatorship over entire continents of nonconsenting, non-European peoples into a skeletal principle of the U.S. legal system. From our present-day, supposedly more enlightened, post-*Brown* racial perspective, *Johnson v. McIntosh* ranks with *Dred Scott* and *Korematsu* as one of the most disturbing examples in legal history of the Supreme Court's unconstrained and unappealable reliance on negative racial stereotypes in its declaration of the reigning and supreme law of the land. If *Johnson v. McIntosh* were to be issued today as a binding legal precedent by the Court, the justices' decision would be regarded as not only being in bad racial taste but as grossly violative of a host of contemporary international human rights standards relative to indigenous tribal peoples.[28]

Every major standard-setting and adjudicative body in the contemporary international human rights system that has examined the rights of indigenous peoples has concluded that states have an obligation to recognize and protect indigenous peoples' cultural survival and the property rights sustaining their continued existence in a postcolonial world. Furthermore, under the evolving norms of the international human rights system in the twenty-first century, states have a clear duty to meaningfully consult with the indigenous communities affected before taking any legal actions interfering with their human rights, most particularly with respect to the lands and natural resources that sustain their cultural integrity and survival as indigenous peoples.[29]

But Marshall's opinion for the Supreme Court in *Johnson* imposed the European colonial-era doctrine of discovery on tribes in a case in which Indians were not even represented before the Court. Furthermore, as judged by contemporary standards at least, through his use of racist language and imagery at critical junctures in his opinion in *Johnson,* Marshall showed himself to be thoroughly bigoted and biased against Indians in a very important case involving their most basic human rights as indigenous peoples. He showed no discomfort or embarrassment at all in using the "s" word, that is, "savages," to describe Indians and to justify their lesser rights under U.S. law in his opinion in *Johnson.*[30] A contemporary reading of this foundational precedent of the Marshall model strongly suggests that the greatest chief justice of all time was also one of the most Indianophobic, racist justices of all time, at least when it came to giving his opinion on Indian rights in the "great case of *Johnson v. McIntosh.*"[31]

Whether Marshall was a "racist," as defined by our own more highly refined, twenty-first-century, post-*Brown* contemporary racial sensibilities, or whether he really meant all the horrible, misinformed things he said about Indians in *Johnson,* however, are questions that are quite beside the point that needs to be made about this foundational precedent of the Supreme Court's Indian law. With respect to the legal principle established by the case, what should really matter to us is that Marshall's early-nineteenth-century opinion for the Court denied Indian tribes the same rights as their European colonizers because Indians were regarded, under the European Law of Nations and the doctrine of discovery, as an inferior race of savages. What should really matter, therefore, in terms of our present-day understanding of Indian rights as interpreted by the Supreme Court, is that *Johnson v. McIntosh* is still the reigning and supreme law of the land in the United States. In fact, unlike *Dred Scott,* its antiquated and discredited nineteenth-century counterpart minority rights decision negating black Americans' rights to citizenship, *Johnson v. McIntosh* and the stereotype-infused model of Indian rights that it incorporates into U.S. law are relied upon frequently and without any form of discomfort, embarrassment, or even qualification as governing the Indian rights decisions of the present-day Supreme Court justices (see chapter 8).

No one presently sitting as a justice on the Supreme Court seems to have the least problem with *Johnson*'s legalized presumption of Indian racial inferiority, its incorporation into U.S. law of a European colonial-era legal doctrine of conquest and colonization, its use of an antiquated racist judicial language of Indian savagery to define Indian rights, or its declaration that the justices can unfortunately do nothing about the resulting white racial dictatorship imposed upon tribes. Marshall's opinion in that 1823 precedent is simply regarded as stare decisis by the justices and by most present-day advocates and scholars of the Court's Indian law as well. Like signs taken for wonders, the rights-destroying, jurispathic force of Marshall's early-nineteenth-century perpetuation of a language of Indian racial inferiority is still regarded as a vital, authoritative precedent in the present-day Supreme Court's Indian law.

Marshall's Opinions in the *Cherokee* Cases

In *Johnson v. McIntosh*, Marshall laid out a model of Indian rights with four clearly identifiable elements organizing its approach to defining the legal relationship between Indian tribes and the United States. This four-part model of Indian rights adumbrated by Marshall would come to exercise a profound and directive impact on the Supreme Court's future Indian law decisions.[32]

First and foremost, the Marshall Model of Indian Rights recognizes the exclusive right of the United States to exercise supremacy over Indian tribes on the basis of the Indians' presumed racial and cultural inferiority. The Marshall model then applies the European colonial-era doctrine of discovery as a regulative legal principle to define the scope and content of that right to white privilege as covering the entire continent of North America. Additionally, the model perpetuates a long-established language of racism to justify the specific set of rights and prerogatives of conquest and privilege under the discovery doctrine. Finally, it absolves the justices for perpetuating the discovery doctrine as part of U.S. law by viewing it as "indispensable" to the European-derived "system" of colonial governmentality "under which the country has been settled."

Chief Justice Marshall continued to apply and refine these basic elements which he first outlined in *Johnson* in his two subsequent controlling opinions for the Supreme Court, *Cherokee Nation v. Georgia*, decided in 1831, and *Worcester v. Georgia*, decided in 1832. Referred to collectively by Indian law scholars and advocates as the *Cherokee* cases, these two seminal decisions completing the Marshall Trilogy were issued by the Marshall Court in direct response to the Cherokee Nation's efforts to prevent the state of Georgia from extinguishing the tribe as a distinct, self-governing society within its borders.

Under the state-controlled form of white racial dictatorship that Georgia sought to impose upon the Cherokees, tribal self-government and territorial rights would be abolished. Stripped of their tribal citizenship and lands, individual Cherokees would be subject to the onerous, racially discriminatory legal regime imposed by Georgia on all "free persons of color" within its sovereign borders. As legally designated second-class citizens of color, they would be unable to testify in "any suit in any court created by the constitution and laws of this state to which a white man may be a party." They would be unable to vote, unable to serve in the state militia, and unable to send their children to Georgia's public schools under the racial apartheid laws that would apply to the Cherokees under state jurisdiction.[33]

The Cherokees, after being rebuffed by President Andrew Jackson and his Democrat-controlled Congress in their pleas for protection of their rights under their treaties negotiated with the United States, turned to the Supreme Court in an effort to block Georgia from extending its racist regime of state laws over the tribe's federally established, treaty-guaranteed reservation.[34] The Marshall Court—and just about everyone else in the United States, including the Cherokees—quite clearly recognized at the time just what Georgia's assertions of state jurisdiction and sovereignty over the tribe's federally reserved territory would mean for the Cherokees, who would be legally treated as "free persons of color under Georgia law if they remained in the state." The "Cherokee codes" were designed as the first strike in an ethnic-cleansing campaign that would enable the state to take control over the immensely valuable Indian lands within its borders and make them available to Georgia's white citizen farmers and plantation owners.[35]

The legalized form of white racial supremacy that Georgia sought to impose upon the Cherokee Nation and its reservation was ultimately designed to force the tribe to accept removal to an Indian Territory beyond the Mississippi River. Today, such ethnic-cleansing activities on the part of any government in the world would be deemed a crime of genocide, punishable by international law. In early-nineteenth-century America, forced relocation and resettlement, in the form of Congress's infamous Removal Act of 1830,[36] was the official, legislated policy of the U.S. federal government toward all the Indian tribes east of the Mississippi River.[37]

Cherokee Nation v. Georgia

In *Cherokee Nation v. Georgia,* the Cherokees filed suit against enforcement of Georgia's laws on their territory under Article III of the Constitution, which granted original jurisdiction to the Supreme Court in suits between "foreign states" and "states" of the Union, such as Georgia.

Before even examining the substantive legal issues involved in the case, Marshall, characteristically,[38] first addressed the jurisdictional question presented by the case. Could the Cherokees and other Indian tribes be regarded as "foreign states" under Article III of the Constitution, and therefore able to bring suit against Georgia under the Court's original jurisdiction? On that precise legal question, Marshall expanded upon his interpretation of the model of Indian rights that he had first laid out in *Johnson* and held against the Cherokees. Indian tribes could not be regarded as "foreign states" as that term is used in the Constitution:

> [I]t may well be doubted whether those tribes which reside within the acknowledged boundaries of the United States can, with strict accuracy, be denominated foreign nations. They may, more correctly, perhaps, be denominated domestic dependent nations.[39]

To reach this legal conclusion that Indian tribes were "domestic dependent nations" rather than "foreign nations" and therefore had no right to a judicial hearing under the Supreme Court's grant of original jurisdiction, Marshall turned directly to the European colonial-era doctrine of discovery that he himself had incorporated into U.S. law in his 1823 opinion in *Johnson.* In that case, the doctrine's principle of white racial superiority was called upon to define the diminished property rights belonging to Indians under U.S. law. In *Cherokee Nation,* Marshall relied upon the doctrine to define a related discriminatory form of inferior *political* status for Indian tribes under the Constitution.

In fact, in *Cherokee Nation,* the doctrine of discovery provides the organizing principles of Marshall's entire reasoning process relative to Indian political rights and status under the Constitution. Indian tribes, according to his model of Indian rights as developed, applied, and expanded upon in this second case of the trilogy, could never be recognized as "foreign" nations under the Constitution. The discovery doctrine's racially discriminatory principle respecting the diminished rights of Indians in their lands inalterably placed the tribes under the superior political sovereignty of the United States. The doctrine, as Marshall carefully explained in *Cherokee Nation,* marked the relationship between Indian tribes and the United States by "peculiar and cardinal distinctions which exist nowhere else." These "peculiar" differences proved, in his opinion, "that the framers of our Constitution had not the Indian tribes in view, when they opened the courts of the union to controversies between a state or the citizens thereof, and foreign states." Unlike those of "foreign states," the tribes' political rights and status, according to Marshall, were defined by reference to the overriding organizing principle of white supremacy embodied in the European colonial-era doctrine of discovery. Indians under U.S. law, *Cherokee Nation* holds, "occupy a territory to which we assert a title independent of their will, which must take effect in point of possession when their right of possession ceases. Meanwhile they are in a state of pupilage. Their relation to the United States resembles that of a ward to his guardian."[40]

This critical passage in *Cherokee Nation* represents the textual source of one of the most important legal principles generated by the Marshall Trilogy and the model of Indian rights that it incorporates into the Court's Indian law. The guardian-ward relationship, announced for the first time by the Court in *Cherokee Nation,* is the source of what is called the "trust doctrine" in Indian law. Under the Marshall model, the trust doctrine is supposed to function as a primary protective principle of Indian rights under U.S. law.[41]

Cherokee Nation's delineation of Indian tribes' "domestic dependent nation" status and of the guardian-ward relationship makes it, along with *Johnson,* one of the most important decisions ever issued by the Supreme Court on Indian rights. The Court's ruling that Indian tribes could not be regarded as "foreign" nations under the Constitution meant that the Cherokees, in Marshall's words, "cannot maintain an action in the courts of the United States." Though Georgia's laws, as pleaded by the tribe, sought "directly to annihilate the Cherokees as a political society, and to seize, for the use of Georgia, the lands of the nation which have been assured to them by the United States in solemn treaties repeatedly made and still in force,"[42] the Constitution, according to the holding of *Cherokee Nation* and the Marshall Model of Indian Rights, literally left them incapable of defending themselves before the Supreme Court from these state-sponsored acts of what Rennard Strickland has called "genocide-at-law."[43]

Cherokee Nation substantially reinforced and expanded upon the basic elements of the model of Indian rights that Chief Justice Marshall had first laid out in *Johnson. Cherokee Nation,* like *Johnson,* expressly recognizes the exclusive right of the United States to establish a racial dictatorship over tribes, regulated by the doctrine of discovery. As "domestic dependent nations," Marshall wrote in *Cherokee Nation,* the tribes were "so completely under the sovereignty and dominion of the United States, that any attempt to acquire their lands, or to form a political connection with them, would be considered by all as an invasion of our territory, and an act of hostility."[44]

As in *Johnson,* Marshall also relied on the rights-destroying jurispathic force of a language of Indian savagery to justify U.S. hegemony over Indian tribes. In *Cherokee Nation,* this long-established language of racism conveniently provides Marshall with the interpretive principle for understanding the Founders' original intent toward Indian tribes in drafting Article III of the Constitution:

> In considering this subject, the habits and usages of the Indians, in their intercourse with their white neighbors, ought not to be entirely disregarded. At the time the Constitution was framed, the idea of appealing to an American court of justice for an assertion of right or a redress of wrong, had perhaps never entered the mind of an Indian or of his tribe. Their appeal was to the tomahawk, or to the government. This was well understood by the statesmen who framed the Constitution of the United States, and might furnish some reason for omitting to enumerate them among the parties who might sue in the courts of the union.[45]

In stating his holding on the rights-destroying, jurispathic force of the Founders' language of Indian savagery on Indian rights in the United States, the chief justice further developed the elemental theme of judicial self-absolution that had been first stated in *Johnson:* The Court cannot be held responsible for perpetuating this "peculiar" form of white racial dictatorship. According to Marshall, "If it be true that the Cherokee nation have rights, this is not the tribunal in which those rights are to be asserted. If it be true that wrongs have been inflicted, and that still greater are to be apprehended, this is not the tribunal which can redress the past or prevent the future."[46]

Like *Johnson, Cherokee Nation* also has to be regarded as one of the most racist decisions ever issued by the Supreme Court. Marshall's controlling opinion for the Court in *Cherokee Nation,* which provided no effective judicial remedy for Indian tribes to protect their basic human rights to property, self-government, and cultural survival under U.S. law, affirmed the racial dictatorship of the United States over Indian tribes, and based its holding on a racist language that described Indians as bloodthirsty, "tomahawk"-wielding savages who were simply too uncivilized to be recognized under the U.S. Constitution as possessing any original right of legal access to the Supreme Court as a "foreign state." Yet *Cherokee Nation* is cited without embarrassment or discomfort as still good law and binding precedent by the present-day justices of the Rehnquist Supreme Court.[47] Signs taken for wonders, and evidence of the continuing jurispathic force of the Marshall model's racist, judicially sanctioned language of Indian savagery in the Supreme Court's Indian rights decisions.

Worcester v. Georgia

The Marshall Model of Indian Rights was completed and significantly refined by Marshall's celebrated opinion in the case of *Worcester v. Georgia.* Marshall's oft-cited and highly revered opinion for the Court in this third and final case of the Marshall Trilogy held that the federal government, and not individual states, possesses the exclusive right to exercise control over Indian affairs.

Following the Supreme Court's decision in *Cherokee Nation,* Georgia convicted two New England Protestant missionaries, William Worcester and Samuel Butler, of violating its laws prohibiting anyone from entering Cherokee territory without a license from the state. An appeal to the U.S. Supreme Court was taken on the white missionaries' behalf by the Cherokees' attorney, former attorney general of the United States William Wirt. The suit challenged Georgia's enforcement of its laws in the Cherokee Nation's territory.

Worcester v. Georgia thus required the Supreme Court to address for the first time the important legal question of whether it was the federal government or an individual state that exercised the superior rights of sovereignty and jurisdiction recognized under the doctrine of discovery. *Worcester* would decide, once and for all, which level of colonial government, state or federal, would have what Marshall had called in *Johnson* the "exclusive right to extinguish the Indian title of occupancy, either by purchase or conquest" under U.S. law.[48]

In *Worcester*'s opening paragraphs, the chief justice carefully reviewed the basic elements of his heretofore incomplete model of Indian rights. He began by drawing upon the by now familiar judicial language of Indian savagery that he had used in *Johnson* to set the stage for his discussion of the origins of the doctrine of discovery in the European colonial era:

> After lying concealed for a series of ages, the enterprise of Europe, guided by nautical science, conducted some of her adventurous sons into this western world. They found it in possession of a people who had made small progress in agriculture or manufactures, and whose general employment was war, hunting, and fishing.[49]

The chief justice then quoted directly from his earlier opinion in *Johnson* to show how the doctrine of discovery had guided the European colonial powers in establishing and extending their respective claims to white racial dictatorship over Indian tribes in America:

> The great maritime powers of Europe discovered and visited different parts of this continent at nearly the same time. The object was too immense for any one of them to grasp the whole; and the claimants were too powerful to submit to the exclusive or unreasonable pretensions of any single potentate. To avoid bloody conflicts, which might terminate disastrously to all, it was necessary for the nations of Europe to establish some principle which all would acknowledge, and which should decide their respective rights as between themselves. This principle, suggested by the actual state of things, was, "that discovery gave title to the government by whose subjects or by whose authority it was made, against all other European governments, which title might be consummated by possession." 8 Wheat. 573.[50]

Worcester's introductory paragraphs also contain the Marshall model's usual concession of judicial impotency to do very much about the wrongs inflicted upon Indians under the doctrine of discovery. Marshall says in *Worcester* that it "is difficult to comprehend the proposition, that the inhabitants of either quarter of the globe could have rightful original claims of dominion over the inhabitants of the other, or over the lands they occupied; or that discovery of either by the other should give the discoverer rights in the country discovered, which annulled the pre-existing rights of its ancient possessors." But always the racial realist in his opinions, he went on to explain, "power, war, conquest, give rights, which, after possession, are conceded by the world; and which can never be controverted by those on whom they descend." Such was "the actual state of things," according to Marshall in *Worcester*.[51]

This prefatory, proto-Foucauldian genealogy of the doctrine of discovery, jurisgeneratively arising out of "power, war, and conquest"[52] is followed by a lengthy and detailed defense of *Worcester*'s principal holding, that the laws of Georgia, according to Marshall's famous declaration, could have "no force" in the Cherokee Nation.[53] In denying Georgia jurisdictional power over the territory of the Cherokee Nation, the Court's holding recognized the federal government's exclusive colonial supremacy and control over Indian affairs under the Constitution and laws of the United States.[54]

In defending this controversial holding, which would elicit defiant responses from Georgia, the other southern states seeking removal of all tribes within their borders, and President Jackson himself,[55] Marshall's *Worcester* opinion provided a far more carefully crafted and nuanced discussion of the precise legal effects of the discovery doctrine on Indian rights than he had initially adumbrated in *Johnson* or *Cherokee Nation*.

The doctrine, according to the more refined and expanded rendition offered up by Marshall in *Worcester,* was a necessary tool of colonial governmentality developed as part of an art of imperial government during the European colonial era. It functioned, in theory at least, as a means of avoiding inconvenient, unnecessary, and debilitating wars for empire in the New World between the competing European colonial powers.[56] As Marshall declared in *Worcester,* in plain rebuttal to the southern states, like Georgia, seeking to expel Indian tribes,[57] the doctrine simply gave to the European nation making a discovery of Indian-occupied land in the New World "the sole right of acquiring the soil and of making settlements on it. It was an exclusive principle which shut out the right of competition among those who had agreed to it." It did not, as his opinion in *Worcester* carefully explained, operate in any way to interfere with the tribes' preexisting rights of self-government, "so far as respected themselves only."[58]

Worcester's more carefully refined delineation of the precise scope and content of the rights acquired by the first European discoverer under the discovery doctrine represents one of the Marshall model's most important statements on the principle of diminished tribal sovereignty in the Supreme Court's Indian law. However, it is worth noting that Marshall's heroic defense of Indian rights to self-government in the United States relies heavily on the jurispathic force of a familiar racial stereotype of Indians as "warlike" savages. Marshall, now the cautious judicial minimalist in his Indian law decisions, found the perfect instrument for proving his case that Georgia's laws could have no force in the Cherokee Nation: the language of Indian savagery given legal authority and validation by the Crown's colonial charters.

Worcester's more refined analysis of retained tribal sovereignty under the Supreme Court's Indian law begins with Marshall's limiting assertion that the Crown, in its relations with the Indian tribes of North America, never claimed any right under the principles of the discovery doctrine to intrude "into the interior of their affairs." Thus, Georgia, whose charter rights within its territorial boundaries derived solely from the Crown's prerogatives of conquest and colonization under the doctrine of discovery, could make no claim to "legitimate power" to govern the Cherokees or interfere in their internal affairs.[59] The discovery doctrine, under this minimalist interpretation, functioned only to constrain the external relations of the tribes with other European colonial nations.[60] It only gave, as Marshall had explained in *Johnson,* "an exclusive right to extinguish the Indian title of occupancy, either by purchase or by conquest," and nothing more, under the European Law of Nations.

Having laid out this detailed and judicially cautious rendition of the tangible, real-world legal effects of the doctrine of discovery on Indian rights, the chief justice then drew upon the jurispathic force of the language of Indian savagery to explain the reasons for recognizing this inherent right of self-government in the tribes. The tribes of America, as *Worcester* explains, were, "fierce and warlike in their character," their "principal occupation" was hunting, and their land was "more used for that purpose than for any other."[61] They were, in other words, too savage and hostile for the Crown to effectively govern them as loyal subjects, obedient to the control of designated English colonial authorities. The colonial charters granted by the Crown to the British North American colonies, the organic legal documents of all the colonial governments in British North America, in fact uniformly recognized the warlike, irreconcilable character of the Indian tribes of North America in an imperial language of Indian savagery that brooked no superior sovereignty over its prerogatives and privileges of discovery and conquest under English law.

The first Crown charter issued to the Jamestown colony had legally empowered and commended the Virginia Company to "bring the Infidels and Savages, living in those Parts, to human civility, and to a settled and quiet Government."[62] Georgia's own Crown charter, its originating, organic text of legal meaning and jurisgenerative governing authority in North America, was cited specifically by Marshall to demonstrate that this immutable principle of the Indian's implacable savage nature was deeply embedded in the legal language of the Crown's charters to the English colonies in North America:

> ". . . and whereas our provinces in North America have been
> frequently ravaged by Indian enemies, more especially that of South
> Carolina, which, in the late war by the neighbouring savages, was laid
> waste by fire and sword, and great numbers of the English inhabitants
> miserably massacred; and our loving subjects, who now inhabit there,
> by reason of the smallness of their numbers, will, in case of any new
> war, be exposed to the like calamities, inasmuch as their whole south-
> ern frontier continueth unsettled, and lieth open to the said savages."[63]

The imperial language of Indian savagery used in this and the other royal charters cited and relied upon at length in *Worcester* demonstrated, at least in Marshall's view, that the Crown had never presumed to consider the Indians as domestic subjects to be governed by royal decree or proclamation. Rather, the Indian tribes of North America were regarded by the Crown as "barbarous nations, whose incursions were feared, and to repel those incursions, the power to make war was given."[64] They were, in other words, lawfully recognized by the Crown as hostile, savage, and violent enemies implacably opposed to England's assertions of sovereignty and dominion over North America under the doctrine of discovery. They were incommensurable others, and only the Crown possessed the power and the right of discovery and conquest over these radically opposed forms of savage humanity.

This was the "actual state of things" at the time the charters were granted. The broadly drawn racial iconography of Indians as fierce, war-loving, and hostile savages contained in those royally generated juris-pathic texts provided the governing legal principles and racial precepts of colonial governmentality, indigenous to British North America, that the Court now had to apply to all questions of Indian rights under the Constitution and laws of the United States.

The Indians were simply too uncivilized and "barbarous" to be brought under the immediate and direct control of any European co-lonial power in North America: "Fierce and warlike in their character, they might be formidable enemies or effective friends." To cement their friendship and cooperation against the other European colonial pow-ers, the English Crown had no choice but to recognize the tribes' actual independence and therefore "their right to self government."[65] At an early point in the Crown's formal relations with the tribes of the origi-nal Atlantic seaboard colonies,[66] limited recognition of Indian forms of self-government was viewed as a convenient operating principle of co-lonial governmentality for North America. It was in the interests of the Crown and its colonies to recognize this fundamental principle through-out British North America as the law of England's colonial empire.

These reasons of state and sovereign self-interest were precisely why the power of dealing with the tribes by treaty under the discovery doc-trine, "in its utmost extent, was admitted to reside in the crown."[67] It was an imperially exercised power made necessary by the conditions of colonial governmentality in a territory occupied by hostile savages but claimed by England's imperial rights of discovery and conquest. Only the Crown possessed the paramount authority under the doctrine of discovery to extinguish the Indians' title of occupancy, by purchase or by conquest, and perfect England's rights to superior sovereignty over North America.

Following the Revolutionary War, as Marshall next explained, the power of exclusive colonial control over Indian affairs recognized in the Crown under the doctrine had devolved to the federal government of the United States: "The treaties and laws of the United States con-template the Indian territory as completely separated from that of the states; and provide that all intercourse with them shall be carried on exclusively by the government of the union."[68] The laws of Georgia, therefore, as Marshall famously declared in *Worcester*, could have no force within the Cherokee Nation.

Worcester significantly expanded and refined the principles of the doctrine of discovery. According to the Marshall model as rendered in *Worcester*, the Indian's savage nature and fierce resistance to English claims of superior sovereignty required a pragmatic, limited recognition of Indian rights to self-government and property. It was also necessary that sovereign supremacy over Indian tribes be centralized in the Crown, which required an ultimate freedom and authority to negotiate with the tribes over the scope and content of those rights. That supreme form of imperial sovereign power over the tribes, *Worcester* holds, was now possessed by the U.S. federal government over all aspects of Indian affairs under the Constitution and laws of the United States.

Worcester v. Georgia completed the Marshall Trilogy and refined the basic elements of the Marshall Model of Indian Rights by fixing the balance of colonial power and control over Indian affairs under the Constitution of the United States in favor of the federal government. In that sense, *Worcester* is rightly regarded as a landmark victory, in theory at least, for Indian rights. Its principle of federal supremacy in Indian affairs theoretically immunizes tribal Indians from many forms of state encroachment on tribal rights and interests.[69] As the *Cherokee* cases demonstrate, state laws directed at Indian country in the past have oftentimes sought to impose highly onerous and sometimes even virulent, genocidal forms of white racial dictatorship upon Indians.[70] From our post-*Brown* racial perspective, however, the problem with this final and most celebrated case of the famous Marshall Trilogy is that it embraces and perpetuates a racist language of Indian savagery to rationalize the recognition of these retained rights of a limited form of tribal sovereignty under the doctrine of discovery. *Worcester*'s primary importance as the third and final case of the Marshall Trilogy is that it underscores the multiplicity of legitimating jurispathic functions performed by the language of Indian savagery in the Marshall model. Signs taken for wonders, *Worcester* reveals how the same basic hybrid image of the Indian as inferior savage with limited rights can be used to justify not only the jurispathic denial but also the Supreme Court's steadfast protection of Indian self-government and property rights under

U.S. law. According to *Worcester*'s authoritative legal interpretation of this European-derived form of colonial governmentality, the U.S. federal government, and no other sovereign power, possesses the exclusive privileges of white racial dictatorship over Indian tribes in the United States.

Conclusion: The Jurispathic Power of the Language of Indian Savagery Perpetuated by the Marshall Model of Indian Rights

We have identified four principal elements of the Marshall Model of Indian Rights as it arises out of *Johnson* and the two *Cherokee* cases.[71] First, the Marshall model is based upon a foundational set of beliefs in white racial superiority and Indian racial inferiority. Second, the model defines the scope and content of the Indian's inferior legal and political rights by reference to the doctrine of discovery and its organizing principle of white racial supremacy over the continent of North America. Third, the model relies on a judicially validated language of Indian savagery to justify the asserted privileges. Finally, the Court's role as a creature and instrument of these originating sources makes it impossible for the justices to do anything meaningful or lasting to protect Indian rights from the continuing rights-denying jurispathic force of the language of racism used to justify the discovery doctrine's racially discriminatory legal principles.

The doctrine of discovery, first incorporated into the Marshall model by *Johnson*'s diminishment of Indian rights to property and self-rule, next applied in *Cherokee Nation* to define an inferior political status for tribes as "domestic dependent" nations under the Constitution, and then finally used by the Court in *Worcester* to justify exclusive federal authority over Indian affairs, provides a powerful illustration of what happens when the justices validate a principle of racial discrimination in one of their legal decisions on minority rights. Just as Justice Jackson predicted in his dissent in *Korematsu*, such a principle then "lies about like a loaded weapon ready for the hand of any authority that can bring forward a plausible claim of an urgent need." *Johnson, Cherokee Nation,* and *Worcester,* as I show in the remaining chapters of this book, have been used repeatedly by the Supreme Court to expand in our law the principle of racial discrimination perpetuated by the doctrine of discovery.

5

The Rise of the Plenary Power Doctrine

Chief Justice Roger Taney's Antebellum Racial Perspective on Indian Rights

As a potent signifier of colonial desire and discipline, the model of Indian rights inaugurated by Chief Justice Marshall's trilogy of Indian law opinions has come to serve a number of important organizing functions in the Supreme Court's Indian law. The model's validation of the discovery doctrine provided the Court and the U.S. government with a devastatingly effective form of rights-denying, jurispathic power. The doctrine of discovery, according to the Marshall model, functions to deny all competing claims to Indian rights that are opposed to the colonial interests of the United States and to the Court's interpretation of its underlying principle of white racial supremacy.

Closely connected to its rights-destroying jurispathic function in the Court's Indian law, the Marshall model's judicial embrace of the discovery doctrine legally reinforces and sanctions long-established racist stereotypes and imagery directed at Indians as a discrete and insular minority group in America. A well-known language of racism that identifies Indians as irredeemable savages now generates important legal

71

consequences and precedents. The Marshall model gives authoritative legal meaning and sanction to the language of racism used to justify the doctrine's regime of legalized racial discrimination and then perpetuates that meaning through the force of stare decisis.

The destructive jurispathic force of the Marshall model is potently evidenced in the post-Marshall nineteenth-century Supreme Court's development of the congressional plenary power doctrine in Indian affairs. This notorious doctrine effectively immunized Congress's legalized racial dictatorship over tribes from any form of meaningful judicial review. Significantly, the plenary power doctrine was generated directly out of the principles of white racial superiority affirmed by the Marshall model's originating precedents in a series of major nineteenth-century Supreme Court decisions that followed the Marshall Trilogy.[1]

The first point of emergence of the plenary power doctrine in the Supreme Court's post-Marshall era can be traced to *United States v. Rogers,* an opinion written in 1846 by Marshall's successor as chief justice, Roger Taney, of "infamous" *Dred Scott* fame. Chief Justice Taney had only briefly discussed Indian rights in *Dred Scott,* citing the jurispathic principles Marshall had derived from the doctrine of discovery to distinguish the rights to citizenship "of the Indian race" from those of Negroes under the Constitution. Indian tribes, Taney wrote in *Dred Scott,* had not historically formed a part of the colonial communities, and had never "amalgamated" with them. Though the Indians were "uncivilized," as *Dred Scott* explained, "the course of events" has brought them "under subjection" to the white race, "and it has been found necessary, for their sake as well as our own, to regard them as in a state of pupilage, and to legislate to a certain extent over them and the territory they occupy." Applying the Marshall model's guardian-ward principle, Taney's opinion noted that Indians could only become naturalized as citizens under the laws of the United States by abandoning their ties to their savage tribes and taking up "abode among the white population."[2] Negroes, of course, were not provided this amalgamating option under the Constitution and laws of the United States, according to the Court's decision in *Dred Scott.*

In *United States v. Rogers,*[3] written a decade prior to his *Dred Scott* opinion, Taney used the Marshall model to define Indian rights for a different jurispathic purpose. *Rogers* adumbrates the basic contours of what will come to be known in the nineteenth-century Supreme Court's Indian law as the congressional plenary power doctrine.[4]

The case involved the federal government's criminal prosecution of a white man, William Rogers, indicted by the federal Circuit Court in Arkansas for the murder of another white man in federally reserved Indian territory. Rogers's defense to his crime was that he was immune from federal prosecution for this alleged murder under a proviso to an 1834 act of Congress extending federal criminal laws over Indian country.[5] The proviso that Rogers relied upon in his defense to the federal charges declared that federal criminal jurisdiction did not "extend to crimes committed by one Indian against the person or property of another Indian." Rogers, a white man, claimed that he had been adopted into the "Cherokee tribe of Indians, and having married a Cherokee Indian woman" under tribal law, had renounced his U.S. citizenship.[6] His novel legal argument to the Court was that, politically speaking, he was an Indian and therefore exempt from the U.S. criminal jurisdiction over non-Indians in Indian territory.

The Taney Court, with the chief justice himself writing the opinion in the case, had no trouble holding unanimously that the proviso applied only to real Indians, not those adopted into the tribe who were racially white.[7] In announcing this holding that only real Indians could be recognized as such under the Marshall model, and not those whites who just want to be considered as Indians, Taney, in broad terms, declared Congress's unbridled power to assert its criminal laws over the Indian territory generally. The chief justice derived this broad power from principles that he declared were "too firmly and clearly established to admit of dispute."[8] These of course, were the principles of white racial supremacy over Indians and their lands affirmed by his predecessor, Chief Justice Marshall, in his famous trilogy of opinions on Indian rights. The indisputable authority of Marshall's principles of Indian rights led Taney to the legal conclusion that where the country occupied by the Indian tribes residing within the territorial limits of the United States "is not within the limits of any state, Congress may by law punish any offence committed there, no matter whether the offender be a white man or Indian."[9]

All the basic elements of the Marshall model adopted by later Supreme Court decisions following the trilogy are deployed by the Court's opinion in *Rogers*.[10] Taney justified Congress's unlimited jurisdictional power over Indian affairs by reprising the Marshall model's rendition of the rights-destroying, jurispathic effects of the doctrine of discovery upon the Indian tribes of the continent. According to Taney:

> The native tribes who were found on this continent at the time of its discovery have never been acknowledged or treated as independent nations by the European governments, nor regarded as the owners of the territory they respectively occupied. On the contrary, the whole continent was divided and parceled out, and granted by the governments of Europe as if it had been vacant and unoccupied land, and the Indians continually held to be, and treated as, subject to their dominion and control.[11]

Having recognized the U.S. rights of conquest under the doctrine, Taney next relied on the jurispathic force of the long-established tradition of negative racial stereotyping of Indians to justify current application of the doctrine's principle of white supremacy over tribes. The United States, Taney explained, had always exercised "its power over this unfortunate race" in what he called a "spirit of humanity and justice," endeavoring "by every means in its power to enlighten their minds and increase their comforts, and to save them if possible from the consequences of their own vices."[12]

Having relied upon the same basic language of Indian savagery that Marshall had used in his famous trilogy of Indian law opinions, Taney also rendered the same type of judicial concession to the controlling and unappealable force of the discovery doctrine in defining Indian rights under U.S. law that Marshall had displayed in his earlier Indian rights decisions. Even if Congress were to decide to exercise its unquestioned power in Indian affairs "otherwise" than in a "spirit of humanity and justice," *Rogers* declared that it ultimately would not matter under the Marshall Model of Indian Rights. There was nothing that the Court could do to protect Indian rights once Congress decided to exercise its broad power under the discovery doctrine: "[W]ere the right and propriety of exercising this power now open to question, yet it is a question for the law-making and political department of the government, and not for the judicial. It is our duty to expound and execute the law as we find it."[13]

Taney's dutiful articulation of the unappealable nature of federal power over tribes under the Marshall model generated a significantly reinforced and strengthened form of legalized dictatorship possessed by the United States under the Supreme Court's Indian law. Taney's stated principle in *Rogers* that Indian affairs are subject to a judicially unreviewable power in Congress would in fact come to play an important organizing role in many of the Supreme Court's major decisions on Indian rights for the remainder of the nineteenth century and into the early decades of the twentieth century as well. At the same time, *Rogers*'s embrace of a language of Indian savagery to justify this judicially unreviewable power perpetuated an important legal tradition in America. As predicted by Justice Jackson in his dissent in *Korematsu* (see chapter 2, "'Like a Loaded Weapon'"), the principle of white racial superiority historically used to justify discrimination against Indian tribes under the doctrine of discovery had been expanded to new purposes in the Supreme Court's Indian law. According to the language of racism used in *Rogers,* Indians, as members of an "unfortunate race," were under the "dominion and control" of the United States.[14]

Crow Dog

Though Taney in *Rogers* had outlined its basic contours and precedential groundings in the Marshall Model of Indian Rights, Indian law scholars and historians usually consider the congressional plenary power doctrine to have originated in two related landmark Supreme Court decisions of the late nineteenth century, *Ex parte Crow Dog* and *United States v. Kagama.*[15] The first case, *Crow Dog,* was decided by the justices in 1883. *Kagama* was then issued by the Court in 1886, upholding Congress's 1885 legislative repeal of *Crow Dog.*[16]

Crow Dog involved a murder committed by Crow Dog, a Brule Sioux Indian, against another member of his tribe, Spotted Tail. As thoroughly documented by Sidney Harring's compelling study of the case, the BIA had been attempting since at least 1874 to get a bill passed by Congress to extend the jurisdiction of federal courts to a list of enumerated felonies committed by Indians against other Indians within "Indian country," federally reserved and protected tribal lands. The BIA was measurably aided in this task by a number of humanitarian and Christian religious organizations closely associated with the "law for the Indians" movement. This reform movement sought to extend the "white man's law" as a civilizing agent over Indians living on the reservation. Congress, however, had failed to act to fulfill the reformers' goal by an express statute. The BIA therefore brought *Ex parte Crow Dog* as a test case to acquire by Supreme Court ruling what it could not achieve through the normal democratic legislative processes of Congress.[17]

Crow Dog's murder of Spotted Tail had been satisfactorily dealt with from the Sioux's perspective by the local customary or common law[18] of the tribe. As the BIA and government prosecutors were all well aware, the families involved had agreed, following a tribal council meeting and mediation by Brule Sioux peacemakers, to a payment of $600, eight horses, and one blanket for the murder of Spotted Tail.[19] The federal prosecutors argued, however, that Crow Dog, a Sioux Indian, could be prosecuted under the same scheme of federal legislation as it had successfully applied to William Rogers, a white man, in *United States v. Rogers*. That legislation, however, had specifically exempted crimes committed by one Indian upon another from federal prosecution. The government argued, nonetheless, that the Sioux Treaty of 1868 required the Sioux to turn over "bad men among the Indians" for crimes committed in their territory. This provision, along with a subsequent agreement in which Congress pledged to secure to the Sioux an "orderly government" by appropriate legislation enacted at some unspecified future date, constituted, according to the government's attorneys, an implicit surrender to the United States of any exclusive sovereign right of the Sioux tribe to criminal jurisdiction over member-on-member crimes.[20]

Justice Stanley Matthews's opinion for a unanimous Supreme Court rejected the government's argument and held that Crow Dog was not subject to federal criminal prosecution for the murder of Spotted Tail. The murder of one Indian by another in Indian country, explained Matthews, was "not an offense under the laws of the United States."[21]

Matthews's analysis of the Sioux's treaty rights in *Crow Dog* shows how firmly embedded the Marshall model had become in the late-nineteenth-century Supreme Court's jurisprudence on Indian rights. Adopting the same approach as Taney had in *Rogers,* Matthews noted that the Sioux's rights under their treaty and any other related agreements ratified by Congress were to be understood by reference to their status as "wards" under the Marshall Model of Indian Rights. In interpreting the legal consequences of this status, Matthews drew upon the jurispathic force of the long-established tradition of stereotyping Indians as savages:

> They were nevertheless to be subject to the laws of the United States, not in the sense of citizens, but as they had always been, as wards, subject to a guardian; not as individuals, constituted members of the political community of the United States, with a voice in the selection of representatives and the framing of the laws, but as a dependent community who were in a state of pupilage, advancing from the condition of a savage tribe to that of a people who, through the discipline of labor, and by education, it was hoped might become a self-supporting and self-governing society.[22]

Though affirming important Sioux rights to self-government, *Crow Dog*'s holding that Indians were not civilized enough to be subjected to the same rules of justice as white people is perfectly consistent with the principles of white racial superiority perpetuated by the Marshall model's judicial embrace of the European colonial-era doctrine of discovery. Writing in a well-known language of Indian savagery, Matthews noted that the Sioux treaties looked to the tribe's

> establishment as a people upon a defined reservation as a permanent home, who were to be urged, as far as it could successfully be done, into the practice of agriculture, and whose children were to be taught the arts and industry of civilized life, and that it was no part of the design to treat the individuals as separately responsible and amenable, in all their personal and domestic relations with each other, to the general laws of the United States, outside of those which were enacted expressly with reference to them as members of an Indian tribe.[23]

Crow Dog has often been viewed by scholars of the Supreme Court's Indian law as a landmark decision upholding Indian rights to self-government, giving a degree of legitimacy and "context to inherent tribal sovereignty."[24] It is important to recognize, however, that the Court's contextual analysis of Crow Dog's right, as a Sioux Indian, to immunity from federal criminal prosecution for the killing of Spotted Tail is justified by Matthews's express reliance upon well-known and widely dispersed late-nineteenth-century racist beliefs about Indians. The reason the Sioux should not be subjected to the white man's law,

Matthews explained, was because they were uncivilized savages. I have previously identified this type of jurispathic, rights-destroying use of a language of Indian savagery as one of the essential elements of the Marshall model (see chapter 4). In *Crow Dog*, Matthews used familiar, long-established stereotypes to deny the federal government's right of criminal jurisdiction over an uncivilized Indian. In *Crow Dog*'s most famous passage, Matthews again used this racist form of discourse to denounce the government's attempt to extend the dominant white society's civilized forms of law

> over aliens and strangers; over the members of a community, separated by race, by tradition, by the instincts of a free though savage life, from the authority and power which seeks to impose upon them the restraints of an external and unknown code, and to subject them to the responsibilities of civil conduct, according to rules and penalties of which they could have no previous warning; which judges them by a standard made by others and not for them, which takes no account of the conditions which should except them from its exactions, and makes no allowance for their inability to understand it. It tries them not by their peers, nor by the customs of their people, nor the law of their land, but by superiors of a different race, according to the law of a social state of which they have an imperfect conception, and which is opposed to the traditions of their history, to the habits of their lives, to the strongest prejudices of their savage nature; one which measures the red man's revenge by the maxims of the white man's morality.[25]

Matthews's approach to interpreting Indian rights under the Marshall model follows what is by now becoming a familiar pattern in the nineteenth-century Supreme Court's Indian law: The negative racial stereotypes used by the dominant society to perpetuate the myth of Indian savagery are expressly being relied upon by the Court to expand the original discriminatory principles of the European colonial-era doctrine of discovery to new purposes. In *Crow Dog*, the expansion of the doctrine's organizing principle of white racial superiority to uphold discriminatory treatment of Indian tribes produced the odd consequence of shielding Indians from the exercise of federal criminal jurisdiction. *Crow Dog*'s victory for Indian tribal sovereignty, in other words, was achieved by the Court's application and extension of the Marshall model's foundational principle of Indian racial inferiority. But as we have seen before in *Worcester,* under the Marshall model the jurispathic force of long-established stereotypes of Indians' racial inferiority can be drawn upon as a justification for protecting as well as for denying important Indian rights of cultural sovereignty and survival (see chapter 4). In this sense, the Marshall Model of Indian Rights functions as a highly flexible tool of colonial governmentality in the Supreme Court's Indian law. It can uphold the discovery doctrine's underlying principle of white racial superiority not only by selectively destroying but also by selectively recognizing and protecting certain types of Indian rights under U.S. law.

It is also important to note that the so-called victory for Indian rights represented by *Crow Dog*'s upholding of Indian tribal sovereignty in the criminal jurisdictional sphere was short-lived. The decision was cited by the BIA as proof that Congress needed to exercise its own jurispathic powers of plenary authority and control over Indian affairs and affirmatively impose federal criminal jurisdiction over the tribes. The Supreme Court's elemental impotency in protecting any remaining rights of the tribes from the imperial privileges asserted by a white racial dictatorship meant that the *Crow Dog* decision could be subsequently repealed by Congress, and there was nothing the justices could do about it under the Marshall Model of Indian Rights. And Congress did just that, by passing the Major Crimes Act of 1885, which effectively overturned the Court's unanimous decision in *Crow Dog*.[26]

Kagama

The Major Crimes Act of 1885, in which Congress reacted to the BIA's lobbying pressure and the supposed "public outcry" over the Court's upholding of tribal sovereignty in *Crow Dog*,[27] extended federal criminal jurisdiction over eight enumerated felony crimes committed by Indians against other Indians in Indian country. The act nullifying *Crow Dog*'s precedent was then applied in a federal criminal prosecution of a California Indian, Kagama, whose tribe did not even have a treaty with the United States. Kagama was indicted under the act for murdering another Indian on his tribe's reservation. He challenged the statute as going beyond Congress's law-making powers under the Constitution's Indian commerce clause.

The Supreme Court's landmark decision in *United States v. Kagama* represents the jurispathic triumph of the Marshall Model of Indian Rights over any competing indigenous legal tradition of unconstrained inherent tribal sovereignty. *Kagama*'s rights-destroying reach did not just extinguish the autonomy and validity of all competing visions of exclusive tribal sovereignty over Indian-on-Indian crime in Indian country. The Court's unanimous opinion in *Kagama* also effectively immunized Congress's plenary power in Indian affairs from any meaningful form of constitutionally based judicial scrutiny or review. The only interpretation of Indian rights that had any definitive legal meaning under *Kagama*'s holding was that of Congress acting under its unquestioned plenary power in Indian affairs according to the Marshall Model of Indian Rights.

The basic constitutional problem confronting the Supreme Court in *Kagama* was that the Major Crimes Act was a federal criminal code asserting felony jurisdiction over Indians in Indian country. Nowhere in the Constitution was Congress given express authority to enact such a law regulating crimes committed by members of Indian tribes on their own reservations. As Justice Samuel F. Miller's opinion for the Court in *Kagama* concedes, "The constitution of the United States is almost silent in regard to the relations of the government which was established by it to the numerous tribes of Indians within its borders." The only significant mention of Indians in the Constitution, Miller noted, was in that "clause which gives congress 'power to regulate commerce with foreign nations, and among the several states, and with the Indian tribes.'" The Court, however, was not buying the government's argument that a criminal code could fit under any plausible definition of Indian commerce:

> [W]e think it would be a very strained construction of this clause that a system of criminal laws for Indians living peaceably in their reservations, which left out the entire code of trade and intercourse laws justly enacted under that provision, and established punishments for the common-law crimes of murder, manslaughter, arson, burglary, larceny, and the like, without any reference to their relation to any kind of commerce, was authorized by the grant of power to regulate commerce with the Indian tribes.[28]

Fortunately for the BIA's late-nineteenth-century colonial fantasy of unilaterally imposing federal criminal jurisdiction over the tribes regardless of express constitutional limitations, Miller's interpretation of the Marshall model in *Kagama* demonstrated that there was no need to engage in such a "strained" construction of the Constitution's Indian commerce clause.[29] In fact, according to the Court's opinion in *Kagama,* the justices didn't need to construe the language of the Constitution at all to justify this congressional exercise of unbridled power over Indian tribes. The Marshall Model of Indian Rights and its underlying principle of the tribes' inferior racial status provided Congress with all the legal authority and justification it needed to enact a criminal code, even without Indian consent, governing Indian-on-Indian crimes in Indian country. According to the Court in *Kagama,* Indian rights were subject to Congress's extraconstitutional power under the Marshall model's guardian-ward principle.

This major transformation in the *Kagama* Court's approach to defining the scope of congressional power in Indian affairs under the Constitution was firmly grounded in well-recognized legal authority.[30] The Marshall model's major precedents were called upon to define and support virtually every aspect of Miller's legal analysis of the unlimited scope of congressional plenary power in *Kagama.*[31]

Miller begins his analysis with a restatement of the foundational principle of white racial superiority embodied in the doctrine of discovery. Reprising the Marshall Model in language that went right to the source of the jurispathic legal principles governing Indian rights in the United States, Miller wrote:

> Following the policy of the European governments in the discovery
> of America, towards the Indians who were found here, the colonies
> before the Revolution, and the states and the United States since, have
> recognized in the Indians a possessory right to the soil over which
> they roamed and hunted and established occasional villages. But they
> asserted an ultimate title in the land itself, by which the Indian tribes
> were forbidden to sell or transfer it to other nations or peoples without
> the consent of this paramount authority.[32]

With the European colonial era's doctrine of discovery providing the foundational racial precepts of his analysis, Miller then specifically cited *Cherokee Nation* and *Worcester v. Georgia* as representing "perhaps the best statement" of the legal rights of Indians in the United States. For good measure, he also directly cited Taney's opinion in *Rogers*[33] as another important precedent of the Marshall model recognizing the unlimited scope of Congressional power in Indian affairs. Stare decisis and the soundness of the holdings in all those leading cases led him to confidently conclude that Congress possessed the unquestioned authority to impose a criminal code over Indians in Indian country, regardless of what the Constitution expressly said or did not say on the matter. Under the Marshall model's guardian-ward principle, Miller declared:

> It seems to us that this is within the competency of Congress. These Indian tribes are the wards of the nation. They are communities dependent on the United States, dependent largely for their daily food; dependent for their political rights. They owe no allegiance to the states, and receive from them no protection. Because of the local ill feeling, the people of the states where they are found are often their deadliest enemies. From their very weakness and helplessness, so largely due to the course of dealing of the federal government with them, and the treaties in which it has been promised, there arises the duty of protection, and with it power. This has always been recognized by the executive, and by Congress, and by this court, whenever the question has arisen.

Miller went on to spell out the justification for this judicially unreviewable, rights-destroying jurispathic power possessed by the United States over tribes in the familiar cadences of the Court's racist nineteenth-century judicial language of Indian savagery:

> The power of the general government over these remnants of a race once powerful, now weak and diminished in numbers, is necessary to their protection, as well as to the safety of those among whom they dwell. It must exist in that government, because it never has existed anywhere else; because the theater of its exercise is within the geographical limits of the United States; because it has never been denied; and because it alone can enforce its laws on all the tribes.[34]

In its holding that Congress did not require express textual authority under the Constitution to enact a criminal code over Indian-on-Indian crimes on the reservation, *Kagama* marks the triumph of the principle of white racial supremacy over Indian tribes under the doctrine of discovery in America, as enforced by the Supreme Court's interpretation of the Marshall Model of Indian Rights. *Kagama,* the nineteenth-century

Supreme Court's landmark case in the development of the Court's plenary power doctrine, "left Indian tribes mere 'wards' of the federal government, totally dependent on the will of Congress, which could assert its political power even to their termination as tribes and the expropriation of their lands without compensation."[35]

Kagama, along with the two other nineteenth-century plenary power cases we have examined leading up to it, *Rogers* and *Crow Dog,* reveals the continuing jurispathic power of the long-established tradition of stereotyping Indians as uncivilized, lawless savages throughout the nineteenth-century Supreme Court's Indian rights decisions. As applied to tribes in these three major Supreme Court opinions on the scope of congressional power in Indian affairs, this racist language of Indian savagery was used to expand the application of the Marshall model's organizing principle of white racial superiority as a justification for discriminatory legal treatment of Indian tribes to new, transformative purposes. The plenary power cases of the post-Marshall, nineteenth-century Supreme Court expansively interpreted the Marshall Model of Indian Rights as placing Indian tribes completely under the control of a judicially unreviewable form of white racial dictatorship. Significantly, Congress's plenary power over Indian tribes was enforced by the justices of the Supreme Court even though no word of textual authority was to be found or cited in the Constitution. All that was needed was the Marshall model of Indian Rights and a familiar and well-known language of racism to justify denying Indian tribes any justice in the courts of their conquerors.

Part III

The Twentieth-Century Post-*Brown* Supreme Court and Indian Rights

> Every American schoolboy knows that the savage tribes of this
> continent were deprived of their ancestral ranges by force and that,
> even when the Indians ceded millions of acres by treaty in return for
> blankets, food and trinkets, it was not a sale but the conquerors' will
> that deprived them of their land.
>
> —Justice Stanley Reed, Tee-Hit-Ton v. United States *(1955)*

The racist precedents and accompanying language of Indian savagery perpetuated by the Supreme Court's interpretation of the Marshall Model of Indian Rights were powerful, organizing forces in justifying the conquest and colonization of Indian tribes throughout the nineteenth century. The rights-destroying jurispathic force of this virulent judicial language succeeded, in roughly half a century's time, in putting Indian tribes completely under the plenary power of Congress as their "guardian." In applying the model's legalized language of Indian savagery, the Supreme Court subjected the most basic human rights of Indian tribal peoples to the whims and abuses of a political process controlled by the white racial dictatorship that ruled America throughout the nineteenth century.

In this part of the book, I show that the same racist nineteenth-century precedents and judicial language can be found organizing and legitimating the Court's treatment of Indian rights in a number of leading twentieth-century cases.

I should first define the terms and theoretical apparatus of the critical perspective I develop in this part of the book on the Supreme Court's twentieth-century Indian law jurisprudence. In analyzing the continuing jurispathic force of the Court's language of Indian savagery in the post-*Brown* era, I use the justices' 1954 *Brown* decision as a primary departure point of cultural reference. That landmark civil rights case has come to be widely recognized as signifying a major constitutional transformation in this country's struggle for racial equality. *Brown* supposedly represents an unequivocal rejection by the twentieth-century Supreme Court of racist nineteenth-century legal precedents, forms of reasoning, and judicial language in its decisions on minority rights under the Constitution.[1] After the *Brown* decision, the long-established tradition of negative racial stereotyping and hostile racist imagery sanctioned by the Court's nineteenth-century decision in *Plessy v. Ferguson* and its "separate but equal" doctrine finally disappears from the way the justices talk about the rights of African Americans.

This post-*Brown* racial paradigm shift, however, which suffices in the main to describe the Supreme Court's stated approach toward defining the rights of black Americans and of virtually every other racial minority group in the United States after 1954, inadequately describes the post-*Brown* Supreme Court's stated racial attitudes in defining the rights of Indian tribal peoples. The justices continued to rely on the same racist precedents and language that had characterized the Supreme Court's Indian rights decisions of the nineteenth century.

Furthermore, this racist judicial language, which post-*Brown* justices relied on and oftentimes even quoted with all its racial excesses and rhetorical flourishes, continued to perform the same legitimating functions it had traditionally performed in the Supreme Court's Indian law. As an integral, organizing part of the Marshall model, this language was used jurispathically by twentieth-century Supreme Court justices to justify the regime of legalized inequality and racialized dictatorial power enforced by the United States over Indian tribes. To borrow once again from the postcolonial perspective of Homi Bhabha, the objective of this discourse remained the same: "to construe the colonized as a population of degenerate types on the basis of racial origin, in order to justify conquest and to establish systems of administration and instruction."[2]

To demonstrate the continuing legal force and racializing objectives of this nineteenth-century language in the post-*Brown* Supreme Court's

Indian law, I examine two of the most important Supreme Court Indian rights decisions of the twentieth century, *Tee-Hit-Ton v. United States,* decided in 1955, the year after *Brown,* and *Oliphant v. Suquamish Indian Tribe,* decided in 1978, nearly a quarter century after *Brown.* In both of these leading cases, the Court jurispathically applied the Marshall model to decide vitally important questions of Indian rights under contemporary U.S. law. Despite the rejection of the nineteenth century's racist precedents and hostile stereotypes directed against blacks and despite the supposed benevolent racial paradigm shift represented by the twentieth-century Supreme Court's landmark civil rights decision in *Brown,* nothing had really changed in the way the justices talked about Indians and their rights. These two important decisions unembarrassedly and unhesitatingly draw on the same legal precedents and language of racism used by the nineteenth-century Supreme Court to deny Indians their asserted rights under U.S. law.

6

What "Every American Schoolboy Knows": The Language of Indian Savagery in *Tee-Hit-Ton*

It would be hard to argue against the proposition that the Supreme Court's 1955 decision in *Tee-Hit-Ton v. United States*[1] was one of the most important Supreme Court Indian rights decisions of the twentieth century, or any century for that matter. The case of the Tee-Hit-Ton Indians specifically involved an unextinguished "aboriginal title" claim[2] to a relatively small amount of territory (350,000 acres of land) in Alaska's Tongass National Forest. But besides that claim, at least according to the government lawyers who argued the case before the justices, *Tee-Hit-Ton* involved potentially as much as *$9 billion* in aggregated just compensation claims asserted against the United States by other similarly situated Indian tribes and groups whose aboriginal property rights in their traditional lands had never been formally extinguished by Congress.[3] And citing that figure, the Supreme Court held in its landmark 6 to 3 *Tee-Hit-Ton* decision that under the European colonial-era doctrine of discovery, Indian tribes are not entitled to just compensation under the Fifth Amendment of the Constitution when their aboriginal property rights are taken and extinguished by the U.S. government.

The Court justified awarding this enormous, $9 billion racial wind-
fall to the U.S. government in *Tee-Hit-Ton* by citing the controlling
legal force of the Marshall model. Justice Stanley Reed, writing for the
majority, held that, under the Constitution, the Tee-Hit-Ton Indians
had no legal rights to just compensation for the taking of their aboriginal homelands because, according to the doctrine of discovery, as Indians, they were to be treated just like the other "savage tribes of this
continent" whose rights have been defined under the Supreme Court's
Indian law. As laid out in "the great case of *Johnson v. McIntosh*," to
quote Reed's own language in *Tee-Hit-Ton*,[4] their occupancy of land
as Indians under *Johnson* was not recognized as a property interest
entitled to just compensation under the Fifth Amendment.

The Tee-Hit-Ton Indians, as the Court described them, comprised
a tiny Tlingit clan of "American Indians of between 60 and 70 individuals."[5] They had occupied their traditional homelands in southeast
Alaska since time immemorial. The whole of Alaska, including the traditional lands of the Tee-Hit-Tons, had been claimed by Russia under
the doctrine of discovery in the mid-eighteenth century, but Russian settlements had always been small and scattered. The czar gladly accepted
the $7 million purchase price for Alaska offered by Secretary of State
William Henry Seward in 1867. By the treaty between the two nations,
Russia conveyed its interest in the vast territory of Alaska—"Seward's
Folly," as it became known—to the United States.[6]

For nearly a century thereafter, there was little pressure to settle
Alaska. Its harsh climate and remote location made it of small interest
to politicians and economic interests in the "lower forty-eight." Consequently, there was little motivation to negotiate treaties with Alaska's
native peoples to extinguish their land claims. During World War II,
however, geological surveys of Alaska revealed its huge potential for
strategically valuable oil and gas reserves. The territory also contained
vast, commercially harvestable timberlands. The only legal impediments
to tapping these abundant natural resources, vital to U.S. national security and economic interests, were the unresolved aboriginal title claims
of Alaska's native peoples to property rights in the territory of Alaska.[7]

To test these aboriginal title claims to Alaska, Congress, by a joint
resolution of August 8, 1947, authorized the federal government to con-
tract for the sale of timber located within the Tongass National Forest in
southeastern Alaska, notwithstanding any claim of possessory "rights,"

including "aboriginal title or occupancy." The congressional resolution
also provided for all receipts from the sale of timber to be maintained in
a special account in the U.S. Treasury until the timber and land rights
were finally determined in a court of law.[8] Essentially, Congress and
the government lawyers involved in the *Tee-Hit-Ton* affair had set up
a test case for the courts to decide the "question of compensation" for
congressionally approved taking of lands occupied in Alaska under "aboriginal Indian use and claim of ownership." To make this intention
perfectly clear, the joint resolution provided expressly that

> [n]othing in this resolution shall be construed as recognizing or deny-
> ing the validity of any claims of possessory rights to lands or timber
> within the exterior boundaries of the Tongass National Forest.[9]

The specifically targeted "claims of possessory rights" in the Tongass
National Forest that the government was testing in this contrived piece
of legislation belonged to the Tee-Hit-Ton Indians.

The tiny band of Tee-Hit-Tons fought all the way to the Supreme
Court in challenging the legality of this congressional action confiscat-
ing the most valuable sustainable natural resource of the lands they
had historically relied on for subsistence and survival. The fact that
their aboriginal property rights were being taken by the United States
without any offer of monetary compensation was obviously of great
concern to the tribe. The Tee-Hit-Tons' constitutionally based claim
for a right of just compensation for their traditional lands, however,
as the Court was made well-aware by government lawyers, held huge
financial consequences that reached far beyond this tiny band of Alaska
Natives. A prior lower court decision had held that Alaskan Native aboriginal property rights were a protected real property interest under
the Constitution. As Justice Reed's opinion in *Tee-Hit-Ton* expressly
noted, that lower court holding, if applied to all the lands claimed by
Alaska's native peoples and similarly situated tribes in the lower forty-
eight states, would, according to the government's figures, expose the
United States to at least $9 billion of just compensation claims.[10]

In 1954, the year following *Brown v. Board of Education,* a six-
justice majority in *Tee-Hit-Ton* denied any form of just compensation
under the Constitution to Alaskan Natives for any of their claimed
property rights.[11] Significantly, the Court's legal justifications for one of
the most important Indian law decisions of the twentieth century relied

upon the European colonial-era doctrine of discovery, the nineteenth-century precedents of the Marshall Model of Indian Rights, and the continuing rights-destroying jurispathic force of a language of racism stereotyping Indians as savages.

The "Rule Derived from *Johnson v. McIntosh*"

Tee-Hit-Ton demonstrates that the basic legal approach of the twentieth-century justices in adhering to the principal elements of the Marshall model had remained wholly unchanged and rigidly static despite the Court's landmark civil rights decision in *Brown,* which it had handed down just the prior term.[12] The doctrine of discovery and the imperial rights of conquest and extinguishment it defined as belonging to the United States continued to control the post-*Brown* Court's racial perspective and reasoning process on Indian rights. According to Reed,[13] it was "well-settled" under U.S. law that after "the coming of the white man to America," Indians lived on their lands only with "permission from the whites." "This position of the Indian" wrote Reed, "has long been rationalized by the legal theory that discovery and conquest gave the conquerors sovereignty over and ownership of the lands thus obtained."[14] Reed's opinion validated this discriminatory legal principle of white racial superiority by specifically citing Chief Justice Marshall's opinion in the "great case of *Johnson v. McIntosh*." That landmark Indian rights decision, Reed explained,

> denied the power of an Indian tribe to pass their right of occupancy to another. It confirmed the practice of two hundred years of American history "that discovery gave an exclusive right to extinguish the Indian title of occupancy, either by purchase or by conquest."[15]

Reed then went on to apply what he called the "rule derived from *Johnson v. McIntosh* that the taking by the United States of unrecognized Indian title is not compensable under the Fifth Amendment." "This is true," he wrote, "not because an Indian or Indian tribe has no standing to sue or because the United States has not consented to be sued for the taking of original Indian title, but because Indian occupation of land without government recognition of ownership creates no rights against taking or extinction by the United States protected by the Fifth Amendment or any other principle of law."[16] There was also the question as to whether this "rule derived from *Johnson v. McIntosh*" could or even should be expanded beyond the lower forty-eight states to apply to any of Alaska's native peoples. Reed simply adopted the long-established stereotype of Indians as savage hunter-gatherers as the governing legal test for deciding whether or not the doctrine of discovery applied to them and their claims for just compensation under the Fifth Amendment:

> From all that was presented, the Court of Claims concluded, and we agree, that the Tee-Hit-Tons were in a hunting and fishing stage of civilization, with shelters fitted to their environment, and claims to rights to use identified territory for these activities as well as the gathering of wild products of the earth. We think this evidence introduced by both sides confirms the Court of Claims' conclusion that the petitioners' use of its lands was like the use of the nomadic tribes of the United States Indians.[17]

In other words, the Tee-Hit-Tons should be treated just like any other group of wandering Indian savages; their rights, if any, under U.S. law are defined by the discovery doctrine. In the language of Indian savagery used by Reed:

> Every American schoolboy knows that the savage tribes of this continent were deprived of their ancestral ranges by force and that, even when the Indians ceded millions of acres by treaty in return for blankets, food and trinkets, it was not a sale but the conquerors' will that deprived them of their land.[18]

Tee-Hit-Ton teaches us the important lesson that a six-justice majority on the post-*Brown* Supreme Court had no problem with relying on racist nineteenth-century precedents and a virulent judicial language of Indian savagery to justify a landmark decision on Indian rights—one with huge financial benefits for the U.S. Treasury to boot. Reed's actively expressed judicial belief that the "tribes of this continent" were savage nomadic hunter-gatherers when the doctrine of discovery was first applied justified both the past colonial aggression by the United States and its continuing racially based imperial privileges over all Indian land. And all of this was perfectly legal, the *Tee-Hit-Ton* majority held, under the Marshall Model of Indian Rights.

"With Congress, Where It Belongs"

Having judicially excused white Americans for taking North America from wandering, savage Indian tribes by conquest and then holding that it was legal under the doctrine of discovery and the Constitution, Reed's opinion in *Tee-Hit-Ton* drew upon another traditional element of the Marshall Model of Indian Rights. Reed concluded the Court's opinion in *Tee-Hit-Ton* by adopting the Marshall model's familiar posture of judicial self-absolution. The Court, as a mere instrument of the white racial dictatorship imposed on tribes by the United States, wasn't responsible for any injustice perpetuated by its decision:

> Our conclusion does not uphold harshness as against tenderness toward the Indians, but it leaves with Congress, where it belongs, the policy of Indian gratuities for the termination of Indian occupancy of government-owned land rather than making compensation for its value a rigid constitutional principle.

In other words, it was the long-established, European-derived system of colonial governmentality respecting Indian property rights adopted under the doctrine of discovery that made the Court rule the way it did in *Tee-Hit-Ton:* "In light of the history of Indian relations in this nation, no other course would meet the problem of the growth of the United States except to make congressional contributions for Indian lands rather than to subject the government to an obligation to pay the value when taken with interest to the date of payment."[19] Even after the Supreme Court's supposed racial paradigm shift in *Brown,* the justices continued to treat one racial minority in America, Indians, as "beggars pleading for decent treatment" under U.S. law.[20]

Beggars before the Justices

As has been previously discussed (see chapter 2, "People of Violence"), the justices, through what Robert Cover has called their "implicit claim to authoritative interpretation," play a critical legitimating role in our society when their legal decisions perpetuate the rights-destroying juris-pathic force of a language of racism. Cover vividly describes the juris-pathic function of the justices: "Confronting the luxuriant growth of a hundred legal traditions, they assert that *this one* is law and destroy or try to destroy the rest." As Cover explains, our adherence as a society "to the judge's interpretation reinforces the hermeneutic process offered by the judge and extends, in one way or another, its social range."[21]

In other words, when a twentieth-century Supreme Court Indian rights decision, such as *Tee-Hit-Ton,* relies upon nineteenth-century precedents and the language of racism perpetuated by the Marshall model to deny Indians their asserted rights under U.S. law, then the justices have declared that it is perfectly legal for the dominant white society to continue to adhere to the same racist system of belief. In so ruling, the justices have given a renewed, twentieth-century legal meaning and powerful form of sanction to a long-established language of racism in America. The principle of white racial supremacy historically used to justify discriminatory treatment of Indians has thus been reinvested, reinforced, and renewed with the force of law. The justices' *legalization of racism* against Indians, by virtue of the Court's final interpretive authority in issuing its landmark opinion in *Tee-Hit-Ton,* is perpetuated as a judicially declared reality for present-day America. According to the familiar stereotype, which "[e]very American schoolboy knows," Indians were savages at "the coming of the white man to America."

As the justices of the Supreme Court tell us, there are important legal consequences and meanings attached to this judicial validation of the language of racism that has been historically directed against Indians in America. The European colonial-era doctrine of discovery and its racist judicial language of Indian savagery will continue to be used as part of the Marshall model to define Indian rights in the twentieth-century Supreme Court's Indian law, even after the landmark civil rights decision of *Brown v. Board of Education.*

7

Rehnquist's Language of Racism in *Oliphant*

As the decision in *Tee-Hit-Ton* clearly illustrates, the twentieth-century Supreme Court's Indian law, even after the landmark civil rights decision in *Brown*, continued to unquestioningly rely on the jurispathic force of the nineteenth-century precedents and hostile judicial language of Indian savagery generated by the Marshall model (see chapter 6). *Tee-Hit-Ton* is not the Court's only post-*Brown* case of major import for Indian rights to display this persistent judicial reliance on racist nineteenth-century precedents and stereotypes. The continuing jurispathic force of the Marshall model's legal mythology of the Indian as an inferior form of savage humanity is evidenced throughout the Supreme Court's 1978 landmark decision in *Oliphant v. Suquamish Indian Tribe*,[1] authored by then associate justice William Rehnquist.

Oliphant is one of the most important Indian law decisions issued by the Supreme Court in the post-*Brown* era, and it unembarrassedly perpetuates the Marshall model's overarching principle of white racial supremacy contained in the European colonial-era doctrine of discovery. It does so through a particularly virulent mode of rights-destroying, jurispathic transmission. *Oliphant,* as written by Rehnquist, cites, quotes, and relies upon racist nineteenth-century beliefs and stereotypes to justify an expansive, rights-destroying, present-day interpretation of the Marshall model. According to *Oliphant,* Indian tribes, as lawless and uncivilized savage peoples, were implicitly divested of any asserted rights that might conflict with the superior sovereign interests of the United States under the discovery doctrine.

Oliphant's "Principle" of "Inherent Limitations on Tribal Power"

The case of *Oliphant v. Suquamish Indian Tribe,* decided by the Supreme Court in 1978, arose out of two separate arrests by Suquamish Indian Tribe police officers for alleged crimes committed on the tribe's reservation, located on the Puget Sound across from the city of Seattle, Washington. Both arrests involved non-Indian defendants who went to U.S. federal district court to challenge the authority of the tribal court to prosecute them for their alleged criminal conduct on the tribe's reservation. The district court and the Ninth Circuit Court of Appeals upheld tribal criminal jurisdiction over both defendants in the case, and the Supreme Court granted certiorari "to decide whether Indian tribal courts have criminal jurisdiction over non-Indians."[2]

The Court, in a 6-to-2 landmark decision written by Rehnquist, held that the Suquamish Indian Tribe could not criminally prosecute non-Indians for crimes committed against tribal police officers trying to keep the peace on the tribe's own reservation during a tribal ceremonial celebration. According to *Oliphant,* Indian tribes had been divested of this particular sovereign power of self-government by their "incorporation" into the United States by operation of the doctrine of discovery. Relying upon this "principle," which he derived from the Marshall model's definition of Indian tribal "status" under the discovery doctrine, Rehnquist wrote that Indian tribes had always been recognized as "diminished" sovereigns under the Supreme Court's Indian law: "Upon incorporation into the territory of the United States, the Indian tribes thereby come under the territorial sovereignty of the United States and their exercise of separate power is constrained so as not to conflict with the interests of this overriding sovereignty."[3] As authority for *Oliphant*'s "principle" of "inherent limitations on tribal powers" over non-Indians on the reservation, Rehnquist directly cited *Johnson v. McIntosh,* the first case of the Marshall Trilogy: "'[T]heir rights to complete sovereignty, as independent nations [are] necessarily diminished.' *Johnson v. McIntosh* 8 Wheat. 543, 574 (1823)."[4]

In applying this newly announced "principle" of the Supreme Court's Indian law, Rehnquist went on to describe "some of the inherent limitations on tribal powers that stem from their incorporation into the United States" under the Marshall Model of Indian Rights. Marshall's decision for the Court in *Johnson v. McIntosh* had denied tribes the "power to dispose of the soil at their own will, to whomsoever they pleased," as Rehnquist explained. In *Cherokee Nation v. Georgia,* Marshall had further observed, as quoted by Rehnquist, that "since Indian tribes are 'completely under the sovereignty and dominion of the United States, . . . any attempt [by foreign nations] to acquire their lands, or to form a political connection with them, would be considered by all as an invasion of our territory, and an act of hostility.'"[5]

According to Rehnquist's expansive interpretation of the legal meanings of these foundational precedents of the Marshall model, the doctrine of discovery functioned to protect the "central" sovereign interests of the United States. Thus, the power to sell their land "to whomsoever they pleased" and to enter into foreign relations were among the rights that Indian tribes had "inherently lost to the overriding sovereignty of the United States" under the doctrine. According to *Oliphant:* "The protection of territory within its external boundaries, is of course, as central to the sovereign interests of the United States as it is to any foreign nation." Further, Rehnquist wrote, there were other sovereign interests that were just as "central" to the United States that the doctrine protected as well. The unprecedented attempt by the Suquamish Indian Tribe to exercise criminal jurisdiction over two non-Indians required the Court to pronounce a newly discovered, third "inherent" limitation on tribal powers stemming from the tribes' "incorporation into the United States" under the Marshall model and the doctrine of discovery.[6]

> But from the formation of the Union and the adoption of the Bill of Rights, the United States has manifested an equally great solicitude that its citizens be protected by the United States from unwarranted intrusions on their personal liberty. The power of the United States to try and criminally punish is an important manifestation of the power to restrict personal liberty. By submitting to the overriding sovereignty

of the United States, Indian tribes therefore necessarily give up their power to try non-Indian citizens of the United States except in a manner acceptable to Congress.[7]

"This principle" that Indian tribes were implicitly divested of their rights to jurisdiction over their territory when those rights conflicted or interfered with the superior rights and interests of the United States under the doctrine of discovery, Rehnquist declared, "would have been obvious a century ago when most Indian tribes were characterized by a 'want of fixed laws [and] competent tribunals of justice.' H.R.Rep. No. 474, 23d Cong., 1st Sess., 18 (1834). It should be no less obvious today, even though present-day Indian tribes embody dramatic advances over their historical antecedents."[8]

Justice Rehnquist's Use of the Nineteenth Century's Racist Language of Indian Savagery and the Marshall Model Precedents in *Oliphant*

It is important to note that the "principle" of inherent limitations on tribal powers announced by the Court for the first time in *Oliphant* relies squarely on Rehnquist's novel interpretation of the jurispathic limitations imposed on Indian rights under the Marshall model and its embrace of the European colonial-era of discovery doctrine. It is also worth noting that Rehnquist defends what he calls the "obvious" nature of this implied principle by quoting from an 1834 House of Representatives report on implementation of the Removal Act. Recall that at that particular moment in American history, Congress was engaged in refining the implementation of the 1830 Removal Act's legislative plan for a massive ethnic-cleansing campaign directed against the Cherokees and the other tribes of the southeastern United States (see chapter 4, "Marshall's Opinions in the *Cherokee* Cases").

In other words, a colonial-era principle of white racial superiority validated by Chief Justice Marshall in the early nineteenth century and a virulent, racist language used by the most aggressive congressional advocates of Indian genocide at the height of the Removal era are given present-day, rights-denying jurispathic force in Rehnquist's 1978 interpretation of Indian rights under U.S. law.

According to the racially recidivist paradigm of Indian rights laid out in *Oliphant,* the beliefs and attitudes of the past, no matter how hostile or racist, must always be given controlling force in interpreting Indian rights in the present day. "Indian law," as Rehnquist writes in *Oliphant,* "draws principally upon the treaties drawn and executed by the Executive Branch and legislation passed by Congress. These instruments, which beyond their actual text form the backdrop for the intricate web of judicially made Indian law, cannot be interpreted in isolation, but must be read in light of the common notions of the day and the assumptions of those who drafted them."[9]

According to *Oliphant*'s expansive, jurispathic paradigm of Indian rights lost to the overriding sovereignty of the United States, the treaties, legislation, and "intricate web of judicially made Indian law" that define Indian rights in America consistently reflect the foundational belief of nineteenth-century white Americans that Indians were a lawless and uncivilized race of savage peoples. Based on that belief, tribal Indians were recognized by Congress, the executive branch, and the federal court system, through various official acts and statements, as possessing inferior legal rights and political status. And in fact, as Rehnquist asserts, these "common notions" and "assumptions" of the past regarding Indian savagery have reflected the actual lived reality of Indian self-government for much of our nation's history. Indians, according to the legal and legislative history lesson Rehnquist carefully narrates in *Oliphant,* were in actuality relatively lawless, unsophisticated, and uncivilized peoples when it came to what white society would call the exercise of criminal jurisdiction on the reservation:

> The effort by Indian tribal courts to exercise criminal jurisdiction over non-Indians is a relatively new phenomenon. And where the effort has been made in the past, it has been held that the jurisdiction did not exist. Until the middle of this century, few Indian tribes maintained any semblance of a formal court system. Offenses by one Indian against another were usually handled by social and religious pressure and not by formal judicial processes; emphasis was on restitution rather than on punishment.[10]

A good part of Rehnquist's opinion in *Oliphant* is devoted to demonstrating that historically speaking, all the official branches of the U.S. government in the nineteenth century steadfastly believed what he himself professes to believe: that Indian tribes, because of their uncivilized lack of "formal" judicial processes, could never be legally imagined as possessing legitimate police power to criminally prosecute non-Indians. And *Oliphant* holds that this racist belief system still has jurispathic, rights-destroying force in defining Indian rights in the present-day United States. This negative nineteenth-century stereotype serves as a confirmatory, dynamically interpreted source of historical authority for the implied limitation on Indian rights of self-government identified in Rehnquist's 1978 Indian rights opinion for the Court in *Oliphant*.

Rehnquist quoted from the 1834 Removal era testimony of Elbert Herring, Andrew Jackson's commissioner of Indian affairs to Congress, for example, to show that the executive branch of the U.S. government recognized the lawless savagery of Indian tribes in nineteenth-century America. According to the individual who was charged with frontline administrative responsibility for carrying out the Jackson administration's ethnic-cleansing campaign against the southern tribes: "With the exception of two or three tribes, who have within a few years past attempted to establish some few laws and regulations among themselves, the Indian tribes are without laws, and the chiefs without much authority to exercise any restraint."[11]

Rehnquist also cited and quoted from the 1834 Western Territory Bill as further authority for his principle of inherent limitations on tribal criminal jurisdiction. In considering that bill, the Removal-era Congress "was first directly faced with the prospect of Indians trying non-Indians." Congress proposed to create in that bill an Indian territory for the tribes it was planning to relocate west of the Mississippi. But as Rehnquist explained in his interpretation of this proposed legislation (which was never passed), "Congress was careful not to give the tribes of the territory criminal jurisdiction over U.S. officials and citizens traveling through the area."[12] Quoting directly from the 1834 House of Representatives report on the proposed legislation, Rehnquist explained that the reasons for this caution by Congress "were quite practical":

"Officers, and persons in the service of the United States . . . must necessarily be placed under the protection, and subject to the laws of the United States. To persons merely traveling in the Indian country the same protection is extended. The want of fixed laws, of competent tribunals of justice, which must for some time continue in the Indian country, absolutely requires for the peace of both sides that this protection should be extended." H.R.Rep. No. 474, 23d Cong., 1st Sess., 18 (1834).[13]

The Removal era's virulent catalog of official government hate speech directed toward Indians as lawless, uncivilized savages was not the only nineteenth-century archive of genocidally inflected white racist attitudes and beliefs raided by Rehnquist in support of the Supreme Court's 1978 opinion in *Oliphant*. The opinion cites and at times even extensively quotes from a host of nineteenth-century racist precedents generated from the Marshall Model of Indian Rights to demonstrate conclusively that the nineteenth-century Supreme Court also believed, along with Congress and the executive branch, that Indian criminal jurisdiction over whites could never have existed under U.S. law. Indians had always been recognized, at least according to these legal precedents, as being too uncivilized and too lawless "to try non-Indians according to their own customs and procedure."[14]

Chapters 4 and 5 have already examined many of the nineteenth-century Marshall model precedents that are cited by Rehnquist as controlling authority in *Oliphant*. The language in these precedents is replete with rhetorical flourishes and quaintly stated references to Indians as an inferior and uncivilized race of peoples, unable to withstand the forces of civilization bearing down upon them and their doomed and vitiated way of life.

Rehnquist's overwhelming preference for these types of racist judicial precedents is reflected in the fact that all but five of the nineteen Supreme Court cases cited in toto in *Oliphant* were issued between the years of 1810 and 1916—the pre–World War I history of the United States, in other words.[15] Only three of the twelve direct quotations taken by Rehnquist from prior Supreme Court opinions are from decisions handed down after the Court's *Brown* decision.[16] The three pre-*Brown* twentieth-century precedents and all the nineteenth-century precedents directly quoted in *Oliphant* uniformly rely upon the familiar judicial language organized around the unquestioning racial belief in Indian tribalism's inferiority and normative divergence from a non-Indian majority society seen as superior.

Overtly racist judicial language, for instance, characterizes the very first Supreme Court case quoted and relied upon by Rehnquist in *Oliphant*,

In re Mayfield, which has already been discussed in the introduction to this book.

> In *In re Mayfield,* the Court noted that the policy of Congress had been to allow the inhabitants of the Indian country "such power of self-government as was thought to be consistent with the safety of the white population with which they may have come in contact, and to encourage them as far as possible in raising themselves to our standard of civilization."[17]

Decided by the Supreme Court in 1891, *In re Mayfield* reflects the typical late-nineteenth-century antagonistic racist belief structure, which held that Indians were an uncivilized and inferior race of peoples and a threat to the safety of the surrounding white population.

As with virtually all of *Oliphant*'s citations to nineteenth-century Marshall model precedents, Rehnquist's use of *Mayfield* and its denigrating racist language functions to support *Oliphant*'s historical analysis of Indian tribes as being far too uncivilized to be allowed to exercise criminal jurisdiction over non-Indians. According to *Oliphant,* the Supreme Court recognized this rights-destroying jurispathic principle in 1891 in its *Mayfield* decision and interpreted Congress's various "actions and inactions in regulating criminal jurisdiction on Indian reservations" as demonstrating what Rehnquist called "an intent to reserve jurisdiction over non-Indians for the federal courts." This 1978 interpretation of the Court's 1891 *Mayfield* decision enabled Rehnquist to assert that "[w]hile Congress never expressly forbade Indian tribes to impose criminal penalties on non-Indians, we now make express our implicit conclusion of nearly a century ago [in *In re Mayfield*] that Congress consistently believed this to be the necessary result of its repeated legislative actions."[18]

Citing and quoting *Mayfield* as a precedent is just one example of Rehnquist's active transmission of a nineteenth-century judicial language of white bigotry into the Indian rights discourse of a major twentieth-century Supreme Court Indian law decision. *Oliphant* encodes many other such virulently jurispathic beliefs through its repeated use of and reliance upon some of the most important and also most racist legal precedents generated by the Marshall model.

In one of the most important parts of his opinion, Rehnquist actually quoted from the 1846 Supreme Court decision in *United States v. Rogers*. *Rogers*, recall, is the case in which Chief Justice Taney helped spawn the constitutionally unconstrained congressional plenary power doctrine (see chapter 5). Rehnquist directly quotes, without qualification or embarrassment, Taney's decision for the proposition that "'Indian reservations are a part of the territory of the United States.' *United States v. Rogers*, 4 How. 567, 571, 11 L.Ed. 1105 (1846). Indian tribes 'hold and occupy [the reservations] with the assent of the United States, and under their authority.'"[19] Signs taken for wonders, according to Rehnquist's interpretation and application of the Marshall model precedents, the antebellum racial reasoning of Roger Taney can still be quoted and relied upon in a 1978 Supreme Court Indian law decision. The author of the infamous *Dred Scott* decision still provides sound (if somewhat incompletely unidentified) legal authority for defining Indian rights in post-*Brown* Supreme Court Indian law jurisprudence.

Oliphant's perpetuation of the racist beliefs of the Supreme Court chief justice reviled by legal historians for writing the infamous *Dred Scott* decision is not, unfortunately, an isolated or aberrant instance of a failure by Rehnquist to carefully sift through the antiquated language of a 132-year-old precedent dusted off by some historically obtuse law clerk in a maze.[20] *Oliphant* is chock-full of extensive citations to and numerous direct quotations from other Marshall model precedents that are replete with antiquated, negative racial stereotypes of Indians. These precedents are elaborated in a robustly articulated judicial language of Indian savagery and inferior rights that has been continuously utilized by the justices to justify the judicially unconstrained white racial dictatorship over Indian tribes since the birth of the Marshall model in the early decades of the nineteenth century.

As has already been noted (in the section "*Oliphant*'s 'Principle' of 'Inherent Limitations on Tribal Power'" above), Rehnquist expressly relied on the first two cases of the Marshall Trilogy, *Johnson v. McIntosh* and *Cherokee Nation v. Georgia*,[21] to support *Oliphant*'s landmark holding that Indian tribes have been implicitly divested of criminal jurisdiction over non-Indians under the doctrine of discovery. Rehnquist cited Chief Justice Marshall's opinion in *Johnson* for support of the following central principle informing the Court's decision in *Oliphant*: "Upon incorporation into the territory of the United States, the Indian tribes thereby come under the territorial sovereignty of the United States and their exercise of separate power is constrained so as not to conflict with the interests of this overriding sovereignty. '[T]heir rights to complete sovereignty, as independent nations [are] necessarily diminished.' *Johnson v. McIntosh*."[22] I have also noted, in the same section, Rehnquist's use of Marshall's opinion for the Court in *Cherokee Nation* to support *Oliphant*'s foundational principle of white racial superiority. Indian tribes, Rehnquist explains, quoting *Cherokee Nation,* are "completely under the sovereignty and dominion of the United States."[23]

Rehnquist used *Worcester v. Georgia,* the third and final landmark case of the Marshall Trilogy, to rebut the Suquamish Tribe's legal argument that because its treaty with the United States was wholly silent on the issue of tribal criminal jurisdiction over non-Indians on the reservation, this important right of tribal self-government had been retained by the tribe under the Marshall Model of Indian Rights. Rehnquist, however, offered a much different, jurispathic interpretation of the language used in the Suquamish tribe's 1855 treaty. According to the interpretive approach spelled out by Rehnquist in *Oliphant,* the tribe's treaty must be read according to the "historical perspective" gained from an understanding of the precise legal meanings of Marshall's judicial language of Indian savagery in *Worcester.*

> While in isolation the Treaty of Point Elliott, 12 Stat. 927 (1855), would appear to be silent as to tribal criminal jurisdiction over non-Indians, the addition of historical perspective casts substantial doubt upon the existence of such jurisdiction. In the Ninth Article, for example, the Suquamish "acknowledge their dependence on the government of the United States." As Mr. Chief Justice Marshall explained in *Worcester v. Georgia,* such an acknowledgment is not a mere abstract recognition of the United States' sovereignty. "The Indian nations were, from their situation, necessarily dependent on [the United States] . . . for their protection from lawless and injurious intrusions into their country." By acknowledging their dependence on the United States, in the Treaty of Point Elliott, the Suquamish were in all probability recognizing that the United States would arrest and try non-Indian intruders who came within their Reservation.[24]

Worcester, as has already been discussed, has long been regarded from the "historical perspective" of Indian law scholars and advocates as a landmark legal victory for Indian rights in the Supreme Court of the United States (see chapter 4). *Worcester's* recognition of inherent tribal sovereignty is also often cited by Indian law scholars and advocates as evidence of Indian law's sometimes contradictory, oftentimes conflicted character. These contradictions in the case law, which recognize Congress's plenary power over tribes *and* inherent tribal sovereignty and rights at the same time, are said to be inevitable given the "actual state of things."[25]

That this so-called legal victory for tribes can be used by a post-*Brown* Supreme Court justice to expand the principle of white racial superiority asserted by the doctrine of discovery, however, teaches us an important lesson about the legal history of racism in America: As *Oliphant* demonstrates, in clear, unconflicted, and noncontradictory fashion, until *Worcester's* underlying principle of white racial superiority is formally repudiated and discredited by the Court, this foundational precedent of the Marshall model will continue to function just as Justice Robert Jackson said it would in his dissent in *Korematsu:* "like a loaded weapon ready for the hand of any authority that can bring forward a plausible claim of an urgent need."

This lesson is illustrated by another leading Marshall model precedent cited in *Oliphant*. Rehnquist also relied heavily on the jurispathic force of the late-nineteenth-century Supreme Court precedent *Ex parte Crow Dog*.[26] Rehnquist used this so-called victory for Indian tribes to lend further support to *Oliphant's* organizing jurispathic principle of implicit divestiture of tribal powers under the doctrine of discovery.

In *Crow Dog*, as discussed in chapter 5, Justice Matthews relied upon racial stereotypes that were widely applied to Indians in the late nineteenth century to reach the 1883 ruling, later repudiated by Congress's passage of the Major Crimes Act of 1885, that federal courts, as stated in *Oliphant*, lacked criminal "jurisdiction to try Indians who had offended against fellow Indians on Reservation land."[27] According to Rehnquist, the *Crow Dog* Court "was faced with almost the inverse of the issue" presented to the justices by the facts of *Oliphant*. In *Oliphant* the "circumstances" were that a twentieth-century Indian tribal court was asserting criminal jurisdiction to try non-Indians who had allegedly committed crimes on the reservation.[28] In *Crow Dog*, a nineteenth-century U.S. federal court was asserting criminal jurisdiction over Indians who committed crimes against other Indians on the reservation.

In the most extensive quotation of any Supreme Court precedent cited in *Oliphant*'s text, Rehnquist offered a heavily edited version of Matthews's stated reasons in *Crow Dog* for exempting an Indian from the criminal jurisdiction of the U.S. federal court under these types of "circumstances." In *Crow Dog,* as quoted by Rehnquist with numerous ellipses, the United States was seeking to extend its

> "law by argument and inference only, . . . over aliens and strangers; over the members of a community separated by race [and] tradition, . . . from the authority and power which seeks to impose upon them the restraints of an external and unknown code . . . ; which judges them by a standard made by others and not for them. . . . It tries them, not by their peers, nor by the customs of their people, nor the law of their land, but by . . . a different race, according to the law of a social state of which they have an imperfect conception. . . ."[29]

Rehnquist concluded his eviscerated quotation of *Crow Dog* with the explanation that the same "considerations"[30] of racial justice that had motivated Matthews and the rest of the Court not to apply the white man's law to the Indian in that 1883 case applied "equally strongly against the validity" of the Suquamish Tribe's contention "that Indian tribes, although fully subordinated to the sovereignty of the United States, retain the power to try non-Indians according to their own customs and procedure."[31]

Rehnquist's elliptical deployment of Matthews's late-nineteenth-century *Crow Dog* opinion to support his own twentieth-century racialized reasoning process for denying Indian tribes criminal jurisdiction over non-Indians illustrates one of the central difficulties in decoding and monitoring the full effects of the nineteenth-century language of Indian savagery used throughout *Oliphant.* As has already been discussed in chapter 5, the "considerations" that motivated the *Crow Dog* Court to exempt an Indian from the criminal jurisdiction of the United States were largely based on Matthews's expressly stated racial stereotypes of Indians as lawless, incommensurable savages. These considerations for not applying the white man's law to the Sioux Indian Crow Dog, in fact, stand out in bold relief if we simply reinsert the words of Matthews's original language of Indian savagery (in brackets in small capitals) that Rehnquist carefully left out of his extensive quotation of this part of the *Crow Dog* opinion:

The United States was seeking in *Crow Dog* to extend U.S.

"law by argument and inference only, . . . over aliens and strangers;
over the members of a community, separated by race, by tradition, . . .
[BY THE INSTINCTS OF A FREE THOUGH SAVAGE LIFE] from the au-
thority and power which seeks to impose upon them the restraints of
an external and unknown code . . . [AND TO SUBJECT THEM TO THE
RESPONSIBILITIES OF CIVIL CONDUCT, ACCORDING TO RULES AND
PENALTIES OF WHICH THEY COULD HAVE NO PREVIOUS WARNING];
which judges them by a standard made by others, and not for them . . .
[WHICH TAKES NO ACCOUNT OF THE CONDITIONS WHICH SHOULD
EXCEPT THEM FROM ITS EXACTIONS, AND MAKES NO ALLOWANCE
FOR THEIR INABILITY TO UNDERSTAND IT]. It tries them, not by their
peers, nor by the customs of their people, nor the law of their land, but
by . . . [SUPERIORS OF] a different race, according to the law of a social
state of which they have an imperfect conception. . . . [AND WHICH
IS OPPOSED TO THE TRADITIONS OF THEIR HISTORY, TO THE HABITS
OF THEIR LIVES, TO THE STRONGEST PREJUDICES OF THEIR SAVAGE
NATURE; ONE WHICH MEASURES THE RED MAN'S REVENGE BY THE
MAXIMS OF THE WHITE MAN'S MORALITY]."[32]

Rehnquist's strategic use of multiple ellipses in his extended quotation
of Matthews's colorful late-nineteenth-century language of racism indi-
cates quite clearly that the "considerations" that motivated the Supreme
Court in *Crow Dog* to exempt an Indian from the strictures of the
white man's criminal law in 1883 do not in fact speak "equally strongly" against subjecting a white person to Indian criminal jurisdiction in
1978. In its efforts to reconstruct *Crow Dog* as a color-blind application of the principle that it is unfair to subject one race of people to the
alien laws and penalties of another race, something important has been
left out of *Oliphant*'s text. Rehnquist's careful elision of *Crow Dog*'s
extensive nineteenth-century catalog of negative racial stereotypes of
Indians obscures the full extent of the discriminatory, racist meanings
of what Matthews is really saying in *Crow Dog*. The reason Indians are
not subject to the white man's civilized system of justice in *Crow Dog* is
because the nineteenth-century Supreme Court racially profiled tribal
Indians as "members of a community, separated by race, by tradition,
[BY THE INSTINCTS OF A FREE THOUGH SAVAGE LIFE]." They were far
too uncivilized and savage to be subjected to criminal prosecution by

"[SUPERIORS OF] a different race." The reason non-Indians are not sub-ject to tribal criminal prosecution, according to the nineteenth-century racial paradigm of Indian rights applied by Rehnquist in the Court's *Oliphant* decision, is because the same basic nineteenth-century racist attitude of Indian cultural inferiority found in *Crow Dog* is now being applied to Indians once again, this time in color-clueless fashion in the twentieth-century Supreme Court's Indian law.[33]

Oliphant compellingly illuminates how the legal force of a racist judicial precedent and its equally racist judicial language of Indian sav-agery are perpetuated and reinforced without any outward signs of dis-comfort or embarrassment by a post-*Brown* Supreme Court justice. By the silent, economizing operations of stare decisis and the sly exercise of the judicial privilege of elision, Rehnquist has revealed what *Crow Dog* now stands for as a supposedly color-blind precedent in the twentieth-century Supreme Court's Indian law: *Crow Dog*, a nineteenth-century "victory" for Indian tribes that supposedly upholds the principle of tribal sovereignty under the Marshall model, is now being used by Rehnquist in *Oliphant* in color-clueless fashion to support the inherent limitations on Indian rights imposed on tribes under the doctrine of discovery.

As if to show that there were no contradictory precedents of the Mar-shall model that didn't support his reasoning, Rehnquist's *Oliphant* opin-ion also used the case that upheld the nineteenth-century Congress's reversal of *Crow Dog, United States v. Kagama*. The Suquamish Tribe's argument that it possessed inherent criminal jurisdiction over non-Indians for crimes committed on the tribe's reservation, Rehnquist wrote, ignored the following principle of the Court's Indian law as laid out in *Kagama*:

> "Indians are within the geographical limits of the United States. The
> soil and people within these limits are under the political control of the
> Government of the United States, or of the States of the Union. There
> exists in the broad domain of sovereignty but these two. There may
> be cities, counties, and other organized bodies with limited legislative
> functions, but they . . . exist in subordination to one or the other of
> these."[34]

Recall that the Court's decision in *Kagama* upheld the Major Crimes Act of 1885 and placed tribes under a highly onerous form of legalized white dictatorship enforced by the congressional plenary power doc-trine. Under *Oliphant*'s twentieth-century interpretation of the Marshall model, *Kagama* now attains renewed legal meaning and new rights-destroying jurispathic force in the post-*Brown* Court's Indian rights decisions. By reason of the principle of white racial superiority upheld in *Kagama* and its perpetuation of the Marshall model's racial profiling of Indians as "wards of the nation,"[35] *Oliphant* holds that the "exercise of jurisdiction over non-Indian citizens of the United States would belie the tribes' forfeiture of full sovereignty in return for the protection of the United States."[36]

Under Rehnquist's twentieth-century interpretation of the Marshall model in *Oliphant,* Indian tribes were in essence getting precisely what they deserved under the nineteenth-century Supreme Court's Indian law. As essentially lawless and uncivilized groups of savages, Indians under the doctrine of discovery were implicitly divested of their inherent sovereign rights "to try non-Indian citizens of the United States except in a manner acceptable to Congress."

The Lesson Taught by *Oliphant*

Indian law scholars and advocates can get very upset when they discuss what they regard as Rehnquist's unprecedented interpretation and abuse of the Marshall model in *Oliphant.*[37] They regard it as one of the worst Supreme Court Indian rights decisions of the twentieth century, or any century, for that matter. *Oliphant*'s principle of tribal powers "inherently lost to the overriding sovereignty of the United States"[38] under the Marshall model, they claim, is absurd and represents an aberration of what Marshall had to say about Indian rights in his trilogy of early-nineteenth-century Indian law opinions.[39]

But the underlying principle of white racial superiority that Rehnquist applies in *Oliphant* as part of his Indian rights paradigm is not at all unprecedented in the Supreme Court's Indian law. *Oliphant*'s principle is generated directly out of and is supported by some of the best-known and most often cited nineteenth-century precedents of the Marshall model. Rehnquist couldn't have written *Oliphant* the way he did, in other words, without the Marshall model's racist nineteenth-century legal discourse of Indian savagery and diminished rights. He needed the precedents and language of the Marshall model to support his expansive interpretation of the continuing jurispathic force of the European colonial-era doctrine of discovery in the Supreme Court's

Indian law. Racist decisions like those of *Johnson, Cherokee Nation, Worcester, Rogers, Crow Dog,* and *Kagama* provided all the precedential authority Rehnquist needed to maintain the discovery doctrine's rights-destroying, jurispathic force in the Supreme Court's post-*Brown* Indian law. It was the Marshall model's underlying approach to defining Indian rights according to a principle of white racial superiority that let him get away with it.

A close examination of *Oliphant*'s expansive legal paradigm of tribal powers "inherently lost to the overriding sovereignty of the United States" reveals, in fact, that Rehnquist's opinion reflects all the basic elements of the Supreme Court's decisions applying the Marshall Model of Indian Rights through two centuries of American legal history.[40] *Oliphant* unquestionably accepts and reinforces the European colonial-era principle of white racial supremacy perpetuated by the doctrine of discovery. Rehnquist's *Oliphant* opinion, for example, directly cites the 1823 case of *Johnson v. McIntosh,* the case that inaugurated the Marshall model and incorporated the doctrine of discovery into U.S. law as a foundational precedent establishing the controlling authority of this principle of legalized racial discrimination in the Court's Indian law.

Rehnquist resorts to the Marshall model's elemental embrace of negative racial stereotyping of Indians throughout his *Oliphant* opinion. He shows no discomfort or hesitancy in relying upon the nineteenth century's overtly hostile and racist language of Indian savagery to justify the Supreme Court's present-day denial of Indian rights to criminal jurisdiction over non-Indians on the reservation, even for serious crimes they commit against tribal police officers enforcing the peace there.

Rehnquist's opinion in *Oliphant* even concludes with the characteristic concession found in so many of the Marshall model precedents: The Court, as an instrument of the white racial dictatorship established under the European colonial-era doctrine of discovery, is powerless to resist the continuing legal force of the Marshall model's overarching principle of racial discrimination:

> We recognize that some Indian tribal court systems have become
> increasingly sophisticated and resemble in many respects their state
> counterparts. We also acknowledge that with the passage of the Indian
> Civil Rights Act of 1968, which extends certain basic procedural rights
> to anyone tried in Indian tribal court, many of the dangers that might

have accompanied the exercise by tribal courts of criminal jurisdiction over non-Indians only a few decades ago have disappeared. Finally, we are not unaware of the prevalence of non-Indian crime on today's reservations which the tribes forcefully argue requires the ability to try non-Indians. But these are considerations for Congress to weigh in deciding whether Indian tribes should finally be authorized to try non-Indians. They have little relevance to the principles which lead us to conclude that Indian tribes do not have inherent jurisdiction to try and to punish non-Indians.[41]

Those principles that Rehnquist is referring to derive directly from the Marshall Model of Indian Rights and its judicial embrace and perpetuation of the doctrine of discovery. According to Rehnquist, these principles require the Court to hold that Indian rights continue to be defined by the overarching metaprinciple of white racial superiority asserted by the discovery doctrine and a judicially validated tradition of negative racial stereotyping of Indians as lawless savages.

The question of whether Rehnquist's supposedly idiosyncratic interpretation of the Marshall model in *Oliphant* somehow distorts Marshall's opinions is really quite beside the point I'm trying to make. My point involves the questions of how we understand and why we continue to apply the Marshall Model of Indian Rights in a post-*Brown*, supposedly color-blind world. The point that needs to be emphasized regarding *Oliphant* is that Rehnquist's application of the Marshall model compellingly demonstrates the continuing and ever-present dangers of a judicially validated vision of Indian rights that relies upon a set of racist nineteenth-century precedents and a closely related racist judicial language of Indian savagery to define the rights of present-day Indian tribes in the United States. The lesson that should be learned from Rehnquist's opinion in *Oliphant* is how the Marshall model can indeed continue to function like a loaded weapon directly aimed at the destruction of Indian rights. Until the Marshall model's underlying metaprinciple of white racial superiority is repudiated by the Court, its racist precedents and language of Indian inferiority lie ready at hand for any justice who can plausibly claim an urgent need to declare the existence of an implicit divestiture of Indian rights under the Supreme Court's Indian law.

8

The Most Indianophobic Supreme Court
Indian Law Opinion Ever

Attempt at a Definition: The Racist Justice

Given the rights-denying, jurispathic application of the Marshall model by Justice Rehnquist in *Oliphant v. Suquamish Indian Tribe,* it's not too difficult to understand why Indian law advocates and scholars get so upset whenever they discuss the opinion. *Oliphant* has to be regarded as one of the most racist Indian law opinions written by a justice of the Supreme Court in the post-*Brown* era, every bit as bad, it can be argued, as Justice Reed's "every American schoolboy knows . . ." majority opinion in *Tee-Hit-Ton,* issued in 1955, the year after *Brown v. Board of Education* was decided by the Court.[1]

But in my opinion, based on close study of the legal history of racism against Indians in America, neither *Oliphant* nor *Tee-Hit-Ton* comes close to being the *most* racist Indian law opinion written by a post-*Brown* Supreme Court justice. Two years after writing *Oliphant,* Rehnquist wrote a lone dissent to the Court's 1980 decision in *United States v. Sioux Nation of Indians.*[2] Rehnquist's dissent in that landmark legal victory for Indian rights is perhaps the most Indianophobic legal opinion *ever* written by a justice of the twentieth-century Supreme Court. In fact, based on what Rehnquist says about Indians in his dissent to *Sioux Nation* and in his majority opinion in *Oliphant,* he has to be ranked right up there with John Marshall and Roger Taney as one of the most racist, Indianophobic justices ever to sit on the Supreme Court, regardless of century.

I recognize the seriousness (and, to some, the spuriousness) of this charge against someone who is probably considered by more than a few Americans as one of the Court's greatest chief justices of all time. In making this charge, however, I rely on the same basic definition of a racist attitude toward Indians that I have used in all my writings where I have discussed and analyzed Rehnquist's legal views on Indian rights.[3] The definition I use is found in Albert Memmi's famous four-part typology of the racist attitude in a colonial context.

Albert Memmi was a Tunisian Jewish writer who produced one of the most important works to emerge out of the post–Word War II decolonization movement, *The Colonizer and the Colonized.*[4] In an essay entitled "Attempt at a Definition," Memmi offered the following definition of racism:

> Racism is the generalized and final assigning of values to real or imagined differences, to the accuser's benefit and at his victim's expense, in order to justify the former's own privileges or aggression.[5]

Memmi theorized four "essential" elements of the "racist attitude" by which European-derived colonial societies operationalized this definition, implementing their exercise of racial rule and dictatorship over non-European races:

1. Stressing *the real or imaginary differences* between the racist and his victim.
2. Assigning *values* to these differences, to the advantage of the racist and the detriment of his victim.
3. Trying to make these differences *absolutes* by *generalizing* from them and claiming that they are final.
4. *Justifying* any present or possible *privilege* by citing these real or imaginary differences between the racist and his victim.[6]

Significantly, all the principal elements of the "racist attitude" identified by Memmi organize themselves around a process that begins with generalizing and essentializing supposedly isolable differences between the racist and the victimized group or groups. This process has been seen at work in the legal history of racism in America as told throughout this book. Memmi shows us how this familiar process of differentiating and discriminating between groups and individuals uses a language of racism made up of well-known negative racial stereotypes and associated imagery to achieve its discriminatory functions within a racist, colonial society.

Memmi's definition of the racist attitude takes this process one step further, hypothesizing that in a colonial society, the language of racism organized around these stereotyped differences will invariably be relied upon to justify any differential treatment between colonizer and colonized groups. In other words, racism in a colonial society will be defined by the use of negative racial stereotypes and racist imagery in order to justify the inequalities enforced by the colonizer over the colonized. As the contemporary postcolonial theorist Homi Bhabha put it, "The objective of colonial discourse is to construe the colonized as a population of degencrate types on the basis of racial origin, in order to justify conquest and to establish systems of administration and instruction."[7]

Bhabha, like Memmi, identifies the recognition of racial differences as central to the justificatory processes of racial dictatorship and rule and therefore as central to the colonizer's law in the colonial society. According to Bhabha, the "difference of colonial discourse as an apparatus of power, at a minimum, turns on the recognition and disavowal of racial/cultural/historical differences."[8]

As members of the colonial society, judges—as demonstrated throughout this book—are all too conversant with this type of racist, stereotypical language and its various modes of articulation (social, cultural, political, economic, and so on). In exercising their jurispathic function in declaring the state's authoritative interpretation on the legal rights and obligations of a particular colonized racial group, judges—as has also been shown throughout this book—will oftentimes attempt to justify the dominant society's acts of racism and violence against the colonized group by using this very same language themselves. Their opinions will, in other words, openly display a racist attitude toward the group, using long-established negative racial stereotypes and racist imagery to justify their differential, discriminatory legal treatment of the group.

Therefore, according to the definition of a racist justice that I use in this book and throughout my other Indian law writings, the reliance upon such traditions of stereotyping and racist imagery in a legal opinion authored by a Supreme Court justice will, as a rule, constitute reliable evidence that an ongoing, hostile, and quite active form of racism on the part of that justice is at work in that opinion. The opinion of a racist justice, regardless of the century or era, will characteristically function jurispathically, invariably denying validity to any competing vision of that group's rights. It will also characteristically rely upon a language of racism to defend the privileges and aggressions of the dominant society against that minority group. Under this definition, Rehnquist's use of a language of racism in his dissent in *Sioux Nation* to elaborate his legal views on Indian rights provides compelling evidence that he is indeed one of the most racist and Indianophobic justices ever to sit on the U.S. Supreme Court.

The *Sioux Nation* Case

The majority opinion in *Sioux Nation*, written by Justice Harry Blackmun, found that Congress had illegally taken the Black Hills in South Dakota from the Sioux Indians in 1877 through a fraudulent treaty and other acts that gave rise to a right of full compensation under the Fifth Amendment's just compensation clause.[9] The case was the largest single judgment award ever confirmed by the Supreme Court in an Indian rights case. The value of the Black Hills at the date of taking as found by the court of claims was over $17 million. Since the United States had recognized the lands taken from the Sioux as belonging to the tribe by treaty, the case was not governed by the *Tee-Hit-Ton* rule for uncompensated takings of congressionally unrecognized Indian title (see chapter 6). Besides the $17 million, the Sioux were also therefore entitled to interest from the United States under the Fifth Amendment takings clause. The total judgment awarded in the *Sioux Nation* case, with that interest added, amounted to over $100 million![10]

Rehnquist's lone dissent to the Court's decision in *Sioux Nation*[11] in particular objected to the majority's conclusion on an important matter of historical interpretation of the factual record in the case. Rehnquist believed that the Sioux had been adequately compensated for the government's taking of the Black Hills in the form of gratuitous daily rations appropriated by Congress following the signing of the fraudulent treaty. The majority's mistaken views on the so-called taking of the Black Hills from the Sioux by the U.S. government in the nineteenth century, Rehnquist wrote in dissent, was unfortunately grounded

> largely on the basis of a view of the settlement of the American West which is not universally shared. There were undoubtedly greed, cupidity, and other less-than-admirable tactics employed by the Government during the Black Hills episode in the settlement of the West, but the Indians did not lack their share of villainy either. It seems to me quite unfair to judge by the light of revisionist historians or the mores of another era actions that were taken under pressure of time more than a century ago.[12]

As Rehnquist noted in his dissent, "different historians, not writing for the purpose of having their conclusions or observations inserted in the reports of congressional committees, have taken different positions than those expressed in some of the materials referred to in the Court's opinion." Criticizing his colleagues in the majority for their own "stereotyped and one-sided impression both of the settlement regarding the Black Hills portion of the Great Sioux Reservation and of the gradual expansion of the National Government from the Proclamation Line of King George III in 1763 to the Pacific Ocean," Rehnquist laid out his version of Indian-white historical relations, relying on historians and stereotypes much different from those of his brethren in the majority to tell his story about what Sioux rights should be recognized by the Supreme Court's Indian law.[13]

Rehnquist first cited Ray Billington, "a respected student of the settlement of the American West,"[14] to tell his version of the history of "the confrontations in the West" between Indians and the U.S. government that led up to the taking of the Black Hills from the Sioux. Rehnquist's dissent quoted from Billington's introduction to *Soldier and Brave; Indian and Military Affairs in the Trans-Mississippi West, Including a Guide to Historic Sites and Landmarks*, which was published in 1963 by the National Park Service and which was probably available at fine ranger stations everywhere at the time of its original publication. As Rehnquist noted, Billington emphasized that the cultural conflicts between Indians

and the United States "were the product of a long history, not a con-
niving Presidential administration."[15] Rehnquist then provided an extended quotation from Billington's introduction:

> "Three centuries of bitter Indian warfare reached tragic climax on the
> plains and mountains of America's Far West. Since the early seven-
> teenth century, when Chief Opechancanough rallied his Powhatan
> tribesmen against the Virginia intruders on their lands, each advance
> of the frontier had been met with stubborn resistance. At times this
> conflict flamed into open warfare: in King Phillips' rebellion against
> the Massachusetts Puritans, during the French and Indian Wars of
> the eighteenth century, in Chief Pontiac's assault on his new British
> overlords in 1763, in Chief Tecumseh's vain efforts to hold back the
> advancing pioneers of 1812, and in the Black Hawk War. . . .
>
> ". . . In three tragic decades, between 1860 and 1890, the Indians
> suffered the humiliating defeats that forced them to walk the white
> man's road toward civilization. Few conquered people in the history of
> mankind have paid so dearly for their defense of a way of life that the
> march of progress had outmoded.
>
> "This epic struggle left its landmarks behind, as monuments to the
> brave men, Indian and white, who fought and died that their manner
> of living might endure."[16]

Rehnquist was not done with quoting large blocks of text from self-
congratulatory histories of the U.S. conquest of Indian tribes during
"three centuries of bitter Indian warfare." His dissent next quoted the
great triumphalist historian of America's discovery and conquest by
Europe, Samuel Eliot Morison.[17] Morison's views provided Rehnquist
with another example of a highly respected American historian whose
work highlighted the cultural differences between white civilization
and the savage Indian tribes of the Plains, such as the Sioux. According
to Morison's version of the "history of the American people" as quoted
by Rehnquist, conflict and brutal warfare were inevitable between these
two very different and opposed races of peoples on the continent:

> "The Plains Indians seldom practiced agriculture or other primitive
> arts, but they were fine physical specimens; and in warfare, once they
> had learned the use of the rifle, [were] much more formidable than the
> Eastern tribes who had slowly yielded to the white man. Tribe warred

with tribe, and a highly developed sign language was the only means of intertribal communication. The effective unit was the band or village of a few hundred souls, which might be seen in the course of its wanderings encamped by a watercourse with tipis erected; or pouring over the plain, women and children leading dogs and packhorses with their trailing travois, while gaily dressed braves loped ahead on horseback. They lived only for the day, recognized no rights of property, robbed or killed anyone if they thought they could get away with it, inflicted cruelty without a qualm, and endured torture without flinching."[18]

Rehnquist then concluded his dissent to *Sioux Nation* with this historiographical flourish:

> That there was tragedy, deception, barbarity, and virtually every other vice known to man in the 300-year history of the expansion of the original 13 Colonies into a Nation which now embraces more than three million square miles and 50 states cannot be denied. But in a court opinion, as a historical and not a legal matter, both settler and Indian are entitled to the benefit of the Biblical adjuration: "Judge not, that ye be not judged."[19]

Rehnquist's selective use of his own preferred, nonrevisionist historical sources on the hostile, savage character of the nineteenth-century Plains Indian tribes in his dissent to the *Sioux Nation* majority opinion teaches us a very important lesson: His reliance on these types of sources to support his counterversion of the "long history" of Indian-white "confrontations" shows the continuing force of the long-established tradition of negative racial stereotyping of Indians. This tradition, as perpetuated by the triumphalist works of "different historians" such as Ray Billington and Samuel Eliot Morison, has clearly influenced the way Rehnquist thinks and talks about Indian rights.

In his illuminating "Theses on the Philosophy of History," written in 1940, a few months prior to his suicide in the face of Hitler's final solution for his race, the German-Jewish writer Walter Benjamin observed:

> There is no document of civilization which is not at the same time a document of barbarism. And just as such a document is not free of barbarism, barbarism taints also the manner in which it was transmitted.[20]

By relying on racial stereotypes and racist imagery culled from such documents of barbarism, Rehnquist's *Oliphant* opinion shows us one of the most dangerous ways a language of racism can be used by a Supreme Court justice. In the hands of a highly Indianophobic justice like Rehnquist, this language can be used to justify and defend the privileges and aggressions of the dominant society against Indian tribes. Indians, according to Justice Rehnquist's judicial opinions in *Oliphant* and *Sioux Nation,* should continue to be treated under our law just as their savage ancestors were by the white racial dictatorship that ruled America in the nineteenth century.

9

The Dangers of the Twentieth-Century
Supreme Court's Indian Rights Decisions

O pinions like those of Justice Reed in *Tee-Hit-Ton* and of Justice Rehnquist in *Oliphant* and *Sioux Nation* teach us the important lesson that a language of racism can continue to possess dangerous,
rights-destroying jurispathic power, even in post-*Brown* America. In
these opinions, racial stereotypes from the nineteenth century were endorsed and accepted as true by twentieth-century justices. These justices
perpetuated a racist and antiquated legal discourse without any signs of
discomfort, embarrassment, or express qualification. In this sense, such
Indianophobic opinions can be read as being much more than just ab-
surdities or aberrations issued in an era of supposedly benevolent racial
paradigm-shifting by the American legal system: They can be read as
unconscious stereotype-congruent responses by twentieth-century justices of the Supreme Court.[1]

Given the dangers such unconscious responses present to the protection of Indian rights, it is important to develop a better understanding of how a post-*Brown* justice could continue to rely on such racist
nineteenth-century language and reasoning in an Indian law opinion without even being conscious of it. Research by social scientists has generated

a broad corpus of work showing how our cognitive thought processes can promote stereotyping and other forms of biased intergroup judgment. The "social cognition approach" to understanding racial discrimination that is developed in this important body of research begins with the view that stereotyping, in the words of Linda Hamilton Krieger, "is nothing special."[2] All of us, in other words, even justices of the Supreme Court, do it from time to time:

> It is simply a form of categorization, similar in structure and function to the categorization of natural objects. According to this view, stereotypes, like other categorical structures, are cognitive mechanisms that *all* people, not just "prejudiced" ones, use to simplify the task of perceiving, processing, and retaining information about people in memory. They are central, and indeed essential to normal cognitive functioning.[3]

The problem with stereotypes, according to social cognition theorists, is that once these categorical ways of looking at the world and others around us are embedded in our minds, they can exert a powerful influence over our intergroup judgments and decision-making processes. Functioning as "person prototypes" or "social schemas," stereotypes become implicit theories, "biasing in predictable ways the perception, interpretation, encoding, retention, and recall of information about other people."[4] These biases, furthermore, operate at the cognitive level, absent any intent or motivation to discriminate against or in favor of certain social groups. They affect our judgment long before the "moment of decision," as we attend to relevant data and interpret, encode, store, and retrieve them from memory. These biases, as Krieger explains, can "sneak up" on decision makers, distorting the factual data that should be relied upon in making a rational, informed decision:

> The notion that decisionmaking is somehow separate from the perceptive, interpretive, and memorial processes that precede it is utterly fallacious. These various processes comprise a functional continuum which is vulnerable to distortion at every point. Thus, discrimination is not necessarily something that occurs "at the moment of decision." Rather, it can intrude much earlier, as cognitive process-based errors in perception and judgment subtly distort the ostensibly objective data set upon which a decision is ultimately based.[5]

Social science research supports the theory that stereotypes can lead to bias and unconscious, unintentional discriminatory attitudes toward certain groups of people. Surveys taken in the post-*Brown* era reveal, for example, that most white Americans ordinarily professed a commitment to nondiscrimination and egalitarian values with respect to things like equal opportunity in education and employment. But the surveys also demonstrated a high level of racial prejudice held by whites generally against certain minority groups, suggesting that although overtly racist attitudes had lost favor, covert, unconscious, and unintentional forms of racism remained pervasive throughout the culture.[6]

Surveys, of course, as any good researcher will admit, can be notoriously unreliable indicators of a person's true beliefs, particularly with regard to matters of race in America.[7] One of the most famous and most-often-repeated types of experiments conducted to determine how white Americans, "deep down," really felt about blacks involved a so-called bogus pipeline. The results of these laboratory experiments suggest that the surveys on white racial attitudes in the post-*Brown* era may actually have underestimated the "true level of white racism."[8]

In the "bogus pipeline" experiments, white subjects were first polled regarding their views on blacks. Typically, half of the subjects were then hooked up to a device described as a sophisticated lie detector. Subjects attached to this "bogus pipeline" routinely admitted to holding far more negative stereotypes than did those merely asked to rate certain racial characteristics. One experiment, for instance, found that the subjects hooked up to the bogus pipeline described blacks as less "honest" and "intelligent" and more "lazy," "stupid," and "physically dirty" than did subjects in the control group, who were not being monitored by the supposed lie detector. Another experiment showed that whites who had been rated as "unprejudiced" in a test on racial attitudes showed a significant reduction of expressed admiration of black public figures when hooked up to the bogus pipeline.[9]

Researchers sought to go even further in developing data on how white Americans felt about certain minority groups, "deep down," by attempting to measure behaviors rather than attitudes. Typically, such experiments were not conducted in a laboratory or college classroom or some professor's comfortable office. They took place in the real world and tested for the presence of discriminatory behavior by observing white subjects in an interracial situation where their conduct, if uninfluenced by racism, would be expected to be similar to their conduct in situations involving only other whites.[10]

Typically, these experiments involved "helping behavior." The subject was engaged in either a face-to-face or a remote encounter with the person needing help. Interestingly, comparison of the experiments involving face-to-face encounters with those involving remote encounters revealed that discrimination against blacks was significantly higher (75 percent versus 32 percent) when whites were able to act on their prejudices in a nonpublic manner, as opposed to when they were engaging in face-to-face, public encounters with blacks. The disparity suggested to researchers that whites in post-*Brown* American society were perhaps being more careful in attempting to avoid discriminatory behavior in public, but that when acting privately or anonymously, most whites were still willing to discriminate against blacks.[11]

In one of the experiments, for example, an envelope was left at an airport phone booth. Inside the envelope was a completed graduate school application and a stamped envelope addressed to the school. There was also a note to "Dad," asking him to please put the application in the mail. Finally, a photograph of the candidate was attached to the application. When white adults picked up the application in the phone booth and inspected it, they were found to be significantly more likely to mail the application when the applicant was white than when the applicant was black.[12]

Other experiments sought to measure nonverbal behavior in testing for racist attitudes. One experiment asked white male students at a prestigious Ivy League college to interview white and black high school students. The high school students who were participating in the experiment had been carefully instructed so that they would all behave similarly when being interviewed by the college students. The findings of the study were most telling: The college students sat further away from the black interviewees than from the white interviewees, made more speech errors in their interviews with the black students, and ended their interviews sooner with black students than with the white high schoolers.[13]

These types of surveys and experiments provide powerful evidence to support the claim made by members of certain minority groups that although overt racism is no longer as evident or as pervasive as it was before *Brown,* covert racist attitudes continue to lurk in the white majority population, right beneath the surface. Primed by long-established stereotypes and unconscious racial beliefs, these attitudes continue to function in modern-day society, ready to be unintentionally triggered by the American racial imagination.

The Language of Indian Savagery in the Twentieth-Century Supreme Court's Indian Law

Indians have long been the subjects of widespread and well-established stereotypes in the American racial imagination. And all of us, from an early age, have been exposed to these racial images of irreconcilable Indian savagery (see chapter 3).

Reed's opinion in *Tee-Hit-Ton* and Rehnquist's opinions in *Oliphant* and *Sioux Nation,* in their use of the racist precedents and language generated by the Marshall model, strongly reflect the traditional stereotypical belief of most Americans, even after the landmark twentieth-century civil rights decision in *Brown v. Board of Education.* Most modern-day Americans continue to believe that Indians were in fact savages at the coming of the white man to the New World.

That this language of racism continues to be so potent in American society is precisely why the Supreme Court's continued adherence to the Marshall model has proved at times to be so dangerous for the protection of Indian rights. Suppose that a post-*Brown* justice has, like most other Americans, been exposed to these stereotypes of Indian racial inferiority at some point in his or her life.[14] For such a justice, the Marshall model and its legal sanctioning of this racist way of thinking and talking about Indians can subvert the rationality of the judicial law-making process when it comes time to decide an important Indian rights case. Instead of turning to the egalitarian principles of racial equality normally applied to all other groups and individuals in post-*Brown* America, the Marshall model justifies deciding an Indian rights case according to an overarching metaprinciple of Indian racial inferiority, represented by the European colonial-era doctrine of discovery. The model, its precedents, and its judicially sanctioned language of racism, in other words, all work to legally validate the tradition of negative racial stereotyping of Indians.

The Post-*Brown* Justice and the Marshall Model of Indian Rights

The Marshall Model in the Hands of a Highly Prejudiced Justice

Let us imagine a post-*Brown* justice who at some point in his or her life has been exposed to the negative racial stereotypes of Indians as savages and who firmly believes that these stereotypes are true. In other words, such a justice holds a derogatory personal belief about Indians—for example, that they were savages "at the coming of the white man"[15] and remained so throughout "the 300-year history of the expansion of the original 13 Colonies into a Nation which now embraces more than three million square miles."[16] We will call such a justice—that is, one who holds such a derogatory personal belief system—"highly prejudiced" toward Indians.[17] This justice not only has an intimate knowledge of negative racial stereotypes of Indian savagery from years of exposure and socialization in the culture of the dominant society, but he or she also endorses and accepts these stereotypes as being historically true. Such a justice believes them to be well-known and established facts, possessing legal significance under the Marshall model and the Supreme Court's Indian law decisions.

In the mind of such a highly prejudiced justice, the Marshall model can generate a highly dangerous form of legal support for that stereotypical view of Indian tribal culture. The model's unqualified endorsement of the doctrine of discovery, its embrace of the European colonial-era metaprinciple of white racial superiority, and its accompanying rights-destroying, jurispathic language of Indian inferiority all work to reinforce the Indianophobic justice's highly prejudiced belief system and biased historical perspective. The model's concession of judicial impotency in ameliorating the effects of the doctrine simply reaffirms what this justice already knows: The Court has no choice but to perpetuate the doctrine of discovery through the silent operations of stare decisis and carefully crafted acts of unappealable judicial elision.

The Marshall Model in the Hands of a Low-Prejudiced Justice

Let us now consider the dangerous, multiform effects of the Marshall model on a much different type of hypothetical justice writing Indian law opinions in the post-*Brown* era. Just because an individual may be aware of certain negative racial stereotypes doesn't necessarily mean that his or her personal beliefs will conform to the stereotypes. In other words, just because a person *knows* about the stereotypes doesn't mean that he or she will in fact apply the stereotypes to an individual.

A justice may, for example, have encountered the traditional stereotypes of Indian savagery, recognized them as inappropriate bases for responding to Indians in present-day American society, and deliberately rejected them. Such a "low-prejudiced" justice[18] holds a much different set of personal beliefs about Indians than does a highly prejudiced justice. Such a justice will be like most Americans in the post-*Brown* era who say they are committed to maintaining an egalitarian, nonprejudiced set of personal beliefs about their fellow citizens, regardless of their race, color, or creed. This commitment will lead the low-prejudiced justice to express these nonprejudiced personal beliefs in a legal opinion, or some other public forum, sometimes in the strongest of terms.[19]

But regardless of the express personal beliefs and commitments of our low-prejudiced justice, the negative racial stereotypes of Indian savagery encountered since the justice's childhood may still not necessarily instantly extinguish themselves in the unbiased judicial mind. Stereotypes are established in children's memories at a very early age.[20] Given the continual reinforcement of stereotypes in the mass media and through other socializing forces, stereotype-congruent responses to these negative racial images may persist long after a person has renounced prejudice. As Armour explains, "Non-prejudiced beliefs and stereotype congruent thoughts and feelings may co-exist within the same individual."[21] Even a low-prejudiced justice, in other words, despite his or her strongly professed nonprejudiced personal beliefs, may be prone to unconscious discrimination and bias. The justice may have developed certain bad habits of thought and action that are primed by pervasive negative racial stereotypes that he or she has encountered over the course of a lifetime in America, pre- and post-*Brown*.

The continuing, pervasive force of such long-established stereotypes is precisely what makes the Marshall model so dangerous when used by a low-prejudiced justice. By virtue of the force of stare decisis in our legal system, the Marshall model sanctions unthinking and unreflective stereotype-congruent responses. A low-prejudiced justice can simply cite a Marshall model precedent to decide an Indian rights case without thinking about it all that much. Unfortunately, the Marshall model says that Indians can be legally treated as supposed hostile savages were treated by the white racial dictatorship that ruled the United States during the nineteenth century.

Instead of engaging the important and difficult questions that frequently arise in the modern Supreme Court's Indian law, particularly when Indians seek to impose their own systems of law and property rights on nonmembers on the reservation, for example, the normally low-prejudiced justice can rely on the Marshall model to guide all judicial inquiry on such issues. The familiar precedents and doctrines of the model, reinforced by centuries of stare decisis, have already clearly defined the diminished rights of Indian tribes under U.S. law.

Why should such a justice take on the challenge of exploring "unfamiliar intellectual terrain"[22] in an Indian rights opinion when the question of the diminished rights of Indian tribal peoples to a "degree of measured separatism"[23] has already been worked out by the precedents of the Marshall model? Stare decisis makes it all too easy for this normally low-prejudiced justice to ignore the unconstrained impulse to decide highly problematic Indian rights claims according to the principles of racial equality and nonsubordination that the Court usually applies in all other types of minority rights cases. This justice will simply rely on the Marshall model, with its fundamental principle of racial discrimination against Indians contained in the doctrine of discovery, to decide on Indian rights cases.

Our legal system, based as it is on continuing fidelity to past judicial precedents, in fact says it's perfectly valid for such a normally low-prejudiced justice to resort to the traditional judicial approach of relying upon nineteenth-century cases that perpetuate and reinforce the familiar stereotypes of Indian savagery with the authority of the Marshall model behind them. Stare decisis tells this justice that it is lawful to apply a European colonial-era principle of white racial superiority, the doctrine of discovery, to Indians—and to no one else in twentieth-century America—even after the landmark civil rights decision in *Brown*. This justice may even feel somewhat regretful about it, but there's really nothing that can be done about the situation, or so this justice will write in his or her Indian law opinion (see chapter 2). The continuing legal force of the Marshall model made this normally low-prejudiced justice do it.

The Marshall Model in the Hands of an Aversive Racist Justice

I have discussed the dangers of the Marshall Model of Indian Rights when used both by a highly prejudiced justice and by a normally low-prejudiced justice. Although these very different justices may be at variance in their personal beliefs about the Indian's perceived inassimilable savage identity, both carry in their memories a long-established and firmly entrenched narrative tradition of negative stereotypes of Indians. Both of these justices will therefore be highly susceptible to the dangers of the Marshall model. Both will have their stereotype-congruent responses to the model's organizing principle of white racial superiority validated and reinforced simply by following stare decisis and by relying upon the racist nineteenth-century precedents and judicial language of Indian savagery generated by the doctrine of discovery, as perpetuated in the Supreme Court's Indian law by the Marshall model.

Let us consider the distinct and pervasive set of dangers presented by a third and final type of hypothetical justice who decides to follow the Marshall model in a given Indian rights case. This type of justice, "deep down," is what researchers of America's post-*Brown* racial imagination refer to as an "aversive racist":[24]

> In contract to "old-fashioned" racism, which is expressed directly
> and openly, aversive racism represents a subtle, often unintentional,
> form of bias that characterizes many white Americans who possess
> strong egalitarian values and who believe that they are nonprejudiced.
> Aversive racists also possess negative racial feelings and beliefs of
> which they are unaware or that they try to dissociate from their non-
> prejudiced self-images.[25]

As has already been noted, most twentieth-century Americans in the post-*Brown* era tend to express an enduring commitment to egalitarian values of racial equality and to profess their nonprejudiced personal beliefs about people of all races to demonstrate the strength and sincerity of this commitment. So, too, the justice who is "deep down" an aversive racist. The negative feelings that the aversive racist justice has for certain minority groups in this country do not necessarily reveal themselves as open hostility or hatred directed at members of those particular groups. Instead, the justice's reactions involve discomfort, uneasiness, sometimes disgust, and perhaps even fear. The aversive racist justice will disfavor most contacts or personal interaction with these groups based on these stereotype-induced reactions. But at the same time, this type of justice would find any suggestion that he or she might actually be prejudiced against certain minority groups a highly aversive notion as well.[26]

The aversive racist justice, in other words, avows the same egalitarian values and beliefs as do most other Americans, sometimes most passionately, but beneath the surface, at the level of the unconscious id, the justice who is an aversive racist really believes in a deeply entrenched racial mythology of "white superiority."[27] The aversive racist justice just doesn't know it, though. Desperately clinging to egalitarian, nonprejudiced values and to a purified self-image as fair arbiter of all minority rights claims that may come before the Court, the aversive racist justice works hard to repress any negative feelings and beliefs about Indians. But these repressed anti-Indian beliefs, because they are a form of what has been called "hidden prejudice,"[28] keep bubbling to the surface, insidiously shaping the way this justice looks at the world. These repressed, anti-Indian racial beliefs can reveal themselves in subtle and even not so subtle ways—for example, in his or her spontaneous reaction, say, to a subversive *Far Side* cartoon about Indians selling Manhattan to the Dutch, or to the fearful thought of Indian tribes exercising criminal jurisdiction over whites on the reservation.

Because aversive racists do not recognize their anti-Indian attitudes, attacking this type of racist attitude in such a justice would be a particularly daunting challenge. To quote Peggy Davis again: "It is difficult to change an attitude that is unacknowledged" (see chapter 1). Further, given that this justice may well be highly offended by the notion that he or she might be an aversive racist, few lawyers would be willing to confront this justice with the fact that he or she harbors "hidden prejudice" against Indian tribes.

These are just some of the reasons why the precedents and judicially sanctioned language of racism perpetuated by the Marshall model can function so dangerously and insidiously when used by the aversive-racist justice. Like the highly prejudiced and low-prejudiced justices, the aversive racist justice will feel totally justified in using the Marshall Model of Indian Rights to deny Indians the same rights to property, self-government, and cultural survival as enjoyed by non-Indians, despite the seeming racial paradigm shift represented by *Brown*. For the justice who is an aversive racist, the Marshall model functions just like a loaded weapon, aimed and ready to discharge the unconscious racist impulses and beliefs that still lie buried deep down. For this justice, the Marshall model will help bring those hidden prejudices against Indians bubbling to the surface. By joining to form a majority with his or her highly prejudiced and low-prejudiced fellow justices on the Court, the justice who is "deep down" an aversive racist can give those hidden prejudices a heretofore unrevealed jurispathic, rights-destroying force in the Supreme Court's Indian law, resulting in a decision that perpetuates a highly dangerous and legally sanctioned principle of racial discrimination against Indian tribal peoples in post-*Brown* American society.

Part IV

The Rehnquist Court's Perpetuation of Racism against Indians

Federal Indian policy is, to say the least, schizophrenic, and this confusion continues to infuse federal Indian law and our cases.

—Justice Clarence Thomas, dissenting, in United States v. Lara

So far, this book has used the Supreme Court's own language and holdings in its Indian rights decisions of the nineteenth and twentieth centuries to examine some of the lessons that can be drawn from a study of the legal history of racism in America and the role of the justices in perpetuating it. One important observation was inspired by the racial imagination of Malcolm X and confirmed by research on racial attitudes during the post-*Brown* civil rights era: Certain well-known languages of racism have flourished throughout American history as part of our national heritage.

One of those still vital and widely disseminated languages is generated by the long-established tradition of stereotyping Indians as an inferior race of savage peoples. The Supreme Court's Indian rights decisions of the past two centuries give ample evidence of the continuing real-world force of this language of racism. Indians have been treated as an inferior colonized race by the Supreme Court, even in important cases decided after the supposed benevolent racial paradigm shift represented by the landmark civil rights decision of *Brown v. Board of Education*.

The Supreme Court's Indian law decisions of the past two centuries illuminate another important lesson derived from our history, one that borrows and builds on Justice Robert Jackson's "loaded weapon" imagery in his famous dissent to the Supreme Court's notorious 1944 *Korematsu* decision. The Marshall model's judicial validation of the doctrine of discovery has indeed functioned in the Supreme Court's Indian rights decisions just as Justice Jackson said it would in his prophetic dissent: "like a loaded weapon ready for the hand of any authority that can bring forward a plausible claim of an urgent need." For nearly two hundred years, the justices have relied on the racist precedents and judicial language perpetuated by the Marshall model to uphold the Court's continuing support of the doctrine of discovery and its legal privileging of white interests and dictatorial power over the most basic human rights of Indian tribal peoples in the United States.

In this final part of the book, I show that the twenty-first-century Rehnquist Court's continuing, unquestioning acceptance of nineteenth-century stereotypes of Indian savagery and lawlessness still presents a dangerous human rights situation for Indian tribes in America. Two cases issued in the twenty-first century by the Rehnquist Court, *Nevada v. Hicks*, decided in 2001, and *United States v. Lara*, decided in 2004, show how a long-established language of racism continues to be employed to support a jurispathic, rights-destroying principle of racial discrimination applied to Indians in America by the doctrine of discovery.

10

Expanding *Oliphant*'s Principle of Racial Discrimination: *Nevada v. Hicks*

A nyone familiar with the workings of our judicial process knows the lesson taught by Judge Benjamin Cardozo's trenchant observation on the "tendency of a principle to expand itself to the limits of its logic" in a legal system such as ours (see chapter 2, "'Like a Loaded Weapon'"). Justice Jackson referred to this basic lesson in his dissent to the Court's 1944 decision in *Korematsu,* where he quoted Cardozo's observation to warn his fellow justices of the dangers of a principle of racial discrimination once approved by the Court as the doctrine of the Constitution: Because of stare decisis, "it has a generative power of its own, and all that it creates will be in its own image."[1]

In this chapter, I use the Supreme Court's 2001 decision in *Nevada v. Hicks*[2] to illustrate this lesson at work in the Rehnquist Court's Indian rights decisions. Justice Antonin Scalia's opinion for the Court in *Nevada v. Hicks* adopts the principle of implicit divestiture of tribal powers announced by Justice Rehnquist's 1978 opinion in *Oliphant* (see chapter 7) and expands it to control *all* exercises of tribal jurisdictional rights, criminal or civil, over all non-Indians on all land on every Indian reservation in the United States. Just as Jackson predicted, *Oliphant,* as expanded by *Nevada v. Hicks,* now possesses the generative power to re-create itself throughout the Rehnquist Court's Indian law decisions of the twenty-first century.

Justice Scalia's Expansion of *Oliphant*'s Principles in *Nevada v. Hicks*

The Supreme Court's landmark 2001 Indian rights decision in *Nevada v. Hicks* involved Floyd Hicks,[3] a former tribal police officer for his tribe, the Fallon Paiute-Shoshone Tribes of western Nevada. On two separate occasions, Nevada state game wardens executed search warrants approved by state and tribal court judges to search Hicks's home on the Fallon Paiute-Shoshone Tribes' reservation land for evidence of an off-reservation crime, the taking of an endangered species—a California bighorn sheep—in violation of Nevada law. No charges were ever filed against Hicks, and two Rocky Mountain sheep's head trophies were returned to him in damaged condition after being certified as not having been taken from an endangered species protected under Nevada law.[4]

Hicks then filed suit in the Fallon Paiute-Shoshone Tribes Tribal Court against the game wardens in their individual capacities and against the state of Nevada, alleging trespass, abuse of process, and violation of constitutional rights remediable under 42 U.S.C. sec. 1983, a federal statute authorizing civil suits against state government officials for violations of civil rights,[5] and under tribal law as well. The tribal court held that it had jurisdiction over Hicks's claims, and the Intertribal Appellate Court affirmed. The state of Nevada then went to U.S. federal district court, seeking a declaratory judgment that the tribal court lacked jurisdiction over the claims arising on the tribe's reservation land. The state's request was denied on the grounds that under principles of federal Indian law contained in the Marshall model's precedents, the state game wardens would have to exhaust their qualified immunity claims as defenses to Hicks's suit in the tribal court.[6] The Ninth Circuit Court of Appeals agreed and affirmed, concluding that the fact that Hicks's home was on tribally owned reservation land was sufficient to support tribal jurisdiction over Hicks's civil claims against the nonmember game wardens arising from their activities on that land.[7]

The Supreme Court, in a six-person majority opinion written by Scalia,[8] held in *Nevada v. Hicks* that the tribal court did not have jurisdiction to adjudicate the state game wardens' alleged tortuous conduct in executing the search warrant for an off-reservation crime on tribal land. Significantly, Scalia repeatedly (three separate times) relied on *Oliphant*'s principle of implicit divestiture of tribal powers lost to the overriding sovereignty of the United States to justify this new and expansive interpretation of *Oliphant*'s precedent for defining Indian rights under the Marshall model.[9]

As Scalia's opinion carefully explained, two earlier Indian rights decisions by the Court, *Montana v. United States,* decided in 1981, and *A-1 Contractors v. Strate,*[10] decided in 1997, had already expanded *Oliphant*'s principles well beyond the criminal jurisdictional sphere. *Montana,* as Scalia noted, had been cited in *A-1 Contractors* as the "pathmarking case" on Indian tribes' regulatory authority over nonmembers.[11] Both *Montana* and subsequently *A-1 Contractors* had held that according to *Oliphant*'s principles, inherent tribal authority to regulate non-Indians through the exercise of *civil* jurisdiction on the reservation had also been implicitly divested by what the Court in *Montana* described as the tribes' "original incorporation into the United States" under the doctrine of discovery.[12] As Scalia noted, *Montana* had held that while "*Oliphant* only determined inherent tribal authority in criminal matters, the principles on which it relied support the general proposition that the inherent sovereign powers of an Indian tribe do not extend to the activities of nonmembers of the tribe."[13] Thus according to the *Hicks* Court's interpretation of *Oliphant*'s principles as applied in *Montana* and *A-1 Contractors,* "where nonmembers are concerned, the 'exercise of tribal power *beyond what is necessary to protect tribal self-government or to control internal relations* is inconsistent with the dependent status of the tribes, and so cannot survive without express congressional delegation.'"[14]

The problem presented to the Rehnquist Court in *Hicks* was that both *Montana* and *A-1 Contractors* had involved attempts by tribes to exercise civil jurisdiction over nonmembers on reservation lands that the tribe no longer exclusively owned or controlled. The Court had denied jurisdiction to the tribes in both these cases, noting especially the nontribal status of the land in each.

In *Montana,* the reservation lands at issue were not owned by the tribe or individual tribal members. Title and ownership to the lands were held by non-Indians. In *A-1 Contractors,* the reservation land involved had been granted out as an easement and right-of-way to the state of

North Dakota by the federal government for purposes of constructing and maintaining a state road.[15] Because the tribes had lost the power to exclude non-Indians—what Justice Ruth Bader Ginsburg's majority opinion in *A-1 Contractors* had called a "gatekeeping right"[16]—over the lands at issue, the Court found in both of these cases that tribal civil jurisdiction had been implicitly divested under *Oliphant*'s principles.[17]

In *Hicks,* however, the tribe still possessed this seemingly talismanic gatekeeping right over the land involved. Hicks's home and yard, as Scalia emphasized in recounting the relevant facts of the case, "*are* on tribe-owned land within the reservation."[18]

Scalia's application of the principles drawn from *Oliphant* as applied by the Court in *Montana* and *A-1 Contractors* sought to show that it didn't matter whether the tribe owned or controlled the land over which it sought to regulate non-Indian conduct. *Oliphant*'s overarching principle of implicit divestiture of tribal sovereignty rights controlled all efforts by a tribe to exercise all forms of jurisdiction over nonmembers, regardless of the status of the land at issue.

> Both *Montana* and *Strate* rejected tribal authority to regulate non-members' activities on land over which the tribe could not "assert a landowner's right to occupy and exclude," *Strate; Montana.* Respondents and the United States argue that since Hicks' home and yard *are* on tribe-owned land within the reservation, the Tribe may make its exercise of regulatory authority over nonmembers a condition of nonmembers' entry. Not necessarily. While it is certainly true that the non-Indian ownership status of the land was central to the analysis in both *Montana* and *Strate,* the reason that was so was *not* that Indian ownership suspends the "general proposition" derived from *Oliphant* that "the inherent sovereign powers of an Indian tribe do not extend to the activities of nonmembers of the tribe" except to the extent "necessary to protect tribal self-government or to control internal relations." *Oliphant* itself drew no distinctions based on the status of the land.[19]

As Scalia interpreted *Oliphant* and the line of precedents following it, the existence of tribal ownership of land is not alone enough to support tribal regulatory jurisdiction over nonmembers who enter upon that land. The tribes, under Scalia's expansive interpretation of *Oliphant*'s line of precedents, must show that tribal authority to regulate state officers who are executing a search warrant related to an off-reservation violation of state law is "essential to tribal self-government or internal relations." According to Scalia, the tribe failed to make this needed showing in *Hicks*, even though reservation land was involved. Nevada's interest in the execution of the warrants was found to be "considerable," whereas the tribe's interest in "self-government" was found to be no more impaired "than federal enforcement of federal law impairs state government." Therefore, Scalia applied what he described as "the general proposition" derived from *Oliphant* that the inherent sovereign powers of an Indian tribe do not extend to the activities of nonmembers as the rule for deciding the case of *Nevada v. Hicks*.[20] Signs taken for wonders, under Scalia's interpretation of the Marshall Model of Indian Rights in twenty-first-century America, Hicks, an Indian tribal member living on his own reservation, could not use his tribe's courts, laws, customs, and traditions to protect himself from acts of trespass, abuse of process, and violation of his constitutional rights allegedly committed by law enforcement officers of the state of Nevada, who had entered upon his home, on tribal land, on two separate occasions to execute a search warrant for a crime he did not commit.

Recall Judge Cardozo's famous maxim on the tendency of a principle to expand itself to the limits of its logic in a legal system that adheres to stare decisis. *Hicks*'s legal conclusion that *Oliphant*'s jurisdictional principles extend to all nonmembers on the reservation, regardless of the status of land, provides compelling evidence of that tendency at work in the twenty-first-century Rehnquist Court's Indian rights jurisprudence. Scalia's 2001 opinion in *Hicks* relies directly upon "the general proposition" derived from *Oliphant*, a 1978 case dealing only with tribal *criminal* jurisdiction over non-Indians, to justify its expansive application of the principle of implicitly divested tribal sovereignty rights to all forms of *civil* jurisdiction over all nonmembers of the tribe, regardless of the status of reservation land.

Scalia's Judicial Acts of Sly Elision in *Hicks*

Besides its significance in demonstrating Cardozo's famous judicial maxim at work, Scalia's majority opinion in *Nevada v. Hicks* also compellingly illustrates one of the principal dangers of the twenty-first-century Rehnquist Court's continuing reliance on the racist precedents and principles generated by the Marshall Model of Indian Rights. We have already seen how Rehnquist's sly exercises of his judicial privilege of elision in *Oliphant*—such as his highly edited, elliptical quotation of the nineteenth-century Marshall model precedent *Crow Dog*—worked to obscure the reinforced racist meanings of that decision in the Supreme Court's twentieth-century post-*Brown* Indian law (see chapter 7). By a similar use of the silent, eviscerating operations of stare decisis, Scalia perpetuated *Oliphant*'s precedent in *Hicks* through this same discreetly executed process of judicial elision.

Only three of the nineteenth-century Marshall model precedents that Rehnquist used to justify his opinion in *Oliphant* are even cited by Scalia in *Hicks*.[21] *Oliphant*, itself, however, as noted in the preceding section, is cited as the controlling modern authority three separate times in *Hicks*. Furthermore, the nineteenth-century judicial language of Indian savagery that *Oliphant* cited, relied upon, and even quoted to support its rights-destroying, jurispathic holding has been eliminated from Scalia's 2001 opinion in *Hicks*. From reading *Hicks*, no one could ever know that *Oliphant* is explicitly grounded in a vision of Indian rights that traces back to the white racial dictatorship exercised by the United States over Indian tribes throughout the nineteenth-century and beyond that to the European colonial era.

The economizing and sanitizing judicial applications of the principle of stare decisis make it unnecessary to rehearse the precedents and justificatory discourse of Indian savagery supporting the foundational principles of white racial superiority validated by *Oliphant*'s 1978 holding. Justice Scalia's elisions in interpreting what *Oliphant* stands for in the Rehnquist Court's twenty-first-century Indian law make those nineteenth-century racist precedents and language disappear as unneeded verbiage in a soundly reasoned judicial precedent. They become, in Scalia's application of the Marshall model in *Hicks*, literally invisible, hidden, lurking beneath the surface. The judicially validated and sanitized language of Indian savagery that originated in the European colonial era and was then perpetuated by *Oliphant* has completely vanished from Scalia's opinion in *Hicks*, submerged in the uncoded conventions and elliptical rules of the Court's citation of Rehnquist's twentieth-century landmark decision on Indian rights, *Oliphant v. Suquamish Indian Tribe*.

Under the Rehnquist Court's interpretation of the Marshall model in *Hicks*, we thus begin to see how Rehnquist's 1978 opinion in *Oliphant* now indeed seems to possess a "generative power of its own."[22] What it creates in the Rehnquist's Court's Indian law is a perpetually reinscribed, judicially validated language of Indian racial inferiority in a modern, sanitized form of color-blind and color-clueless legal discourse.

Fearful Hybridities: Justice Souter's Jurispathic Use of the Marshall Model in His Concurring Opinion in *Nevada v. Hicks*

Nevada v. Hicks can be used to teach a number of important lessons about the dangers of the Supreme Court's continuing reliance on the racist precedents perpetuated by the Marshall model of Indian rights. Justice David Souter's separate concurring opinion in the case[23] underscores one such lesson, that judges in our legal system, as Robert Cover once wrote, are "people of violence": "Confronting the luxuriant growth of a hundred legal traditions, they assert that *this one* is law and destroy or try to destroy the rest."[24]

Souter's concurring opinion in *Nevada v. Hicks* teaches us that the justices of the Rehnquist Court must be watched very closely whenever they rely upon the precedents of the Marshall model in any of their important Indian rights opinions. Like Souter, they may be using the Marshall model to justify the jurispathic destruction of Indian rights in response to a deep-down fear that Indian tribal courts are inferior to "American courts."[25] Souter's concurring opinion in *Nevada v. Hicks* shows that there are justices on the twenty-first-century Rehnquist Court who see nothing wrong with using the same negative racial stereotypes of Indians that the nineteenth-century Supreme Court used to justify denying important Indian rights of self-government over the reservation.

As written by Scalia, the Court's majority holding in *Nevada v. Hicks* was expressly "limited to the question of tribal-court jurisdiction over state officers enforcing state law." The reach of *Hicks*'s holding, as Scalia noted, left "open the question of tribal-court jurisdiction over non-member defendants in general."[26]

In concluding the Court's opinion, however, Scalia specifically referred to Souter's separate concurrence in *Hicks,* which was joined in by Justices Clarence Thomas and Anthony Kennedy. According to Scalia, although the majority had "avoided" the broad question of tribal court jurisdiction over nonmember defendants in general, "[a]s Justice Souter's separate opinion demonstrates, it surely deserves more considered analysis."[27]

Souter's concurring opinion in *Hicks,* admiringly noted by Scalia, drew upon a diverse archive of nineteenth- and twentieth-century Supreme Court legal precedents, and included several quotations lifted from the most favorable contemporary legal literature on modern-day tribal courts, to argue for the adoption by the Supreme Court of a general "rule that, at least as a presumptive matter, tribal courts lack civil jurisdiction over non-members." According to Souter's "more considered analysis," his general rule for deciding all Indian rights claims to tribal jurisdiction over nonmembers "would thus make it explicit that land status within a reservation is not a primary jurisdictional fact."[28] In other words, under Souter's interpretation of the Marshall model, it makes no real difference whether Indians own the land upon which they assert jurisdiction over nonmembers because Indian tribes presumptively lack all jurisdiction over nonmembers.[29]

Souter believed it was necessary to apply this broad, prophylactic rule to all exercises of tribal court civil jurisdiction over nonmembers based upon his stated fears of the "special nature of [Indian] tribunals" and the "risk of substantial disuniformity in the interpretation of state and federal law" by tribal courts.[30] In other words, it was Souter's racial fears of a strange, alien form of legal hybridity perpetuating itself in Indian country that made him write his separate concurring opinion the way he did in *Nevada v. Hicks.*

Souter's jurispathic concurrence raises an important and difficult issue that has vexed the post-*Brown* Supreme Court's Indian law decisions: What sovereign powers should Indian tribes be recognized as possessing over nonmembers under the Marshall Model of Indian Rights?[31] The Supreme Court has long recognized that Indian tribes are not subject to the Constitution's Bill of Rights in exercising their lawfully vested governmental powers over the reservation.[32] In 1968, Congress modified that rule somewhat in passing the Indian Civil Rights Act (ICRA),[33] but as Rehnquist recognized in his 1978 opinion for the Court in *Oliphant,* the ICRA does not afford the identical protections to a criminal defendant in tribal court.[34] For example, Indian criminal defendants are entitled to legal counsel, but not to appointed counsel, in tribal court proceedings under the ICRA.[35] In enacting the ICRA,

Congress decided not to apply the Supreme Court's landmark 1963 ruling *Gideon v. Wainwright,* which held that an indigent defendant in a state court criminal prosecution has the right to appointed counsel under the Sixth Amendment,[36] to Indian tribal court criminal prosecutions. Put quite simply, Congress was unwilling to fund the mandate of a right to appointed counsel under the ICRA, and the tribes certainly didn't have the money, as Congress knew.[37]

As for civil jurisdiction, in the same year it decided *Oliphant,* 1978, the Court also decided *Santa Clara Pueblo v. Martinez.*[38] *Santa Clara* held that in passing the ICRA, Congress, in the exercise of its plenary power in Indian affairs under the Marshall model, chose not to waive tribal sovereign immunity from suit in federal or state courts for civil rights actions brought under the statute. Under *Santa Clara*'s ruling, therefore, litigants in tribal court have no direct right of appeal to a non-Indian court once they are found to be lawfully under an Indian tribe's civic jurisdiction.[39]

There are thus any number of legitimate questions that the justices might ask in deciding whether an Indian tribe possesses jurisdictional authority over nonmembers on its reservation under the Marshall Model of Indian Rights. For example, in considering the question of whether the Fallon Paiute-Shoshone Tribes Tribal Court should have civil adjudicatory jurisdiction over alleged torts committed against tribal members by state law enforcement officers who pursue off-reservation violations of state law on the Fallon Paiute-Shoshone Tribes reservation, it is certainly legitimate for the justices to ask, What process is due these nonmember defendants? What process will they actually get? What common law immunities and defenses, if any, can be raised by the state game wardens in the Fallon Paiute-Shoshone Tribes Tribal Court?[40] Are there any precedents or decisions on this point that have been issued by the tribal court on the reservation? Instead of engaging with these types of legitimate questions about the exercise of tribal court civil jurisdiction over nonmembers, however, Souter's concurring opinion chose instead to urge a general rule that tribal courts presumptively lack civil jurisdiction over nonmembers. Under the jurispathic precedents perpetuated by the Marshall model and the force of stare decisis in the Supreme Court's Indian law, Souter's reliance on *Oliphant* and the cases expanding its principles provided all the justification he needed for his "general jurisdictional presumption."[41]

Citing the Court's 1981 decision in *Montana,* which had expanded *Oliphant*'s principle of implicit divestiture of tribal criminal jurisdiction over non-Indians to the civil jurisdictional sphere, Justice Souter noted:

"[T]hough *Oliphant* only determined inherent tribal authority in criminal matters, the principles on which it relied" support a more "general proposition" applicable in civil cases as well, namely that "the inherent sovereign powers of an Indian tribe do not extend to the activities of non-members of the tribe."[42]

To lend further support to his interpretation of Indian rights under the Marshall model, Souter also relied upon the Rehnquist Court's 1990 decision in *Duro v. Reina,* which had expanded *Oliphant*'s principle to include implicit divestiture of tribal criminal jurisdiction over non-member Indians committing crimes on a tribe's reservation. Though *Duro* was overturned by Congress the year after it was issued by the Court,[43] Justice Souter quoted Justice Kennedy's opinion in that case in support of his belief that the "ability of nonmembers to know where tribal jurisdiction begins and ends, it should be stressed, is a matter of real, practical consequence given '[t]he special nature of [Indian] tribunals,'"[44] As Souter stated, Indian courts "differ from traditional American courts in a number of significant respects."[45] He then went on to list some of the normative differences and divergences between tribal courts and "American courts": "To start with the most obvious one, it has been understood for more than a century that the Bill of Rights and the Fourteenth Amendment do not of their own force apply to Indian tribes."[46]

Souter's concurrence noted other "significant" differences between Indian tribal courts and non-Indian "American courts."[47] The ICRA,[48] he explained, "makes a handful of analogous safeguards enforceable in tribal courts." But, he continued, quoting *Oliphant*'s dismissive characterization of that act's protections, "the guarantees are not identical."[49] He drew from some of the more recent legal literature on modern-day tribal courts to help illustrate the normative hybridity of contemporary tribal justice systems, generally speaking. He quoted, for instance, from a 1998 law review article authored by Nell Jessup Newton, one of the country's most respected Marshall model Indian law scholars, and a strong advocate for tribal justice systems and protection of Indian rights, as noting "a definitive trend by tribal courts toward the view that they ha[ve] leeway in interpreting the ICRA's due process and equal protection clauses and need not follow the U.S. Supreme Court precedents 'jot-for-jot.'"[50] Having identified this possibility of interpretive divergence from the Court's normative hegemony over the monistic meanings of the U.S. Constitution's due process and equal protection clauses, Souter stated his belief that his preference for a legal presumption against tribal court civil jurisdiction "squares with one of the principal policy considerations underlying *Oliphant,* namely, an overriding concern that citizens who are not tribal members be protected . . . from unwarranted intrusions on their personal liberty." In other words, according to Souter's interpretation of the Marshall model, the "special nature of [Indian] tribunals" would render all tribal efforts to assert jurisdiction over U.S. citizens who are not members of the tribe "an unwarranted intrusion on their personal liberty" and would therefore be in violation of the "policy considerations underlying *Oliphant.*"[51]

According to Souter, his general presumption against subjecting nonmembers of the tribe to these irregular, hybrid forms of tribal justice holds "practical importance."[52] Citing a publication by a leading national organization of tribal court judges in the United States as authority, Souter stated that the "resulting law applicable in tribal courts is a complex mix of tribal codes and federal, state, and traditional law, which would be unusually difficult for an outsider to sort out." Given this difficulty, he explained, nonmembers on the reservation should be able to anticipate tribal jurisdiction by reference to a fact "more readily knowable than the title status of a particular plot of land."[53] To show how important this ability to anticipate tribal jurisdiction was to non-Indians, he cited "[o]ne further consideration":

> It is generally accepted that there is no effective review mechanism in place to police tribal courts' decisions on matters of non-tribal law, since tribal-court judgments based on state or federal law can be neither removed nor appealed to state or federal courts. The result, of course, is a risk of substantial disuniformity in the interpretation of state and federal law, a risk underscored by the fact that "[t]ribal courts are often 'subordinate to the political branches of tribal governments.'"[54]

Signs taken for wonders: We have seen this type of judicial concern over the normative differences between Indian tribal justice systems and what is taken to be the superior form of justice meted out by "American courts" expressed before in the Supreme Court's Indian rights decisions. Throughout the nineteenth century, the justices on the Court regularly expressed these types of recurrent concerns about the lawless, uncivilized, inferior nature of Indian tribal justice systems in justifying their Indian rights decisions and opinions (see chapters 4 and 5). Even as Indian tribes adapted themselves to an alien, colonially imposed way of life on Indian reservations, as they struggled to maintain their dignity as human beings and their self-governing rights under the watchful surveillance of the army, missionaries, and BIA agents, the nineteenth-century Congress, executive branch officials, and Supreme Court uniformly regarded them as not measuring up to the dominant society's standards for the administration of justice on the reservation.[55]

According to Homi Bhabha, "The social articulation of difference, from the minority perspective is a complex, on-going negotiation that seeks to authorize cultural hybridities that emerge in moments of historical transformation."[56] Tribal courts are today recognized by tribal advocates, legal scholars, and other important legal commentators as important jurisgenerative institutions that enable Indian tribes to revive and assert a robust and rights-affirming Indian vision of justice based on indigenous American tribal values of human dignity and respect for the equality of all races in America.[57]

Souter's rights-denying, jurispathic approach in *Hicks* to all Indian claims to "tribal-court jurisdiction over non-member defendants in general" illustrates precisely why the justices of the twenty-first-century Rehnquist Court must be watched very closely whenever they use the precedents of the Marshall model, no matter from what era or century, in any of their Indian rights opinions. The tendency of the Marshall model's principle of racial discrimination to expand itself to the limits of its own legal logic is particularly intensified by the long-established tradition of stereotyping Indians as lawless, less civilized peoples. As Souter's concurring opinion in *Nevada v. Hicks* demonstrates, a justice on the Rehnquist Court may respond to an Indian tribe's claim of rights-reviving jurisgenerative authority over the reservation by using the Marshall Model of Indian Rights to perpetuate the same basic stereotypes of Indian racial inferiority and lawlessness that the justices of the nineteenth century used. For this type of justice, the Marshall model functions just like a loaded weapon, to be used for the jurispathic destruction of a fearful form of legal hybridity in America.

11

The Court's Schizophrenic Approach to Indian Rights: *United States v. Lara*

I set out an axiom at the beginning of this book: "A winning courtroom strategy" for protecting Indian rights cannot be organized around nineteenth-century racist legal precedents and an accompanying form of legal discourse that stereotypes tribal Indians as lawless, uncivilized savages (see the introduction, the section "A Winning Courtroom Strategy"). Some Indian law scholars and advocates, of course, reject this axiom, knowing that there are famous Indian law cases decided by the Supreme Court that Indians, in fact, have "won."[1] I concede that the cases that support their legal faith in the Marshall Model of Indian Rights are some of the most important Indian rights cases ever decided by the justices. Nineteenth-century cases such as *Worcester v. Georgia* and *Ex parte Crow Dog*,[2] which were indeed "won" by tribes (see chapter 4, "*Worcester v. Georgia*," and chapter 5, "*Crow Dog*"), provided foundational precedents for many of the great Supreme Court Indian rights victories of the post-*Brown* era. Cases such as *Williams v. Lee* (1959), upholding tribal court jurisdiction over civil suits involving contracts executed on the reservation by tribal members; *Morton v. Mancari* (1974), upholding Indian hiring preferences in the BIA; and *Santa Clara Pueblo v. Martinez* (1978),[3] upholding tribal sovereign authority over membership and other matters of internal control and self-government on the reservation, are all grounded firmly in the Marshall model, and all affirm important tribal rights to a degree of "measured separatism" in America (see the introduction, on the right to a degree of "measured separatism" asserted by Indian tribes).

In 2004, the Supreme Court decided another case "won" by Indians that can be cited to support the continuing use of the Marshall model to protect Indian rights in twenty-first-century American society. In *United States v. Lara,* the Rehnquist Court held that Congress, under the Constitution's plenary grants of authority over Indian affairs, has the power "to enact legislation that both restricts and, in turn, relaxes those restrictions on tribal sovereign authority."[4] Specifically, the legislation upheld in *Lara* was the so-called *Duro*-fix enacted in 1991 by Congress in reaction to a Supreme Court decision that Indians had lost the prior year, *Duro v. Reina. Duro v. Reina* held that tribes, under the principle of *Oliphant,* had been implicitly divested of criminal jurisdiction over nonmember Indians who commit crimes on the reservation.[5] The 2004 *Lara* decision, written for the Court by Justice Stephen Breyer, upheld this 1991 legislative reversal of the 1990 *Duro* decision and the constitutionality of Congress's recognition and affirmation of the inherent sovereign power of Indian tribes to exercise criminal jurisdiction over *all* Indians on the reservation. Significantly, Breyer's opinion for the Court used the Marshall model to get the job done.

In affirming this very important tribal right to a degree of measured separatism, *Lara* has been hailed as a significant legal victory for Indian tribes.[6] *Lara* demonstrates quite clearly that the Marshall model can be made to work to produce a winning courtroom strategy for protecting important Indian rights before the twenty-first-century Rehnquist Court. In *Lara,* at least, the Marshall model, with what one noted Indian law scholar has called its "necessary tension between inherent tribal sovereignty and Congress's plenary power," seems to provide Indian law with the strength it needs to protect Indian rights in the Supreme Court. *Lara* shows how the seemingly "contradictory tenets" of the Marshall model respecting congressional plenary power and tribal sovereignty can work together to assure "that neither the power nor the sovereignty will carry the full force it might were the other not recognized."[7]

An unreconciled form of legal hybridity may well be the best that Indians can hope for from the white man's Indian law, given the realities of the necessarily continuing, subordinated position of Indian tribes as colonized peoples in the United States. Indian law, after all, as Chief Justice Marshall reminded us, deals with "the actual state of things."[8] No one can deny that Indian law, as elaborated by the Marshall model, has worked well enough to keep tribal Indians around much longer than the Founders would ever have thought possible under the system of colonial governmentality they created for Indian tribes in America (see chapter 3). Given the legal history of racism in America, a racial realist might argue that Indians should take the Marshall model and make its "contradictory," tension-filled vision of Indian rights work for them even better in the Supreme Court's twenty-first-century Indian law. This is the only model of Indian rights the Supreme Court has ever accepted, and given the force of stare decisis in our legal system, it might make sense to commit ourselves fully to making the Marshall model be the best that it can be at protecting Indian rights in America (see the introduction, especially on racial realism).

Perhaps it is possible to develop an approach to protecting Indian rights that uses the Marshall model with a "delicate" touch[9] when it comes to deciding cases involving important Indian rights to property, self-government, and cultural integrity and survival. But the problem with any approach to protecting Indian rights that relies upon the principle of racial discrimination perpetuated by the Marshall model is that those rights are never really safe under the Supreme Court's Indian law. The model's acceptance of the European colonial-era doctrine of discovery and its foundational legal principle of Indian racial inferiority licenses Congress to exercise its plenary power unilaterally to terminate Indian tribes, abrogate Indian treaties, and extinguish Indian rights, and there's nothing that Indians can legally do about any of these actions. Under the Marshall model, such actions by Congress are all regarded as political questions, not subject to Supreme Court judicial review.[10]

As for the Supreme Court, we have seen that when Indians do manage to get a hearing before the justices in their effort to protect their rights, even seemingly great legal victories, such as the nineteenth-century Supreme Court decisions in *Worcester* and *Crow Dog*, can be turned against tribal interests, and the principle of racial discrimination they uphold can be cited to deny important tribal rights in a later case. Thus, Scalia can cite the 1832 decision in *Worcester v. Georgia,* one of the most important Indian rights victories ever issued by the Supreme Court, to support his jurispathic, rights-denying reasoning in the twenty-first-century Indian rights decision *Nevada v. Hicks.* Rehnquist can cite *Crow Dog,* another important Supreme Court legal victory for tribes, and throw *Worcester* in too, in order to uphold his rights-destroying principle of implicit divestiture of tribal powers under his much-criticized interpretation of the Marshall model in his 1978 opinion *Oliphant v. Suquamish Indian Tribe.*[11]

Like the other precedents generated by the Marshall Model of Indian Rights, *Lara,* along with *Worcester, Crow Dog, Oliphant,* and *Hicks* (all of which, by the way, are cited in Breyer's *Lara* opinion),[12] now comes to assume the familiar function of all the justices' Indian law opinions that uphold the principle of racial discrimination embodied in the doctrine of discovery. *Lara* represents another loaded weapon in the Supreme Court's Indian law, ready for the justices to use in justifying some future exercise of Congress's judicially unappealable plenary power over Indian tribes.

The *Lara* Decision

In *Lara,* the Rehnquist Court was asked to consider a 1991 congressional statute "recogniz[ing] and affirm[ing]" the "inherent" authority of an Indian tribe to bring a criminal misdemeanor prosecution against an Indian who was not a member of that tribe.[13] As Breyer's majority opinion in *Lara* noted, the Court had previously held in its 1990 decision, *Duro v. Reina,* that under the precedent established by *Oliphant,* Indian tribes did not possess this inherent power over nonmember Indians committing crimes on the reservation. Tribal criminal jurisdiction over Indians not members of the tribe had been implicitly divested under *Oliphant*'s reasoning, according to Kennedy's majority opinion for the Supreme Court in *Duro v. Reina.*[14]

Duro was met by an outpouring of protests by Indian tribes and expressions of concern on the part of federal prosecutors about the serious jurisdictional gaps arising out of the decision with respect to enforcement of criminal law against nonmember Indians in Indian country.[15] Congress responded the very next year by enacting the *Duro*-fix, the statute at issue in the *Lara* decision, which "recognized and affirmed" what Congress declared to be "the inherent power of Indian tribes" to exercise criminal jurisdiction over *all* Indians who commit crimes on the reservation.[16]

It was the fate of Billy Jo Lara, an enrolled member of the Turtle Mountain Band of Chippewa Indians in North Dakota, to be the first Indian prosecuted by another tribe under the *Duro*-fix and to have his case heard on appeal before the Supreme Court. Lara lived with his wife, a member of the Spirit Lake Tribe, and his children on the Spirit Lake Reservation. He had been excluded from the reservation after several incidents of serious misconduct. When he ignored the exclusion order, federal officers stopped him and arrested him. During the course of his arrest he struck one of these federal officers. The Spirit Lake Tribe then prosecuted Lara in the Spirit Lake Tribal Court for "violence to a policeman." Lara pleaded guilty and served ninety days in jail for his crime.[17]

After Lara's tribal court conviction, the federal prosecutor decided to charge him in federal district court with the federal crime of assaulting a federal officer. This similarity between the two crimes, Breyer noted, would *"ordinarily"* have brought Lara under the protection of the Fifth Amendment's double jeopardy clause, which states that the government may not "subject" any person "for the same offence to be twice put in jeopardy of life or limb."[18] But under the Court's prior constitutional law precedents, the double jeopardy clause does not bar successive prosecutions brought by separate sovereigns. Thus, under this "dual sovereignty" doctrine, if a single criminal act by a person violates the laws of North Dakota, for example, and at the same time also violates the laws of the United States as enacted by Congress, that person has committed two distinct "offenses" and can be prosecuted and jailed separately for each.[19] The Constitution's double jeopardy clause does not apply to separate prosecutions by the two distinct forms of sovereignty, federal and state, established and recognized by that founding text at the creation of the Republic.

In 1978 (the same year it decided *Oliphant*), the Supreme Court extended this dual sovereignty doctrine to Indian tribes in *United States v. Wheeler,* holding that an Indian tribe acts as a separate sovereign when it prosecutes its *own members.*[20] In *Duro v. Reina,* however, the Court refused to extend *Wheeler*'s holding to tribal criminal prosecutions over *nonmember* Indians. Relying on *Oliphant,* the Court ruled in *Duro* that a tribe no longer possessed *inherent or sovereign authority* to prosecute such individuals.[21]

It was soon after the *Duro* decision that Congress in effect overturned the Court's decision and enacted the *Duro*-fix, specifically authorizing a tribe to prosecute Indian members of a different tribe for on-reservation crimes.[22] Significantly, in permitting an Indian tribe to bring certain tribal prosecutions against nonmember Indians, Congress did not purport to delegate the federal government's own federal power to prosecute crimes on an Indian reservation. Rather, the statute specifically makes reference to the tribes' own "'powers of self-government,'" as including "the inherent power of Indian tribes, hereby recognized and affirmed, to exercise criminal jurisdiction over *all* Indians," including nonmembers.[23]

Even at the time of its passage, serious questions were raised about the constitutionality of the congressional *Duro*-fix, and about whether, indeed, Congress possessed the constitutional authority to reverse a Supreme Court decision on the scope of inherent tribal sovereignty under the Marshall model.[24] If Congress indeed did lack such authority, then the federal legislation restoring tribal criminal jurisdiction over all Indians on the reservation could be regarded as a form of delegation of federal authority, and the dual sovereignty doctrine would not apply to successive prosecutions by a tribal government and the federal government for the same offense. This result would have undermined one of the primary purposes of the *Duro*-fix, which was to provide tribes and the federal government with the prosecutorial flexibility they said they needed to effectively administer criminal justice in Indian country. Given that Indian tribes under the ICRA are limited to the imposition of jail sentences of no more than one year for violations of tribal law, Congress recognized that there may be occasions where dual prosecutorial power might better assure effective law enforcement on the reservation.[25]

Breyer's majority opinion for the Court in *Lara* began its analysis of the *Duro*-fix legislation by describing the law as an attempt by Congress "to adjust the tribe's status. It relaxes the restrictions, recognized in *Duro*, that the political branches had imposed on the tribes' exercise of inherent prosecutorial power." Breyer framed the question before the Court in *Lara* as "whether the Constitution authorizes Congress to do so." Breyer answered that question by holding for the Court "that Congress does possess the constitutional power to lift the restrictions on the tribes' criminal jurisdiction over nonmember Indians as the statute seeks to do."[26]

Breyer based his legal analysis in *Lara* on precedents drawn primarily from the Marshall model[27] to show that the Constitution grants Congress broad general powers to legislate with respect to Indian tribes. According to Breyer, these "plenary and exclusive powers" have been traditionally identified by the court as originating in the Indian commerce clause and the treaty clause.[28]

Besides these sources, Breyer also cited "the first century of America's national existence," when Indian affairs "were more an aspect of military and foreign policy than a subject of domestic or municipal law."[29] Thus, the Constitution's "adoption of preconstitutional powers necessarily inherent in any Federal Government, namely powers that this Court has described as 'necessary concomitants of nationality,' also serve as the source of Congress' great powers to regulate and modify the status of tribes."[30]

Having squarely located the source of the federal government's "preconstitutional powers" over Indian tribes as arising out of affairs of state, war, conquest, and territorial integrity, Breyer went on to note that Congress,

> with this Court's approval, has interpreted the Constitution's "plenary" grants of power as authorizing it to enact legislation that both restricts and, in turn, relaxes those restrictions on tribal sovereign authority. From the Nation's beginning Congress' need for such legislative power would have seemed obvious. After all, the Government's Indian policies, applicable to numerous tribes with diverse cultures, affecting billions of acres of land, of necessity would fluctuate dramatically as the needs of the Nation and those of the tribes changed over time. And Congress has in fact authorized at different times very different Indian policies (some with beneficial results but many with tragic consequences).[31]

Breyer then cited a series of Marshall model precedents involving congressional decisions to recognize or to terminate the existence of individual tribes as evidence of this "plenary" power possessed by Congress to make "major policy changes in the metes and bounds of tribal sovereignty."[32] Indeed, as Breyer noted, Congress's power over Indian affairs is so great and unconstrained, as interpreted by the Supreme Court under the Marshall model, that it has restored previously extinguished tribal status by re-recognizing a tribe whose tribal existence it previously had terminated. Furthermore, Congress, as Breyer explained, has exercised its plenary power over Indian affairs by conferring U.S. citizenship upon all Indians,[33] and by granting tribes "greater autonomy in their inherent law enforcement authority" by increasing the maximum criminal penalties tribal courts may impose upon tribal members under the ICRA.[34]

Calling the change in tribal jurisdictional power approved by Congress in the *Duro*-fix a limited one, concerning "a power similar in some respects to the power to prosecute a tribe's own members," Breyer was careful to note that *Lara* did not raise the more difficult issue of "potential constitutional limits on congressional efforts to legislate far more radical changes in tribal status." The *Duro*-fix did not interfere with the power or authority of the state governments, Breyer said, and the Court's decision in *Lara* did not have to "consider the question whether the Constitution's Due Process or Equal Protection Clauses prohibit tribes from prosecuting a nonmember citizen of the United States."[35]

As for the Court's prior holdings in *Oliphant* and *Duro*, which had held that the power to prosecute nonmembers was an aspect of the tribes' external relations and hence part of the tribal sovereignty that was divested by treaties and by Congress, those cases, Breyer explained, reflected the Court's view of the tribes' retained sovereign status *"as of the time* the Court made them. They did not set forth constitutional limits that prohibit Congress from changing the relevant legal circumstances, *i.e.,* from taking actions that modify or adjust the tribes' status."[36]

Although *Lara* can most certainly be claimed as a "victory" for Indian rights, it is important to recognize that the 7-to-2 decision by the Rehnquist Court characteristically affirms the basic elements of the Marshall model, though thoroughly cleansed of any of the embarrassing or anachronistic racist language or imagery from the nineteenth century that has been so often used by the Court in the past to justify Congress's plenary power over Indian tribes. Significantly, the Court in *Lara* recognizes the exclusive power possessed by the United States to make "major policy changes in the metes and bounds of tribal sovereignty," whether tribes give their consent or not, without making any reference to the foundational principles of racial inferiority supporting U.S. powers over tribes under the Marshall model.

This twenty-first-century "victory" for Indian tribes thus affirms a nineteenth-century form of white racial dictatorship exercised by Congress over Indians, grounded upon precedents of the Marshall model upholding congressional plenary power under the doctrine of discovery. In other words, the victory in *Lara* upholds a long-established principle of racial discrimination against Indians under the Constitution and laws of the United States, thereby perpetuating the same legal discourse of racial and cultural inferiority, cleansed of its more offensive racist stereotypes and images, that the Court has used for the past two centuries in its Indian rights decisions. Breyer's statement in *Lara* that "the Constitution does not dictate the metes and bounds of tribal autonomy" means that under the Marshall model, no judicially enforceable protections for tribal sovereignty are to be found in that document. Congress has the power to take actions that "modify or adjust" tribal sovereign powers, and nothing in the Supreme Court's Indian law decisions suggest "that the Court should second-guess the political branches' own determinations" on the question of the scope of tribal authority.[37]

Given the broad language of its holding on the scope of congressional plenary power in Indian affairs, it is worth asking why anyone would regard *Lara* as a great victory for Indian tribes. True, the decision upholds important tribal rights of self-government in the area of criminal jurisdiction, but at the cost of affirming Congress's judicially unappealable, jurispathic, rights-destroying racial power over tribes, a power that traces its origins and trajectory to the European colonial era. According to the *Lara* decision, nothing in the Constitution or the Marshall model prevents Congress from using its plenary power over Indian tribes to completely destroy Indian rights in America. In fact, *Lara* can be cited as precedent for support of any future attempt by the Congress of the United States to exercise such all-encompassing, rights-destroying jurispathic power under the Court's interpretation of the Marshall model. In this sense, *Lara,* like all the precedents of the Marshall model upholding the principle of racial discrimination embodied in the doctrine of discovery, now also functions "like a loaded weapon" in the Supreme Court's Indian law. The precedent it establishes now stands ready to be used by some future justice who wants to justify the jurispathic destruction of Indian rights under what the Marshall model views as Congress's unquestioned plenary power in Indian affairs.

The "Schizophrenic" Nature of the White Man's Indian Law:
Justice Clarence Thomas's Separate Concurrence in *United States v. Lara*

United States v. Lara was the first major "victory" for Indian tribes issued by the twenty-first-century Supreme Court. This final section of the chapter examines Justice Clarence Thomas's separate concurrence in *Lara*[38] to underscore what I believe is one of the most important lessons that can be learned about relying on the Marshall model's "tensions" and "contradictory tenets" to develop a "winning courtroom strategy" for protecting and upholding important Indian rights to a degree of measured separatism before the present-day Supreme Court.

According to Thomas's concurrence in *Lara,* the Marshall model's precedents on tribal sovereignty, as interpreted and enforced by Congress and the Court since the early nineteenth century, have helped to create a "schizophrenic" body of case law. Thomas's prescription for this base malady affecting the Supreme Court's decisions on tribal sovereignty is to "confront" what he says are the "tensions" in the Marshall model and resolve "the confusion reflected in our precedent." As Thomas writes, "As this case should make clear, the time has come to reexamine the premises and logic of our tribal sovereignty cases."[39]

If Thomas is ultimately successful in getting his colleagues on the Court to confront the "confusion" created by the Marshall model's "schizophrenic" precedents on tribal sovereignty, a winning courtroom strategy for protecting Indian rights had better recognize the important lesson already discussed respecting the Rehnquist Court: There are justices on the Court today who see nothing wrong with using the same negative racial stereotypes of Indian tribes that the justices of the nineteenth century used to justify their jurispathic destruction of a fearful form of legal hybridity (see chapter 10, "Fearful Hybridities"). Such a strategy for protecting Indian rights before a Supreme Court justice who wants to "reexamine the premises and logic" of the Supreme Court's tribal sovereignty cases, in other words, must develop an approach for convincing that justice not to use the same stereotypes that have distorted the rationality of the Supreme Court's decision-making process in the past when it comes time to decide difficult and complex questions of Indian rights now and in the future.

Justice Thomas began his concurrence in *Lara* by stating his express disagreement with the *Lara* majority's holding "that the Constitution grants to Congress plenary power to calibrate the metes and bounds of tribal sovereignty."[40] In Justice Thomas's view, "the tribes either are or are not separate sovereigns, and our federal Indian law cases untenably hold both positions simultaneously":

> It seems to me that much of the confusion reflected in our precedent arises from two largely incompatible and doubtful assumptions. First, Congress (rather than some other part of the Federal Government) can regulate virtually every aspect of the tribes without rendering tribal sovereignty a nullity. Second, the Indian tribes retain inherent sovereignty to enforce their criminal laws against their own members.[41]

Thomas turned to Black's Law Dictionary to illustrate his point about the contradictory nature of tribal sovereignty as conceptualized under the Marshall model: "The sovereign is, by definition, the entity 'in which independent and supreme authority is vested.'" According to this dictionary definition of sovereignty, Thomas argued, tribes cannot logically be regarded as sovereigns: "It is quite arguably the essence of sovereignty not to exist merely at the whim of an external government." While conceding that states can have their sovereignty diminished by Congress, Thomas explained that the states of the Union are part of a "constitutional framework" that recognizes their sovereignty and "specifically grants Congress authority to legislate with respect to them." The tribes, according to Thomas, are not part of the constitutional order, and their sovereignty is in no way guaranteed by the Constitution.[42]

Thomas traced the Court's "schizophrenic" approach to tribal sovereignty as originating in the foundational precedents of the Court's Indian law; Chief Justice Marshall, in other words, was to blame. He first cited Marshall's opinion in *Cherokee Nation v. Georgia* to show how tribes are not sovereign in the sense that foreign nations are sovereign: "[Y]et it may well be doubted whether those tribes which reside within the acknowledged boundaries of the United States can, with strict accuracy, be denominated foreign nations. They may, more correctly, perhaps, be denominated domestic dependent nations."[43] He then quoted Marshall's opinion in *Worcester,* to show that the Court early on recognized tribes as "independent political communities, retaining their original natural rights," and possessed of the power to "mak[e] treaties."[44] According to

Thomas, these Marshall model precedents prove that federal Indian law "is at odds with itself." The federal government, Thomas explained, simultaneously claims power to regulate virtually every aspect of the tribes through ordinary domestic legislation, yet at the same time, it also maintains that the tribes possess "sovereignty." "Federal Indian policy is, to say the least, schizophrenic, and this confusion continues to infuse federal Indian law and our cases."

> The Court should admit that it has failed in its quest to find a source of congressional power to adjust tribal sovereignty. Such an acknowledgement might allow the Court to ask the logically antecedent question *whether* Congress (as opposed to the President) has this power. A cogent answer would serve as the foundation for the analysis of the sovereignty issues posed by this case. We might find that the Federal Government cannot regulate the tribes through ordinary domestic legislation and simultaneously maintain that the tribes are sovereigns in any meaningful sense. But until we begin to analyze these questions honestly and rigorously, the confusion that I have identified will continue to haunt our cases.[45]

Like the scholars and advocates who embrace the Marshall model's contradictory tenets and tensions, Justice Thomas recognizes that the Supreme Court's Indian law "is at odds with itself," and that the source of the "confusion" that haunts the Court's cases traces to Chief Justice Marshall's contradictory Indian law precedents.

The legal history of racism as perpetuated by the Supreme Court's Indian law decisions over the past two centuries teaches us that the justices have never really carried out an honest and rigorous analysis of Indian rights under the Constitution and laws of the United States. Their decision-making process for defining the scope and content of Indian rights in America has been distorted by their use of a long-established language of Indian savagery and racial inferiority in their Indian law opinions. If Thomas succeeds in his quest of convincing his colleagues on the Court to "reexamine the premises and logic" of the Marshall model's precedents on tribal sovereignty, Indian tribes and their lawyers had better be sure they have a winning courtroom strategy to counter the continuing jurispathic force of that language on the Rehnquist Court's Indian rights decisions.

Conclusion

The Fifth Element

I began this book with a lesson taught by a *Far Side* cartoon: A person's response to a long-established language of racism will depend on the particular stereotypes he or she holds about certain types of people. In the conclusion to this book, I want to return to this fundamental lesson. But in returning to this basic point about the power of stereotypes to shape our responses to certain types of people, I want to apply it in a much different context and to a much different group of people. I want to explore how this lesson applies to the present-day justices of the Supreme Court.

Many Indian law scholars and advocates believe that as a group, the justices of the Rehnquist Court are prejudiced against Indians when it comes to deciding certain types of Indian rights cases under the Marshall model, particularly in situations where important interests and values of the non-Indian society are involved.[1] Based on this belief about the justices, some of these Indian law scholars and advocates argue that the present-day Supreme Court is not likely to change its racial paradigm of Indian rights anytime soon. In fact, their typical response to this racially hidebound image of the Rehnquist Court as being irredeemably

161

anti-Indian is to tell Indian tribes to avoid the justices if at all possible.[2] In essence, their strategy is to try to prevent the justices from using the Marshall model to further destroy Indian rights and to set another bad precedent in an important Indian rights case. If a tribe's lawyer must go to the Supreme Court, they say, for example, to defend a victory for Indian rights in a lower court decision, that lawyer shouldn't even think of confronting the justices with the racist judicial language of Indian savagery they rely upon in their opinions. Such a confrontational approach is regarded as a waste of time that can never translate into "a winning courtroom strategy." Challenging the justices about their racial attitudes toward tribes might only make things worse for Indians, they fear (see the introduction). What if the Rehnquist Court justices were to get really mad at being called racists for using the Marshall Model of Indian Rights the way they do?

Unfortunately, the legal history of racism in America and the Supreme Court's role in perpetuating it demonstrates that Indian tribes can't afford to stereotype the justices of the Rehnquist Court or any court in America as being too prejudiced to protect their rights. Indians, given the present-day racial reality of their situation as a relatively small, historically subordinated minority group in America, have no choice but to try to convince the justices of the Supreme Court that their basic human rights to property, self-government, and cultural survival need legal protection, all the time, without exception, even when those rights significantly conflict with the interests and values of the dominant society. The continuing existence of Indian tribalism in America depends on confronting the justices with this reality. It is and always has been for Indians in the United States, the "actual state of things."

The justices, I argue, must be confronted with the fact that they are perpetuating a particularly bad habit when they continue to rely upon the racist nineteenth-century precedents and accompanying judicial language of racism generated by the Marshall model in their present-day Indian rights opinions. By upholding a long-established tradition of negative racial stereotyping of Indians as lawless, uncivilized savages, a tradition that traces back to an era of white racial dictatorship and conquest in America, the justices are denying Indians their most basic human rights, and they are using colonial-era legal precedents to do so. The justices need to be confronted with the racist way they are deciding Indian rights cases in twenty-first-century America.

This postcolonial approach to Indian law asserts that the justices need to be directly confronted with the fact that a Supreme Court decision on Indian peoples' most important human rights is an action that ought to involve a great deal of serious thought, instead of unconscious racial stereotyping. Because Indian rights cases can evoke powerful racial fears that non-Indian interests and values will be trammeled or denied under the measured degree of separatism and self-rule sought by Indian tribes under U.S. law (see chapter 9), the justices must be made alert to the ever-present dangers of unconscious racism and hidden prejudice against Indians in the way that they approach thinking and writing about Indian rights in their opinions. The egalitarian principles of racial equality and fundamental justice that are applied by the Court in all its other minority rights cases may appear to be in conflict and tension with the types of rights Indians want protected under the Constitution and laws of the United States. Given the seemingly problematic, contradictory, and even what Justice Thomas called "schizophrenic" nature of so many Indian rights claims (see chapter 11), the justices need to be confronted with the fact that their habitual reliance on the Marshall model perpetuates a long-established tradition of stereotyping Indians as a savage, lawless race of legal inferiors. In adopting a postcolonial approach to Indian law, the justices must be very careful about using nineteenth-century racist precedents, stare decisis, and slyly crafted acts of judicial elision to justify their reliance on this judicially sanctioned language of racial inferiority as a convenient means for denying these seemingly problematic Indian rights claims to a degree of measured separatism in America.

The confrontational approach I'm arguing for doesn't mean that Indians will win all the time when they bring their cases before the justices of the Supreme Court. It means that the Court (along with tribal advocates and Indian law scholars) must stop using a language of racism to talk, think, and write about the problematic nature of Indian rights claims in a postcolonial world.

The reason I urge this confrontational approach with the justices is that I believe that as a group and as individuals, they are, or at least ought to be, presumed capable of changing their antiquated racial paradigm when it comes to deciding Indian rights cases. I believe that when the justices are confronted with the way the legalized racial stereotypes of the Marshall model can be used to perpetuate an insidious, jurispathic, rights-destroying form of nineteenth-century racism and prejudice against Indians, they will be open to at least considering the legal implications of a postcolonial nonracist approach to defining Indian rights under the Constitution and laws of the United States.

The approach that I put forward here builds upon the substantial body of empirical and theoretical research conducted during the post-*Brown* era that demonstrates that the cognitive biases that can give rise to prejudice and racist attitudes can operate in an unconscious, automatic, uncontrolled fashion (see chapter 9). Research on these social cognition processes also shows that if these biases are to be controlled, we must make a conscious effort at "mental correction."[3] We must make a commitment, in other words, to breaking this type of "bad habit."[4] As Linda Hamilton Krieger has explained, intergroup discrimination that arises from an individual's cognitive biases or prejudices

> does not result from a conscious intent to discriminate, it is an un-
> welcome byproduct of otherwise adaptive cognitive processes. But,
> like many unwanted byproducts, it can be controlled, sometimes even
> eliminated, through careful process re-engineering. Cognitive biases
> in intergroup perception and judgment, though unintentional and
> largely unconscious, can be recognized and prevented by a decision-
> maker who is motivated not to discriminate and who is provided with
> the tools required to translate that motivation into action. Seen in this
> way, disparate treatment does not necessarily manifest discriminatory
> motive or intent, but a motive or intent not to discriminate must be
> present to prevent it.[5]

The strategy of confrontation and "mental correction" that I urge upon tribal advocates and Indian law scholars is intended to appeal particularly to those justices on the Rehnquist Court who consider themselves committed to a form of "color-blind" decision making when it comes to protecting minority rights under the Constitution and laws of the United States.[6] Just because a decision maker lacks discriminatory motivation doesn't mean that he or she isn't affected by various sources of cognitive bias (see chapter 9). In fact, a self-styled color-blind decision maker may well be influenced by innumerable sources of cognitive bias and not even know it:

> For even if this decisionmaker's conscious inferential process is color-blind, the categorical structures through which he collects, sorts, and recalls information are not. In a culture in which race, gender, and ethnicity are salient, even the well-intentioned will inexorably categorize along racial, gender, and ethnic lines. And once these categorical structures are in place, they can be expected to distort social perception and judgment. Our decisionmaker is not colorblind; he is simply "color-clueless," likely unaware that his perceptions, judgments, and decisions are being distorted by cognitive sources of intergroup bias.[7]

Along with a strategy of confrontation that seeks to convince the color-blind (or perhaps color-clueless) justice of the need to engage in a process of "mental correction" when it comes to thinking, talking, and writing about Indians, I urge Indian law scholars and advocates to ask the Court to re-imagine a much different vision of how Indian law can work to better protect Indian rights. This postcolonial vision of Indian rights seeks to return Indian law to its origins, as it were, as reflected in what I have labeled the neglected Fifth Element of the Marshall Model of Indian Rights. This reconstructed version of the Marshall model uses the twenty-first century's discourse of indigenous human rights in contemporary international law, as opposed to a nineteenth-century language of racism, to analyze and decide the seemingly contradictory, problematic, and even "schizophrenic" nature of Indian rights claims to a degree of measured separatism under U.S. law.[8]

A growing number of Indian rights advocates and legal scholars in fact have argued for an approach that looks to contemporary international human rights law as a source of legal protection for Indian rights in the United States. They point to the developing body of contemporary international human rights norms and standards recognizing and upholding the collective rights of indigenous peoples to cultural integrity, lands and resources, and self-determination as a model for deciding Indian rights claims in this country. According to James Anaya:

> The new indigenous rights norms are grounds upon which indigenous peoples may appeal to decisionmakers within the international human

rights [system]. The norms may even be invoked in purely domestic adjudicative settings. In many countries, as in the United States, domestic tribunals may invoke international treaty and customary norms as rules of decision. Alternatively, international norms may be used to guide judicial interpretation of domestic rules. Indeed, the genesis of United States legal doctrine concerning Native peoples is in the international law of the colonial period. It would be appropriate for the United States doctrine to again cross paths with the relevant international law.[9]

Philip Frickey has specifically appealed to Indian law advocates and scholars and to the Court, urging them all to draw upon contemporary international law norms respecting indigenous peoples' human rights in an effort to decolonize Indian law. He outlines an approach to protecting Indian rights that draws upon international law "as an important framework for constitutional interpretation throughout the field of federal Indian law."[10] Like Anaya and other advocates of this human rights approach to protecting Indian rights in the U.S. legal system, Frickey believes that the contemporary Supreme Court should revive Marshall's judicial reliance upon international law as a source of relevant interpretive authority for deciding Indian rights cases in America.

Considered together, these two complementary strategies suggest the possibility of a new, postcolonial model for protecting Indian rights before the Supreme Court. This model focuses first on confronting the justices with the racist stereotypes and patterns of thought they perpetuate in relying on the Marshall model's precedents. Once convinced of the need to recognize and repudiate the continuing force in the American racial imagination of the Marshall model's judicial language of Indian savagery, the justices then need to be convinced of the usefulness of reviving the long-neglected fifth element of the Marshall model, which looks, as Marshall did, to contemporary international law for guidance in defining the basic rights of tribal Indians as indigenous peoples. But before Indian law scholars and advocates can begin to apply this new type of postcolonial model of Indian rights, they need to be disabused about their own stereotyped perceptions of the twenty-first-century Court's capacity for "mental correction" and of how contemporary international law works to protect indigenous peoples' human rights.

The "Mental Correction" Approach for Combating Unconscious Racism against Indians in the Supreme Court's Indian Law Decisions

The "mental correction" approach for combating unconscious racism in the Court's Indian law decisions draws heavily from the work of social cognition researchers and theorists who describe the way we perceive others in the world as involving a categorization process. According to these theorists, when we are called upon to judge another person's behavior, we first take information received about that individual and process, interpret, and encode it. In other words, we categorize that individual. As Jody Armour explains this categorization process in his book *Negrophobia and Reasonable Racism,* whenever we are asked to judge another person's behavior, we are "unlikely to perform an exhaustive search of memory for all potentially relevant categories, compare the behavior to each such category, and then characterize the behavior in terms of the category with the best fit."[11] Rather, we are more likely to base our judgment on the most readily accessible category retrieved from memory at that moment in time. In other words, we rely on a stereotype, for example, of black male youths being prone to violence or of Arabs being potential suicide bombers.

This notion that our social judgments can be "captured" or "primed" by the mental categories about certain groups that are encoded in our minds, usually at a very young age, means that certain organizing, telltale "cues" of group membership, particularly those involving race, can in fact serve to trigger the trait categories that are derived from our long-established familiarity with a negative racial stereotype.[12] In this sense, it can be said that the stereotype functions just like a loaded weapon, primed and ready to go off whenever we encounter members of certain groups associated with that stereotype (see chapter 1). As William James, at the very beginnings of modern psychology, recognized in his classic nineteenth-century text *Principles of Psychology:* "[A]ny sequence of mental action which has been frequently repeated tends to perpetuate itself; so that we find ourselves automatically prompted to *think, feel,* or *do* what we have been accustomed to think, feel or do, under like circumstances, without any consciously formed *purpose,* or anticipation of results."[13] So "prompted," there is a strong likelihood, at least according to this Jamesian foundational psychological insight, that we will be led to systematically view the behaviors of members of the group according to the categories derived from our familiarity with a negative racial stereotype. Researchers have found in fact that a person's anticipation of a trait category increases the chances that he or she will process and encode ambiguous information as being in that category.[14]

Using a social cognition approach, let us suppose a hypothetical justice who is presented with a Supreme Court case that involves, let us say, the exercise of tribal court jurisdiction over a nonmember of the tribe. Let us also say, for the sake of argument, that this exercise of tribal sovereign authority will be under the control of an Indian tribal court judge and an all-Indian jury. It is quite possible, at least according to a social cognition approach to racial discrimination, that this justice will view the anticipated behavior of that Indian tribal court judge and that all-Indian jury according to the most readily accessible category available to the justice. Given the insidiously ubiquitous, continuing, and controlling force of the long-established tradition of stereotyping Indians as savages, there is a distinct possibility that this justice will view the anticipated behavior of all Indian tribal court judges and all Indian jury members by referring to the stereotype of Indians as being more lawless and less civilized than non-Indians. There is a possibility, in other words, for this justice to view the anticipated behavior of the Indian tribal court judge and all-Indian jury as raising what Justice Souter referred to as "an unacceptable risk of substantial disuniformity in the interpretation of state and federal law," given the "special nature of [Indian] tribunals." This justice will accordingly feel compelled to render a judgment congruent with that stereotype, and it is thus highly possible that he or she will fall into the discrimination habit and rule against Indian tribal rights to jurisdiction over nonmembers in this type of case. And because of the Marshall model precedents, the workings of stare decisis, and sly, color-clueless acts of judicial elision, this justice can do so in his or her Indian rights opinion without ever even having to use the "s" word, or any of those other embarrassing, anachronistic racial stereotypes that haunt the Court's past Indian law decisions. All this justice has to do, for example, is hold that under the precedent established by *Oliphant,* this specific Indian right that this particular tribe is claiming in the present day was implicitly divested by the European colonial-era doctrine of discovery as interpreted and enforced by the Marshall Model of Indian Rights.[15]

It is fair to ask at this point: How, then, do we combat the unconscious discrimination tendencies that lurk in such a justice? How do we prevent such a justice from unintentionally falling into the discrimination habit?

Research suggests that the first step that must be taken is getting the justice to engage in a process of mental correction. In order to avoid stereotype-congruent responses, a justice who rejects the negative racial stereotypes perpetuated by the Marshall model precedents and the doctrine of discovery must be convinced of the need to make a personal decision to intentionally inhibit the automatically activated stereotype. This justice must instead activate his or her nonprejudiced, egalitarian personal belief structure. Through what the noted social psychologist Patricia G. Devine has described as a rigorous, self-policing process of "intention, attention, and effort,"[16] this justice will have to consciously work at controlling any stereotype-congruent response (for example, "because Indians were savages, and for all I know, still might be, they shouldn't be trusted to exercise criminal jurisdiction over nonmembers of their tribe"). He or she will then have to follow up on the intent to replace that habitual response with one grounded in nonprejudiced personal standards (for example, "I should decide Indian rights cases by a more consciously attentive resort to principles that do not reflect or perpetuate nineteenth-century negative racial stereotypes of Indians as lawless and uncivilized savages"). This justice will have to pay close attention to the precedents and language used in his or her opinion on Indian rights (for example, "are the precedents and language I'm using generated out of a stereotype of Indians as savages, thereby perhaps prompting a stereotype-congruent response on my part in deciding this case?"). In other words, this justice will have to make a conscious effort to decide Indian rights cases before the Court without habitually relying on a judicially validated language of racism directed at Indians (for example, "I must take on the judicial challenge of developing and articulating a more fair and less racially biased approach to Indian rights cases, one that reflects my personal beliefs in the egalitarian principles of racial equality and fundamental justice that ought to apply to all individuals and groups in post-*Brown* American society, regardless of race, color, creed, or the fact that they are Indians").

This approach to combating the unconscious discrimination tendencies that may lurk in the mind of a particular justice when it comes to deciding Indian rights cases is based on the belief that the justices of the Supreme Court are indeed capable of changing their racial paradigms about Indian rights. Getting the justices to shift their approach to Indian law from a model originating in the European colonial-era doctrine of discovery to one more congruent with twenty-first-century egalitarian notions of racial equality and fundamental human rights is simply a matter of mental correction, to be brought about by confronting them, individually and as a group, with their bad habits of thinking, talking, and writing about Indians as if they are lawless savages.

To assume that the justices of the Supreme Court are incapable or unwilling to engage in this type of effort at mental correction is, according to the definitions we've been using in this book, just another form of harmful stereotyping with dangerous consequences for Indians and Indian rights in America. The decision not to confront the justices with the way they use the Marshall model, in this sense, can itself be viewed as a stereotype-congruent response on the part of Indian law advocates and scholars, one that permits an insidiously pervasive, long-established language of racism to be perpetuated against Indians.

A Postcolonial Approach to Protecting Indian Rights

It's at this point that we need to supplement our approach to decolonizing the Supreme Court's Indian law. Once the justices have been convinced of the need to change the way they talk, think, and write about Indian rights, something else must be offered to fill the void left by the central organizing and sustaining role of the language of Indian savagery and racist legal precedents perpetuated by the Marshall model. Filling that void is perhaps the greatest challenge confronting Indian rights lawyers, scholars, advocates, and the Court itself today. The challenge is made all the more difficult by the fact that Indian rights claims to a measured degree of separatism, as we have noted, raise a host of difficult conceptual questions in our legal system.

Recall our discussion of the highly problematic nature of Indian rights cases for the justices and my "singularity thesis" for protecting Indian rights that I laid out at the beginning of this book (see the introduction). The thesis asserts that the group rights claims made by Indian peoples today are much different from the types of individual rights claims asserted before the Supreme Court in such landmark civil rights cases as *Brown v. Board of Education*. As Charles Wilkinson has written: "The most cherished civil rights of Indian people are not based on equality of treatment under the Constitution and the general civil rights laws."[17] Ultimately, what Indians are seeking from the Court is something much different. They are arguing for the right to a degree of "measured separatism," and as I have already explained in the introduction, this aspiration to a group right of cultural self-determination situates Indian rights questions upon difficult and very "unfamiliar intellectual terrain" for the justices of the Supreme Court and for most other Americans as well.[18] The unique types of autochthonous rights that Indians want protected under U.S. law are inherently problematic for the justices in a way that the less-novel types of individualized rights that most other minority groups want protected by the Court are not.

Even if Indian law scholars and advocates confront the justices with the racist judicial language of savagery embedded in the Marshall model, and if a majority on the Court agrees on the need to find some other way to talk, think, and write about Indian rights, what alternative language can be made available to them that can meaningfully address the difficult conceptual questions raised by Indian rights claims to a degree of measured separatism? It's challenging enough for the justices to consciously engage and creatively adapt their normal egalitarian responses when highly unfamiliar Indian rights claims to a degree of measured separatism are presented to the Court, and only Indians are affected, such as in the *Lara* case (see generally chapter 11). When tribes seek to engage in activities or assert rights that seem wholly contrary to the personal liberty interests[19] and even the values of non-Indians in the dominant society, what compelling legal arguments can be formulated and presented to convince the justices that our legal system should tolerate such potentially threatening, unprecedented forms of legal hybridity? Where can Indian rights advocates and scholars turn to in their search for an alternative vision of Indian rights that still carries a degree of precedential validity and normative compatibility with the justices' egalitarian commitments to racial justice? The postcolonial approach to Indian rights that I argue for tells the justices to turn to the heretofore neglected fifth element of the Marshall model and to use the contemporary international law of indigenous peoples' human rights as an interpretive backdrop for aiding judicial understanding of Indian rights claims in America.

Let us hypothesize a group of present-day Supreme Court justices who must decide a difficult Indian rights case. After having been confronted with what the Court has been doing in its Indian law decisions for the past two centuries, at least five of them have finally come to recognize, individually and as a group, the dangers of using the Marshall model's nineteenth-century racist precedents and language of Indian savagery in their Indian rights decisions. They have expressly vowed not to perpetuate negative racial stereotypes of Indian racial and cultural inferiority in any of their Indian rights opinions in the future. They simply will no longer allow these types of habitually relied upon, legalized racial stereotypes of Indian savagery and lawlessness to influence and bias their judgments on Indians and their rights. They all agree, as a group of self-professed nonprejudiced justices, that they want all future Indian rights decisions to be based on their shared personal commitment to racial justice and egalitarian values. They commit themselves to developing a postcolonial approach to Indian rights cases suitable for use by the justices of the twenty-first-century Supreme Court.

The problem confronting this group of postcolonially inclined Supreme Court justices is that they are not quite sure how their shared egalitarian principles might apply to an Indian rights claim to a degree of measured separatism for tribes in a truly postcolonial, totally decolonized U.S. society. Where can these justices turn in interpreting Indian rights claims without habitual reliance on the racist precedents and stereotypical language of the Marshall model?

They can turn to an approach that uses international law just as Marshall did, that is, "as an important framework for constitutional interpretation"[20] of Indian rights. In reviving this fifth element of the Marshall model, these justices can be made to feel perfectly justified in returning to an important, originary jurisprudential source of Indian rights law that was relied upon by John Marshall himself in thinking and talking about Indian rights in his famous nineteenth-century trilogy of Indian rights cases.

As has already been discussed in chapter 4, the Marshall Model of Indian Rights itself traces its origins to Marshall's nineteenth-century conceptions of the contemporary international law that he and the other justices of his era authoritatively recognized as controlling the most important questions of Indian rights in America. It was, after all, the European Law of Nations that made Marshall apply the doctrine of discovery the way he did to Indian tribes in *Johnson v. McIntosh* and the *Cherokee* cases. There was, in other words, in addition to the four elements of the Marshall model that have already been identified, a fifth element of the model that exercised a profound influence upon the Supreme Court's original approach to defining Indian rights under the Constitution and laws of the United States. As Professor Frickey has written:

> [T]he Supreme Court in the Marshall trilogy embraced pre-constitutional notions of the colonial process, rooted in the law of nations, involving both inherent tribal sovereignty and a colonial prerogative vested exclusively in the centralized government.[21]

As Frickey noted, the legal doctrinal source of U.S. power over Indian tribes traces to the contemporary international law of Marshall's day. A group of present-day justices who therefore recognize that the sole legal justification for the enormous racial power possessed by the United States over tribes originates in international law can feel totally justified in continuing to rely upon that source of law as an "important framework" for interpreting Indian rights in their present-day Indian rights opinions. In other words, the precedent established by the Marshall Trilogy would support these justices in their use of contemporary international law principles in a present-day Court decision on Indian rights. These justices would just be following the judicial example set by Marshall himself in these foundational early-nineteenth-century Indian rights opinions for the Court.[22]

The Fifth Element: The Use of Contemporary International Law Norms in the Supreme Court's Marshall Model Indian Law Decisions

Today, in fact, international law has a good deal to say to the justices of the twenty-first-century Supreme Court about the duties and responsibilities of states toward the protection of the fundamental human rights of indigenous peoples. For starters, international law, as it is now understood and practiced, has repudiated the use of European colonial-era legal doctrines and principles of racial discrimination as a basis of justification for a state's violation of indigenous peoples' human rights.[23]

Contemporary international law's more egalitarian response to indigenous peoples' human rights claims can be located in the emerging norms applied in the international human rights process to indigenous tribal peoples in the Americas and elsewhere around the world. One of the most notable features of the contemporary international human rights regime has been the recognition that indigenous peoples are subjects of international legal concern. A discrete body of international law upholding important collective rights of indigenous peoples has rapidly developed around this core organizing concern with the protection of indigenous peoples' human rights.[24]

This core concern is reflected in a growing number of important legal and political developments in the field of indigenous peoples' human rights. After years of political activism and lobbying, for example, indigenous peoples succeeded in convincing the International Labour Organization (ILO) to promulgate a new multilateral treaty—ILO Convention No. 169 of 1989 (ILO 169)[25]—protecting the rights of indigenous peoples. This first-ever, postcolonial-era international treaty on the human rights of indigenous peoples, contains detailed human rights standards recognizing indigenous peoples' rights to property, self-government, cultural integrity and survival, and other important rights. ILO 169 has now been ratified and is binding on several states, in the Americas and elsewhere, that have agreed to its terms. The establishment of the U.N. Working Group on Indigenous Populations in 1982 and that group's promulgation of the Draft U.N. Declaration on the Rights of Indigenous Peoples, which is presently under review by the U.N. Commission on Human Rights, have focused even greater international attention and concern on the protection of indigenous peoples' rights.[26]

The Draft U.N. Declaration on the Rights of Indigenous Peoples, as developed by the working group, provides further evidence of the increasingly widespread international recognition of and respect for indigenous peoples' human rights. The Draft Declaration reflects years of discussions and debate in a U.N.-sponsored standard-setting process in which both states and indigenous peoples from throughout the world have taken part. Its proposed provisions on indigenous peoples' basic human rights include detailed statements of recognized rights which member states of the United Nations are obligated to respect and protect in their dealings with indigenous peoples. For example, Article 26 of the Draft Declaration affirms indigenous peoples' rights to land and resources in the following terms:

> Indigenous peoples have the right to own, develop, control and use the lands and territories, including the total environment of the lands, air,

waters, coastal seas, sea-ice, flora and fauna and other resources which they have traditionally owned or otherwise occupied or used. This includes the right to the full recognition of their laws, traditions and customs, land-tenure systems and institutions for the development and management of resources, and the right to effective measures by States to prevent any interference with, alienation of or encroachment upon these rights.[27]

The type of international standard-setting activity represented by ILO 169 and the U.N. Draft Declaration concerning the rights of indigenous peoples has in turn significantly influenced the work of other U.N. human rights bodies and regional international organizations. The U.N. Human Rights Committee and the U.N. Committee on the Elimination of Racial Discrimination now regularly apply the prevailing understandings of indigenous peoples' human rights that are reflected in the newly articulated standards. These bodies cite and rely upon these standards and norms in their own monitoring of human rights situations involving indigenous groups around the world.[28] The emerging international legal discourse of indigenous human rights also now affects the lending processes of the World Bank, the Inter-American Development Bank, the European Union, and the domestic legislation and policies and judge-made law of states throughout an increasingly globalized modern world legal system.[29] All of these important international legal developments reflect the ever-increasing interdependencies, ever-improving communications technologies, and burgeoning international institutions that characterize the contemporary international legal system and its human rights regime of universally declared norms and related enforcement procedures, as applied to indigenous peoples throughout the world.[30]

The Inter-American Human Rights System

At the regional level in the Americas, with the world's largest population of indigenous tribal peoples, the inter-American system for the protection of human rights, which functions within the Organization of American States (OAS), has responded in progressive and meaningful fashion to the human rights concerns of indigenous peoples. The OAS is the regional intergovernmental organization for the Americas, and it includes among its thirty-five members the United States as well as all the other sovereign states of the Western Hemisphere. The OAS Charter includes a separate agreement, the American Declaration of the Rights and Duties of Man (the American Declaration),[31] which contains the express human rights guarantees binding upon all members of the OAS.[32]

As the founding constitutional document of the organization, the OAS Charter, along with the American Declaration, is regarded under widely recognized principles of international law as a binding treaty for those states (like the United States) that sign on to it and agree to its terms. Member states of the OAS thereby undertake explicit international legal treaty obligations, including the obligation to uphold the human rights of their inhabitants and to submit their performance to the scrutiny of the Inter-American Commission on Human Rights (IACHR, or the Inter-American Commission), an organ of the OAS created to promote the observance and defense of human rights.[33]

The OAS human rights system has drawn upon the emerging international legal discourse of indigenous human rights as an important legal framework for the interpretation of indigenous peoples' basic human rights in the Americas. An examination of how the inter-American system of human rights has used contemporary international human rights law to define the scope and content of indigenous peoples' rights under the OAS Charter and the American Declaration shows one of the important ways that international law is supposed to "work" in a postcolonial world legal order: as an integrative, progressive force in encouraging international concern and a convergence of international opinion on the content of indigenous peoples' human rights under principles of international law.

As explained by Anaya, this type of "norm-building" activity gives rise to the expectations of the international community that these basic human rights belonging to indigenous peoples will be recognized and protected by states. The pervasive assumption of the international human rights system is that the articulation of norms concerning indigenous peoples is an exercise in identifying standards of conduct imposed upon states that are *required* to uphold widely shared values of human dignity. Accordingly, indigenous peoples' rights typically are regarded as, and can be demonstrated to be, derivative of already widely accepted, generally applicable human rights principles.[34]

In the United States, of course, where law students usually don't study much international law and where most people dismiss its relevance to their own government's conduct and policies, the pervasive belief is that international law doesn't work very well at all.[35] Many lawyers and law students I know will say they think international law is a waste of time for Indian people, sheer "folly."[36] It lacks effective enforcement mechanisms, hegemons like the United States appear to pay little attention to it,[37] pariah states like Saddam Hussein's Iraq wantonly violate it, and the Supreme Court rarely relies upon it in cases that really matter; these are a few of the typical comments I've heard lawyers and my own students make over the years about international law's ineffectiveness as a system for protecting human rights and enforcing its norms and strictures. Even international law scholars admit that it can be difficult to grasp the workings of the international legal system. As Mark W. Janis has explained, unlike most domestic legal systems,

> where courts, agencies, and other formal organs of dispute settlement or rule application are all more or less coordinated in an integrated and hierarchical legal system, international legal process displays a complexity that may verge on anarchy. The different and sometimes uncoordinated ways in which matters are handled in international law often seem to defy the very idea of any international legal "system" at all.[38]

But, as noted by Janis and many other scholars, diplomats, and practitioners who have closely examined and participated in the contemporary international legal system, international law actually does work at times to achieve its goals. It cannot be denied that over the past several decades, ever-increasing interdependencies, ever-improving communications technologies, burgeoning international institutions like the United Nations, the OAS, and the World Trade Organization, and many other multifaceted processes have all contributed to the growing influence of international law as a constitutive, functioning component of the modern world's political and legal order.[39] Today, states and nonstate actors—including transnational corporations, international lending organizations, international nongovernmental organizations (NGOs), and even the most radicalized liberation movements—use international law to exert influence and pressure on the domestic legislation, national policies, and judicial decision-making processes of nation-states. In fact, the U.S. Supreme Court in recent times has relied on international law in at least two cases that have really mattered, at least from an international human rights perspective.[40]

The emergence of international human rights law as an integrative, progressive force in the world has been called one of the most important and revolutionary developments of our era.[41] International human rights law has proven itself to be increasingly capable and effective in directly and indirectly influencing the domestic laws and policies of states that desire acceptance and integration into the contemporary international political and legal order. By articulating a vision of universal norms and basic values of human dignity governing every state's conduct toward its citizens, the international human rights system "seeks to expand the competency of international law" over spheres of human activity previously regarded as reserved to the asserted prerogatives of the sovereign nation-state.[42] It does so through the work of numerous international organizations, such as the United Nations and the OAS and their subsidiary organs and standard setting processes. Lawyers and advocates, NGOs, government representatives, and international diplomats all contribute to this complex process of transnational jurisgenesis. The legal articulation of developing human rights norms and values seeks to define human rights law as more than just existing state practice. It aims toward what Anaya has called "the prescriptive articulation of the expectations and values of the *human* constituents of the world community."[43]

The reasons that the contemporary discourse of international human rights has assumed an increasing role in regulating instances of egregious state conduct against human rights are relatively simple and easy to understand. They have as much to do with pragmatism and self-interest as with the morality of protecting human rights or whether international human rights law is really law.[44] The major participants in the contemporary international political and legal order rely heavily on domestic and regional stability and international and multilateral harmonization of interests and goals. Human rights law has had "an important socializing impact on the human community" because governments, even the most self-interested ones, increasingly take human rights considerations into account in developing their foreign policy.[45] Diplomats as well as multinational corporations have little difficulty in recognizing that a nation's oppression of its own people is a sign of weakness and instability. More and more, the benefits of political and economic linkages with other countries are determined according to an instrumental calculus that includes the critical dimension of human rights. As Thomas Buergenthal has explained:

> Governments now know that there is a political and economic price to be paid for large-scale violations of human rights. That knowledge affects their conduct, not because they have suddenly become good or altruistic, but because they need foreign investment or trade, economic or military aid, or because their political power base will be seriously weakened by international condemnation.[46]

International law works, then, much differently from the way domestic law in the United States—for example a statute passed by Congress or a Supreme Court decision interpreting that statute—works to protect importantly regarded rights. The approach of the OAS Inter-American Commission on Human Rights in defining indigenous peoples' human rights in the Americas, for example, shows us how the modern international human rights system actually does function and perform as an authoritative system of law, once called into action in an effort to protect human rights.

As the consultative body to the OAS with respect to human rights matters, the Inter-American Commission's multiple functions within the OAS system include consideration of individual complaints regarding specific violations of human rights contained in the American Declaration by any member state of the organization, preparation and publication of reports and on-site observations of general human rights situations within a given country, and general promotion of human rights, including the preparation of studies, reports, and publications on themes related to human rights. In terms of its methodological approach, the model of indigenous human rights developed by the commission in its investigations of human rights complaints, country reports, and other activities draws primary support from the broad body of international human rights law developed during the post–World War II era to define the scope and content of the human rights possessed by indigenous peoples under widely recognized principles of international law. Under the "evolutive" approach developed by the Inter-American Commission in interpreting the American Declaration, international human rights developments that have occurred over the past several decades are incorporated and relied upon in giving legal precedent and support to the commission's jurisprudence on indigenous peoples' human rights under the OAS Charter and the American Declaration.[47]

In developing its analysis of indigenous peoples' fundamental human rights under the principles and norms of the American Declaration and the OAS Charter, the commission has drawn support from a broad range of precedents generated by the contemporary international human rights system. The commission has stated, in fact, that it views and interprets the American Declaration "as an embodiment of existing and evolving human rights obligations of member states under the OAS Charter":

> [I]n interpreting and applying the [American] Declaration, it is neces-
> sary to consider its provisions in the context of international and inter-
> American human rights systems more broadly, in light of developments
> in the field of international human rights law since the [American]
> Declaration was first composed and with due regard to other relevant
> rules of international law applicable to Member States against which
> complaints of violations of the [American] Declaration are properly
> lodged.[48]

In other words, the commission's interpretation of indigenous peoples' human rights under the American Declaration seeks to define the scope and content of the human rights belonging to indigenous peoples under generally recognized principles of contemporary international law.

Indigenous Peoples' Rights to Property within the Inter-American Human Rights System

In its efforts to make the inter-American legal system more responsive to indigenous human rights claims, the commission has focused its attention on a core set of human rights principles and values protected under the American Declaration. One of the commission's most significant contributions to the progressive development of indigenous peoples' human rights under contemporary principles of international law has been its focus on defining the unique scope and content of indigenous peoples' rights to property under the American Declaration.[49]

Article 23 of the American Declaration affirms the right of every person to "own such property as meets the essential needs of decent living and helps maintain the dignity of the individual and the home." In developing the contemporary international understanding of this basic human rights norm[50] under the American Declaration and of how it applies specifically to indigenous peoples, the commission has turned to a number of authoritative sources of international law. For example, it has invoked the opinions and decisions of the Inter-American Court on Human Rights and the American Convention on Human Rights for guidance and persuasive authority in interpreting the American Declaration. The American Convention is a separate and binding human rights treaty promulgated by the OAS in 1978; it essentially adopts the basic human rights provisions outlined in the earlier American Declaration.[51] OAS member states that sign the American Convention, however, bind themselves by treaty obligation to the jurisdiction of the Inter-American Court. The Inter-American Commission has said that the Inter-American Court and its interpretation of the American Convention represents, "in many instances, an authoritative expression of the fundamental principles set forth in the American Declaration."[52]

Like the American Declaration, the American Convention protects the right to property as a human right. Article 21 of the convention provides in clear and unequivocal terms: "Everyone has the right to the use and enjoyment of his property." The Inter-American Court has interpreted the right to property under the convention's Article 21 as it applies to indigenous peoples in the Americas for the first time in its historic decision in the case of the *Mayagna (Sumo) Awas Tingni Community v. Nicaragua*, issued in 2001.[53] The landmark *Awas Tingni* decision has since been adopted by the Inter-American Commission as authoritative precedent on indigenous peoples' right to property in subsequent cases finding OAS member states in violation of Article 23 of the American Declaration.[54]

The *Awas Tingni* case originated in events growing out of Nicaragua's revolution and the Contra wars of the late 1970s and early 1980s. In 1983, the Inter-American Commission found the Sandinista government of Nicaragua responsible for human rights abuses committed against the Miskito Indians during the early years of Nicaragua's civil war. The commission urged the Sandinista government to respond to the Miskito demands for political autonomy by establishing "an adequate institutional order as part of the structure of the Nicaraguan state."[55]

The commission's recommendations were instrumental in leading the Sandinista government to sit down at the negotiating table with

Miskito leaders, culminating in the enactment in 1987 of the Autonomy Statute, which set up regional governments for the Miskito and other communities of Nicaragua's Atlantic coast. Nicaragua also promised in its law to establish a process for demarcating and titling indigenous communal lands.

In 1996, the commission, after years of delay on the part of the Nicaraguan government in acting on its promises and duly enacted laws to secure indigenous land rights, received a petition filed by the Awas Tingni indigenous community of the Atlantic Coast of Nicaragua. The community's human rights complaint charged Nicaragua with failure to take steps necessary to secure the land rights of the Mayagna (Sumo) indigenous community of Awas Tingni and other indigenous communities in the Atlantic Coast region of Nicaragua under the autonomy accords. The case was triggered by Nicaragua's grant of a logging concession to a Korean company in traditional communal lands belonging to the Awas Tingni indigenous community.[56]

In 1998, the commission ruled favorably on the merits of the petition filed by the Awas Tingni community and recommended appropriate remedial action. Because Nicaragua is a party to the American Convention on Human Rights and has also recognized the jurisdiction of the Inter-American Court, the commission based its decision and reasoning in the *Awas Tingni* case on the express terms of the American Convention.[57]

The commission specifically found that Nicaragua was "actively responsible for violations of the rights to property, embodied in Article 21," by granting the logging concession to the Korean company "on Awas Tingni lands, without the consent of the Awas Tingni Community."[58] The commission also found that Nicaragua had not "demarcated the communal lands of the Awas Tingni Community or other communities, nor has it taken effective measures to ensure the property rights of the Community on its lands." These omissions, in the commission's opinion, constituted a violation of the right to property contained in Article 21 and also Articles 1 and 2 of the convention, which oblige states to take the necessary measures to give effect to the rights contained in the convention.[59]

In 2001, with Nicaragua continuing in its unlawful refusal to demarcate Awas Tingni and other indigenous traditional lands as required by its own constitution and laws, the Inter-American Commission itself took the case to the Inter-American Court of Human Rights in accordance with Article 51 of the American Convention. In support of Awas Tingni's claim, the Inter-American Commission argued to the Inter-American Court that both the logging concession and the ongoing failure of Nicaragua to demarcate indigenous land constituted violations of the right to property affirmed in Article 21 of the American Convention.[60]

In September 2001, the Inter-American Court issued its landmark decision in the *Awas Tingni* case, affirming the human rights of indigenous peoples in the Americas to their traditional lands and holding that Nicaragua had violated the Awas Tingni community's rights to property as enshrined in the American Convention on Human Rights.[61] The Court imposed a $50,000 fine, "as reparation for immaterial damages," and directed that it be invested by Nicaragua in public works and services for the benefit of the Awas Tingni Community. It also awarded $30,000 for legal costs associated with the proceeding. The Court further ordered Nicaragua to adopt within its domestic legal system all measures necessary "to create an effective mechanism for delimitation, demarcation, and titling of the property of indigenous communities, in accordance with their customary law, values, and customs." Finally, Nicaragua was ordered to officially recognize, demarcate, and issue title for those lands belonging to the members of the Mayagna (Sumo) Community of Awas Tingni and told by the Court that "until that delimitation, demarcation, and titling has been done, it must refrain from any acts that might lead the agents of the State itself, or third parties acting with its acquiescence or its tolerance, to affect the existence, value, use or enjoyment of the property located in the geographic area where members of the Mayagna (Sumo) Community of Awas Tingni live and carry out their activities."[62] The Court in effect enjoined Nicaragua from interfering with Awas Tingni property rights until the mapping and titling of Awas Tingni lands is carried out, thus providing the government an incentive to move the process along in a fair and effective manner.

The Developing Jurisprudence

Because the Inter-American Court possesses the power to require states that have consented to its jurisdiction (as has Nicaragua) to take remedial measures for the violation of human rights, the *Awas Tingni* case establishes an important legal precedent on indigenous land rights under inter-American and international law. The case has already attracted significant attention worldwide from indigenous, environmental, and human rights groups, as well as influential media coverage.[63] Most significantly, and of greatest importance in terms of applying the precedent created by the *Awas Tingni* case in the inter-American human rights system, the Inter-American Commission has specifically relied upon the Inter-American Court's interpretation of the right to property belonging to indigenous peoples in two subsequent cases.[64] The commission found that OAS member states had violated the property rights protected under Article 23 of the American Declaration in *Mary and Carrie Dann v. United States*,[65] and *Maya Indigenous Communities of the Toledo District v. Belize*.[66] In both these cases, the commission, as part of its "evolutive" approach, also relied upon sources of international human rights law outside the inter-American system. The commission has found support for the recognition of indigenous peoples' property rights as human rights in contemporary international law in ILO 169 and in the reports and activities of the U.N. Human Rights Committee and the U.N. Committee on the Elimination of Racial Discrimination in interpreting the rights to property of indigenous peoples in the inter-American human rights system.[67]

Besides generating jurisprudence through its reports and investigations of specific human rights situations involving indigenous peoples in the Americas, the commission has sought to focus critical attention and scrutiny on indigenous peoples' human rights under international law in its own standard-setting activities. The commission has given its own interpretation of indigenous peoples' right to property under international law in its Proposed American Declaration on the Rights of Indigenous Peoples:

1. Indigenous peoples have the right to the legal recognition of their varied and specific forms and modalities of their control, ownership, use, and enjoyment of territories and property.
2. Indigenous peoples have the right to the recognition of their property and ownership rights with respect to lands, territories, and resources they have historically occupied,

as well as to the use of those to which they have historically had access for their traditional activities and livelihood.[68]

In its multifaceted efforts to define the scope and content of indigenous peoples' human rights in the Americas, the commission has also examined and commented upon relevant state practice respecting the protection of indigenous peoples' human rights at the domestic level. It has cited municipal legislation, judicial decisions, and constitutional reforms.[69] Together with developments in the field of international human rights law, such examples of domestic legal practice give rise to what the commission regards as obligations of customary international law that apply more generally throughout the inter-American system. According to the human rights model employed by the commission in its activities focused on defining the scope and content of indigenous peoples rights in the Americas, the convergence of international opinion on the content of indigenous peoples' human rights gives rise to expectations that those rights will be upheld, regardless of any formal act of assent to the articulated norms. Thus, according to this approach, if an OAS member state's property-law regime, for example, does not give full effect or protection to indigenous peoples' property rights under the OAS Charter, it is not excused from protecting indigenous rights to property recognized by the Inter-American Commission under Article 23 of the American Declaration.[70]

The commission's "evolutive" approach to interpreting indigenous peoples' fundamental human rights under the American Declaration shows one of the most important ways that international law works to protect human rights. The commission's model of indigenous human rights law draws on authoritative sources of international law such as the American Declaration, Inter-American Court's jurisprudence on indigenous peoples rights under ILO 169, the U.N. Draft Declaration on the Rights of Indigenous Peoples, the OAS Proposed Declaration on the Rights of Indigenous Peoples, decisions of such U.N. human rights monitoring bodies as the U.N. Human Rights Committee and the U.N. Committee on the Elimination of Racial Discrimination, and state practice. Taken together, these sources provide the commission with highly relevant evidence of a larger body of increasingly consistent norms and practices at the international and domestic levels, norms and practices that recognize the rights asserted by indigenous peoples as human rights protected under general principles of international law.

Thus, based on its interpretations of the American Declaration and the American Convention as well as other authoritative sources of international law, the Inter-American Commission has consistently recognized in its human rights decisions that indigenous peoples have rights to the protection of their traditionally occupied lands and natural resources. At a minimum, these rights obligate member states, including the United States, to consult with the indigenous groups concerned regarding any decision that may affect their interests and to adequately weigh those interests in the decision-making process. The Inter-American Commission has interpreted this obligation as inclusive of the right to just compensation under principles of international law and of the right to effective judicial remedies as well. These are among the human rights that are recognized within the Inter-American human rights system as belonging to indigenous peoples in the Americas.[71]

It is important to note that the commission's approach to defining the scope and content of indigenous peoples human rights under the American Declaration is no novel or radical application of international law. The commission's jurisprudence builds upon well-recognized principles of international law as theorized and practiced during the post–World War II era, which hold that multilateral processes and individual state practice can work to generate consensus about customary international law. According to this view, consensus arises when a preponderance of states and other authoritative actors converge upon a common understanding of customary international law norms. Future behavior in conformity with the norms on the part of states is then generally expected. The traditional points of reference for determining the existence and contours of customary norms include the relevant patterns of actual conduct of state actors. As Anaya explains:

> actual state conduct, however, is not the only or necessarily determinative indicia of customary norms. With the advent of modern intergovernmental institutions and enhanced communications media, states and other relevant actors increasingly engage in prescriptive dialogue. Especially in multilateral settings, explicit communication may itself bring about a convergence of understanding and expectation about rules, establishing in those rules a pull toward compliance, even in ad-

vance of a widespread corresponding pattern of physical conduct. It is thus increasingly understood that explicit communication, of the sort that is reflected in the numerous international documents and decisions cited by the Commission, builds customary rules of international law. Conforming domestic laws and related practice reinforces such customary rules of international law. Non-conforming domestic practice may undermine the apparent direction of the international norm-building practices, but only to the extent that the international regime eventually accepts non-conforming behavior as legitimate.[72]

Thus, according to the Inter-American Commission's interpretation, although contemporary international and domestic practice may vary in terms of recognition and protection of indigenous peoples' human rights, it nonetheless entails a sufficiently uniform and widespread acceptance of core principles and values of human dignity to constitute identifiable norms of customary international law. The relevant practice of states and international institutions demonstrates, to the commission's satisfaction, at least, that, as a matter of customary international law, states must recognize and protect indigenous peoples' basic human rights according to the obligations established by the American Declaration and the inter-American human rights system.

The commission, as is evidenced by the growing list of international law sources it relies upon, is not alone in its interpretation of indigenous peoples' human rights under contemporary international law. In addition to the many documents and actions that affirm the above principles, examination of the active engagement of international human rights bodies demonstrates the broad acceptance of these basic principles in the realm of international practice beyond the Americas as well. The U.N. Human Rights Committee, the U.N. Committee on the Elimination of Racial Discrimination, the relevant organs of the International Labour Organization, and other human rights bodies and international organizations apply these same basic and prevailing understandings of indigenous peoples' rights when they monitor human rights situations involving indigenous peoples, when they consider complaints brought by specific indigenous groups, or when they take other actions recognizing indigenous peoples' human rights.[73]

Every major international body that has considered indigenous peoples' rights during the past decade, for example, has acknowledged the crucial importance of lands and resources to the cultural survival of indigenous peoples and communities. They have also recognized the critical need for governments to respect and protect the varied and particular forms of land tenure defined and regarded as property by indigenous peoples themselves. In addition to the international human rights institutions mentioned above, as previously noted, the World Bank and the European Union have pronounced and acted in favor of these rights.[74] Indigenous peoples and their rights over land and natural resources, together with their related rights arising out of their modes of self-governance over their communal property rights, have been discussed, debated, and acknowledged at a multitude of international meetings and conferences sponsored by the United Nations, the OAS, and other intergovernmental organizations during the past several decades.[75] In their numerous oral and written public statements at these meetings, states have concurred or acquiesced in the essential elements of the principles of indigenous peoples' human rights; these principles now find expression as internationally binding legal obligations on all nations in the contemporary political and legal world order, including the United States, whether the justices of the Supreme Court know it or not.[76]

My brief attempt to outline an international human rights model for protecting Indian rights in the United States suggests that international law has begun to make important contributions to the progressive development of indigenous peoples' rights in the world. In the Americas, the inter-American human rights system has worked to articulate a highly refined set of legal norms and juridical principles that speak to the concerns and aspirations of indigenous peoples without resort to colonial-era doctrines justifying racial discrimination against indigenous peoples or to a language of racial inferiority and cultural subordination. Contemporary international human rights discourse, with its focus on core human values of racial equality and equal dignity under the law, is used instead to analyze the complex and difficult questions raised by indigenous peoples' rights claims in a postcolonial world.

Internationalizing the Justices' Understanding of Federal Indian Law

Suppose a justice of the U.S. Supreme Court has been confronted with the undeniable fact that the racist nineteenth-century precedents and accompanying language of racism generated by the Marshall Model of Indian Rights perpetuate a dangerous, legalized form of racial discrimination against Indian people. Suppose this justice decides to stop using the juris-pathic, rights-destroying, legalized racial stereotypes of Indian savagery sanctioned by the precedents of the Marshall model and the Supreme Court's Indian law. This justice makes the conscious decision to find another way of talking, thinking, and writing opinions about Indians and their rights under the Constitution and laws of the United States.

Before adopting the legal discourse of indigenous peoples' human rights under international law and making the commitment to closely scrutinize the precedents of the Marshall model for their potential to perpetuate racial discrimination, this justice will want to know what authority and precedents can be cited to the other justices on the Court for this seemingly radical departure from the Court's long-established approach to deciding Indian rights. Why, such a justice would likely ask, should I use international law as a check upon the Marshal model?

Philip P. Frickey, in his article "Domesticating Federal Indian Law," makes the following argument for recognizing the force of "the emerging international law concerning the rights of indigenous peoples" as an important, constitutive part of modern federal Indian law as interpreted under the Constitution:

> [T]he Constitution is inextricably linked to international law on issues of Indian affairs. Thus, the interpretation not only of the existence and nature of congressional power, but its constitutional limits as well, must be informed by international law, including the evolving component of it concerning the rights of indigenous peoples. On this understanding, the emerging international law concerning the rights of indigenous peoples becomes more than simply a set of externally derived norms that do not bind the United States without its formal consent. Instead, these norms have true linkage to our Constitution and provide a domestic interpretive backdrop for both constitutional interpretation and quasi-constitutional interpretive techniques, such as canons for construing federal Indian treaties and statutes.[77]

Frickey's argument, based on constitutional law, for "internationalizing" our understanding of federal Indian law[78] finds firm support in the foundational precedents of the Court issued by Chief Justice Marshall and by his fellow Founders' statements on Indian rights.

In *Worcester v. Georgia,* for example, Marshall makes it absolutely clear that his model of Indian rights "inextricably" links international law to the Constitution "on issues of Indian affairs."[79]

As Marshall carefully explains in *Worcester,* the "actual state of things" at the time of the West's "discovery" of the New World was one of intense competition for land and empire between the great imperial powers of Europe.[80] It was from this original position of European imperial ambition and desire for land and riches possessed by other peoples that the principle of first discovery emerged as part of the European Law of Nations:

> The great maritime powers of Europe discovered and visited different parts of this continent at nearly the same time. The object was too immense for any one of them to grasp the whole; and the claimants were too powerful to submit to the exclusive or unreasonable pretensions of any single potentate. To avoid bloody conflicts, which might terminate disastrously to all, it was necessary for the nations of Europe to establish some principle which all would acknowledge, and which should decide their respective rights as between themselves. This principle, suggested by the actual state of things, was, "that discovery gave title to the government by whose subjects or by whose authority it was made, against all other European governments, which title might be consummated by possession." 8 Wheat. 573 [citing *Johnson*].[81]

Having firmly established the origins of the discovery doctrine in the customary practices and international law of the European colonial era, Marshall went on in *Worcester* to specify the related norms that were generated out of this principle of first discovery under the European Law of Nations:

> This principle, acknowledged by all Europeans, because it was the interest of all to acknowledge it, gave to the nation making the discovery, as its inevitable consequence, the sole right of acquiring the soil and of making settlements on it. It was an exclusive principle which shut out the right of competition among those who had agreed to it; not one which could annul the previous rights of those who had not agreed to it. It regulated the right given by discovery among the European discoverers; but could not affect the rights of those already in possession, either as aboriginal occupants, or as occupants by virtue of a discovery made before the memory of man. It gave the exclusive right

to purchase, but did not found that right on a denial of the right of the possessor to sell.[82]

Marshall's *Worcester* opinion also relied upon international law (what he calls "the common law of European sovereigns")[83] to counter Georgia's primary argument for asserting jurisdiction over the Cherokees. Georgia's politicians had defended the state's Cherokee codes and other actions aimed at bringing about the tribe's demise as within its colonial charter rights derived from the English Crown. As Marshall explained, this interpretation was wholly contrary to the European Law of Nations:

> Soon after Great Britain determined on planting colonies in America, the king granted charters to companies of his subjects who associated for the purpose of carrying the views of the crown into effect, and of enriching themselves. The first of these charters was made before possession was taken of any part of the country. They purport, generally, to convey the soil, from the Atlantic to the South Sea. This soil was occupied by numerous and warlike nations, equally willing and able to defend their possessions. The extravagant and absurd idea, that the feeble settlements made on the sea coast, or the companies under whom they were made, acquired legitimate power by them to govern the people, or occupy the lands from sea to sea, did not enter the mind of any man. They were well understood to convey the title which, according to the common law of European sovereigns respecting America, they might rightfully convey, and no more. This was the exclusive right of purchasing such lands as the natives were willing to sell. The crown could not be understood to grant what the crown did not affect to claim; nor was it so understood.[84]

Marshall concluded his analysis of Indian rights under principles of international law in *Worcester* with one final act of supreme judicial refutation of Georgia's charter-based argument for jurisdiction over the Cherokees, grounded in a well-respected contemporary international law source: In citing the eminent Swiss jurist Emmerich de Vattel, Marshall was relying upon one of the Founders' most favored authorities on the contemporary international law of their day:[85]

> The actual state of things at the time, and all history since, explain these charters; and the king of Great Britain, at the treaty of peace,

could cede only what belonged to his crown. These newly asserted titles can derive no aid from the articles so often repeated in Indian treaties; extending to them, first, the protection of Great Britain, and afterwards that of the United States. These articles are associated with others, recognizing their title to self government. The very fact of repeated treaties with them recognizes it; and the settled doctrine of the law of nations is, that a weaker power does not surrender its independence—its right to self-government, by associating with a stronger, and taking its protection. A weak state, in order to provide for its safety, may place itself under the protection of one more powerful, without stripping itself of the right of government, and ceasing to be a state. Examples of this kind are not wanting in Europe. "Tributary and feudatory states," says Vattel, "do not thereby cease to be sovereign and independent states, so long as self government and sovereign and independent authority are left in the administration of the state." At the present day, more than one state may be considered as holding its right of self government under the guarantee and protection of one or more allies.[86]

Marshall, as we have already noted, was a leading member of the founding generation, so respected by his peers, in fact, that he was asked to take on the critical task of convincing the Virginia legislature to ratify the Constitution of 1787 (see the introduction). Marshall was in good company among the Founders in turning to the contemporary international law of the day as an interpretive framework for understanding Indian rights under the Constitution and laws of the United States. Thomas Jefferson, for example, while serving as President Washington's secretary of state in 1792, replied as follows to the British minister who asked him what he understood to be the American position on Indian rights to the soil under the doctrine of discovery:

> We consider it as established by the usage of different nations into a kind of *Jus gentium* [Law of Nations] for America, that a white nation settling down and declaring that such and such are their limits, makes an invasion of those limits by any other white nation an act of war, but gives no right of soil against the native possessors.[87]

Jefferson consistently abided by this interpretation of Indian rights under principles of international law that applied to America in his official acts as secretary of state and later as president. Washington's secretary of war, Henry Knox, one of the original signers of the Declaration of Independence, a Revolutionary War general and hero, and, along with Washington, a primary architect of the Founders' first Indian Policy, also cited principles of international law in his official statements on Indian rights under U.S. law. Washington himself, despite his views on the ultimately doomed fate of "the Savage as the Wolf," believed that the principles of international law, as defined by the customary practice of European nations, ought to guide his actions as president when it came to questions of Indian affairs and policy.[88]

In other words, a justice who wants to use contemporary international human rights law principles as an interpretive framework for defining Indian rights under the Constitution is really no radical at all. This justice in fact can feel quite comfortable about it; not only Chief Justice Marshall, the greatest chief justice of all time, but his fellow Founders as well originally intended for the U.S. government, in all its branches, to use international law as an interpretive framework in defining Indian rights under the Constitution and laws of the United States.

Let us now return to our hypothetical group of justices who have been asked to decide a difficult Indian rights case, like the one decided, for example, by the Rehnquist Court in 2005, *City of Sherrill v. Oneida Indian Nation*. In *Sherrill*, an 8-to-1 majority of the justices ruled that an Indian tribe could not revive its "ancient sovereignty" by purchasing parcels of historic reservation land now located within the borders of a non-Indian local government. The Court therefore rejected the tribe's argument that the parcels it now owns are exempt from local tax rolls. Significantly, in her opinion for the Court, Justice Ruth Bader Ginsburg specifically noted the "doctrine of discovery" and Marshall model precedents in commencing the Court's analysis of Indian rights in the case.[89] Not surprisingly, under the Marshall model as applied by Ginsburg for the Rehnquist Court in *Sherrill*, Indian rights lost out in the case.

How would this difficult type of case come out in the hands of our group of hypothetical justices who have been confronted with the dangers of using the Marshall model's racist precedents and language of Indian savagery in a modern-day Supreme Court opinion on Indian rights? They understand the jurispathic force of the racial stereotypes justifying the European colonial-era doctrine of discovery and have vowed to be extremely careful in citing or relying upon anachronistic legal doctrines from a period of white racial dictatorship in America. These justices, however, have also recognized the authority of Marshall *and* the Founders' original intent on the question of using contemporary international law principles as a framework for interpreting Indian rights under the Constitution. They also recognize that contemporary international law respecting indigenous peoples' human rights better reflects their own egalitarian principles of racial equality and equal justice and the basic constitutional norms and values of the U.S. legal system, much more so than in the Marshall model's racist judicial precedents and language of Indian savagery upholding the doctrine of discovery. They recognize, for example, that the Inter-American Commission on Human Rights, in its interpretations of contemporary international human rights law as applied to the rights of indigenous peoples, has found the following general international legal principles to be applicable to indigenous peoples in the Americas:

- The right of indigenous peoples to legal recognition of their varied and specific forms and modalities of their control, ownership, use, and enjoyment of territories and property.
- The recognition of their property and ownership rights with respect to lands, territories, and resources they have historically occupied.
- Where property and user rights of indigenous peoples arise from rights existing prior to the creation of a state, recognition by that state of the permanent and inalienable title of indigenous peoples relative thereto and of their right to have such title changed only by mutual consent between the state and respective indigenous peoples when they have full knowledge and appreciation of the nature or attributes of such property. This also implies the right to fair compensation in the event that such property and user rights are irrevocably lost.[90]

Our hypothetical justices, in other words, in deciding a case like *Sherrill*—or any other Indian rights case, for that matter—can cite the commission's authoritative interpretation of contemporary international law as applied to indigenous peoples' human rights as a useful, though certainly not controlling, guide to deciding Indian rights claims in a twenty-first-century Supreme Court Indian law decision. This group of justices can use the authoritative legal precedents issued by the commission as well as other international legal precedents in their opinion as providing an "interpretive backdrop" for applying the types of egalitarian principles of racial equality and equal justice that ought to govern the Supreme Court's Indian rights decisions in twenty-first-century America.[91] They can do this without any degree of discomfort or embarrassment, much less hesitation, because, consistent with stare decisis, using international law to help traverse the "unfamiliar intellectual terrain" presented by the novel and admittedly problematic human rights claims of Indians to a degree of measured separatism in America actually perpetuates a long-established legal tradition in the Supreme Court's Indian law. Signs taken for wonders, these justices can say to any of the other justices on the Court who might dissent from adopting such a human rights approach to Indian rights cases that the precedent established by Chief Justice Marshall's use of contemporary international law for authoritative guidance in defining Indian rights under the Constitution and laws of the United States lets them do it.

Notes

Introduction

1. See "Document 6: Peter Schagen Announces Purchase of Manhattan Island [November 5, 1626]," in *New York and New Jersey Treaties,* ed. Barbara Graymont (1985), vol. 7 of *Early American Indian Documents: Treaties and Laws, 1607–1789,* general editor, Alden T. Vaughan (Washington, D.C.: University Publications of America, 1979), 17. The most respected Indian law scholar of the twentieth century, Felix Cohen, had this to say about the famous story of the Indians giving Manhattan away for next to nothing to the Dutch: "The sale of Manhattan Island for $24 is commonly cited as a typical example of the white man's overreaching. But even if this were a typical example, which it is not, the matter of deciding whether a real estate deal was a fair bargain three hundred years after it took place is beset by many pitfalls. Hindsight is better than foresight, particularly in real estate deals." Felix S. Cohen, "Original Indian Title," *Minnesota Law Review* 32 (1947): 36.

2. See Robert A. Williams, Jr., "Gendered Checks and Balances: Understanding the Legacy of White Patriarchy in an American Indian Cultural Context," *Georgia Law Review* 24 (1990): 1022–27 (discussing Indian humor).

3. See Alexander Cockburn, "Gary, Is It Really Goodbye?" *Nation* 260, no. 1 (January 2, 1995): 7. Cockburn notes that a Larson cartoon often depends "on

a pun, a historical allusion, a surrealist nightmare, a narrative—unstated—stretching both back and forward from the precise freeze-frame of the cartoon itself." Larson himself is quoted by Cockburn as offering his own "unresearched knee-jerk analysis" of what makes his *Far Side* cartoons so funny: "The key element in any attempt at humor is conflict. Our brain is suddenly jolted into trying to accept something that is unacceptable. The punch line of a joke is the part that conflicts with the first part, thereby surprising us and throwing our synapses into some kind of fire drill."

4. Hundreds of treaties were negotiated between tribes and the United States. See Charles J. Kappler, ed., *Indian Treaties, 1778–1883* (New York: Interland, 1972); Vine Deloria, Jr., and Raymond J. DeMallie, *Documents of American Indian Diplomacy: Treaties, Agreements, and Conventions, 1775–1979* (Norman: University of Oklahoma Press, 1999). The colonial period is covered by a multivolume set edited by Alden T. Vaughan, *Early American Indian Documents: Treaties and Laws, 1607–1789,* which actually relates the famous treaty for the sale of Manhattan (see the works cited in note 1). See also Robert A. Williams, Jr., *Linking Arms Together: American Indian Treaty Visions of Law and Peace, 1600–1800* (New York: Oxford University Press, 1997).

5. See the works cited in note 4.

6. Professor Sheri Lynn Johnson employs the term "racial imagery" to refer to "any word, metaphor, argument, comment, action, gesture or intonation" that suggests, for example, that a person's race or ethnicity "affects his or her standing as a full, capable, and decent human being" or affects the likelihood that he or she would "choose a particular course of conduct." In the context of a criminal trial, Johnson argues that a person should be presumed to be using racial imagery "from the unnecessary use of a racially descriptive word" or "where any comparisons to animals of any kind are made." Finally, she argues that where a person who uses racial imagery disclaims any racial intent (e.g., "I'm not a racist"), either contemporaneously or at a later date, nonetheless, such disavowal "shall have no bearing upon the determination of whether his or her remarks or actions constitute a use of racial imagery." Sheri L. Johnson, "Racial Imagery in Criminal Cases," *Tulane Law Review* 67 (1993): 1799–1800.

7. The belief that "races" are biological has exercised a powerful hold on the American racial imagination. See generally Christine B. Hickman, "The Devil and the One Drop Rule: Racial Categories, African Americans, and the U.S. Census," *Michigan Law Review* 95 (1997): 1161–1265. Biologists and geneticists, however, uniformly reject the notion that racial divisions reflect fundamental genetic differences. Science has established that there are no genetic characteristics possessed, for example, by all blacks but not by nonblacks. Nor is there a gene or gene cluster common to all whites but not to nonwhites. See

Ian F. Haney López, "The Social Construction of Race: Some Observations on Illusion, Fabrication, and Choice," *Harvard Civil Rights–Civil Liberties Law Review* 29 (1994): 1–62. In fact, there is greater genetic variation within those groups of people typically categorized as black and white than there is between them. Contemporary scholars cite this scientific research to argue that, in the words of Henry Louis Gates, "races, put simply, do not exist" (quoted in López, "The Social Construction of Race," 26). From this rejection of biological race as an "illusion," other scholars, like Kwame Anthony Appiah, go on to argue that the concept of "race" as it plays out in American history and contemporary society, that is, within the American racial imagination, is in reality "a metonym for culture." See generally Kwame Anthony, *In My Father's House: Africa in the Philosophy of Culture* (London: Methuen, 1992), 18. This "biologizing of culture," to use Appiah's terminology, to describe what we mean by "race" in America in turn is criticized as an incomplete description of "the everyday manifestations of race and racism" that are encountered by certain groups of people in our contemporary society (see López, "The Social Construction of Race," 18). López, for example, argues that race "must be viewed as a social construction," that is, as a process of competing societal forces in which certain gross morphological features that are taken to define race—for example, kinky hair, "flat" noses, "slanted" eyes—are reified in social thought to produce the "races" (27–28). López, following Michael Omi and Howard Winant, uses the term "racial formation" to describe this process by which racial meanings arise in America. See Michael Omi and Howard Winant, *Racial Formation in the United States: From the 1960s to the 1990s,* 2nd ed. (New York: Routledge, 1994). In this book, I use the term "race," particularly when referring to "American Indians," as a "metonym for culture" but also as a product of the American racial imagination in its biologizing moments of categorization and fabrication of what Indians really "look like." As such a product, this view of race, as Omi and Winant have written, asserts that "the truth of race is a matter of innate characteristics, of which skin color and other physical attributes provide only the most obvious, and in some respects most superficial indicators" (64). The complex processes of racial formation in America and the way those processes help shape the construction of the American racial imagination are discussed further in chapter 1.

8. H. J. Ehrlich, *The Social Psychology of Prejudice* (New York: Wiley, 1973), 35.

9. On the idea that racism is an indelible and ineradicable part of the history and cultural heritage of the United States, see chapter 1.

10. *Johnson v. McIntosh,* 21 U.S. 543, 577, 590 (1823). On *Johnson's* importance in the Supreme Court's Indian law jurisprudence, see chapter 4. For a sample of the hagiographic tradition on Marshall's influence in U.S. constitutional

law, the classic text remains Albert J. Beveridge, *The Life of John Marshall* (Boston: Houghton Mifflin, 1919). For a recent, well-written, well-researched, and certainly more nuanced prize-winning version, but one still firmly within the tradition (as evidenced by its inspiring title), see R. Kent Newmyer, *John Marshall and the Heroic Age of the Supreme Court* (Baton Rouge: Louisiana State University Press, 2001).

11. *Cherokee Nation v. Georgia,* 30 U.S. 1, 15, 18 (1831).

12. *Worcester v. Georgia,* 31 U.S. 515, 543 (1832). See Charles Wilkinson, *American Indians, Time, and the Law: Native Societies in a Modern Constitutional Democracy* (New Haven: Yale University Press, 1987), 30 (describing *Worcester* as the "dominant opinion" in the field: "[F]actors of personality, history, pragmatism, and philosophy have locked together to make *Worcester* an enduring artifice, almost a physical presence. The case is continually cited in the modern Indian law decisions").

13. See Newmyer, *John Marshall and the Heroic Age of the Supreme Court.* Indian interests and rights lost out in *Johnson v. McIntosh* and *Cherokee Nation v. Georgia,* and prevailed, in theory at least if not in the final outcome of the case, in *Worcester v. Georgia.* See chapter 4.

14. See Robert A. Williams, Jr., "The Algebra of Indian Law: The Hard Trail of Decolonizing and Americanizing the White Man's Indian Jurisprudence," *Wisconsin Law Review,* 1986: 219–99 (hereinafter "The Algebra").

15. *Ex parte Crow Dog,* 109 U.S. 556, 571 (1883).

16. *United States v. Kagama,* 118 U.S. 375, 382, 384, 384 (1886). See Wilkinson, *American Indians, Time, and the Law,* 24.

17. See, e.g., *Nevada v. Hicks,* 533 U.S. 353, 363–64 (2001), discussed in chapter 10; *United States v. Lara,* 541 U.S. 193, 206 (2004), discussed in chapter 11. *Kagama* also was cited in then Justice Rehnquist's majority opinion in *Oliphant v. Suquamish Indian Tribe,* 435 U.S. 191, 211 (1978), the modern Court's most important precedent on tribal jurisdiction, which has been consistently followed in subsequent decisions on that issue by the Rehnquist Court. See chapter 7.

18. On the concept of the United States as a "racial dictatorship," see Omi and Winant, *Racial Formation in the United States,* 65–66, 67: "For most of its existence both as European colony and as an independent nation, the U.S. was a *racial dictatorship.* From 1607 to 1865 . . . most non-whites were firmly eliminated from the sphere of politics. After the Civil War there was the brief egalitarian experiment of Reconstruction which terminated ignominiously in 1877. In its wake followed almost a century of legally sanctioned segregation and denial of vote, nearly absolute in the South and much of the Southwest, less effective in the North and far West, but formidable in any case."

19. "Out of Tupelo, Mississippi, out of Memphis, Tennessee, came this green, sharkskin-suited girl chaser, wearing eye shadow—a trucker-dandy white boy who must have risked his hide to act so black and dress so gay. This wasn't New York or even New Orleans, this was Memphis in the fifties. This was punk rock. This was revolt. Elvis changed everything—musically, sexually, politically. In Elvis, you had the whole lot, it's all there in that elastic voice and body. As he changed shape, so did the world." Bono, "Elvis Presley," in "The Immortals," special issue, *Rolling Stone,* no. 946, April 15, 2004, 68. As Richard Welch writes in his essay "Rock 'n' Roll and Social Change," *History Today* 40, no. 2 (February 1990): "[O]ne of the most profound cultural changes in American history is seldom credited for what it was and did. In the mid-1950s this enormous cultural revolution swept aside prevailing notions of American popular music, blended black and white musical traditions and integrated black performers into the pantheon of musical superstars in an unprecedented fashion. In such a way, this revolution both presaged and encouraged the desegregation movement of the 1956–64 period. More generally, this revolution created a music which became the common property not only of two generations of Americans, but millions throughout the world, creating the most ubiquitous, and perhaps, most influential form of American popular culture. The revolution was rock 'n' roll" (32). As Welch writes, the person who started this revolution was Elvis Aaron Presley, described by Sun Record Company producer Sam Phillips as "the most introverted person that came into that studio" (35). Presley, Welch explains, "was a loner, heavily attached to his mother and [he] had few real friends. He compensated for his isolation by listening to everything that came out of the radio. He was, in fact, a repository for almost every musical form in America, white country, black blues, black and white gospel and Tin Pan Alley crooning" (ibid.). In August 1954 Phillips recorded "That's All Right Mama" at the Sun Records studio in Memphis, Tennessee. The revolution had begun, a product of the miscegenated hybridity achieved by Presley's groundbreaking fusing of the musical traditions of blacks and white southerners. This new type of music defiantly rejected the racial conventions of America in the '50s (ibid., 35–36). As Welch concludes his essay, "The powerful black element in the music heralded new possibilities in interracial relations. Certainly rock 'n' roll made possible greater acceptance, appreciation, and a wider audience for black culture. But ultimately the triumph of rock 'n' roll signaled the coming of age of a new generation, one whose norms, culturally, intellectually, and politically, often stood in sharp contrast to those of the generation immediately preceding it. The strength of the rock 'n' roll generation's break with previous attitudes, which first manifested itself musically, would reach full fruition in the social and political upheavals of the sixties" (39).

20. *Brown v. Board of Education,* 347 U.S. 483 (1954).

21. On the effects of *Brown* on twentieth-century American racial consciousness and the post-*Brown* Supreme Court's Indian rights decisions, see part III.

22. See Derrick Bell, *And We Are Not Saved: The Elusive Quest for Racial Justice* (New York: Basic Books, 1987).

23. In fact, the era of *Brown* was generally awful for Indians in terms of federal policy toward tribes. The Bureau of Indian Affairs (BIA), led by Dillon S. Myer, who had served previously as director of the War Relocation Authority, the Japanese-American detention camp program of World War II, was told by a joint congressional resolution, passed in 1953, to terminate the federal supervision and control of tribes "as rapidly as possible" (67 Stat. B132). The "termination" policy, enacted into law the year prior to the Court's landmark civil rights decision in *Brown,* was administered with vigor and disastrous consequences for the more than one hundred tribes singled out by the bureau for termination throughout the 1950s. See "The Algebra," 219, 220–23; David H. Getches, Charles F. Wilkinson, and Robert A. Williams, Jr., *Federal Indian Law: Cases and Materials,* 5th ed. (St. Paul, Minn.: West Group, 2004), 199–216 (hereinafter *Federal Indian Law*).

24. *Tee-Hit-Ton v. United States,* 348 U.S. 272 (1955). *Tee-Hit-Ton* and its holding are discussed in chapter 6.

25. Ibid., 289–90.

26. The scholarly literature criticizing *Oliphant* is immense and intensely negative in tone and analysis. See, e.g., Wilkinson, *American Indians, Time, and the Law,* 61; David H. Getches, "Conquering the Cultural Frontier: The New Subjectivism of the Supreme Court in Indian Law," *California Law Review* 84 (1996): 1595–99; Peter C. Maxfield, "*Oliphant v. Suquamish Tribe:* The Whole Is Greater Than the Sum of the Parts," *Journal of Contemporary Law* 19 (1993): 396. See also "The Algebra," 267.

27. See, e.g., *Nevada v. Hicks,* 353, 358, 359, 376; *Strate v. A-1 Contractors,* 520 U.S. 438, 445, 449 (1997); *South Dakota v. Bourland,* 508 U.S. 679, 686n7 (1993); *Duro v. Reina,* 495 U.S. 676, 682, 692, 696, 684–89 (1990); *Brendale v. Confederated Tribes and Bands of Yakima Indian Nation,* 492 U.S. 408 (1989); *Montana v. United States,* 450 U.S. 544, 549, 563n12, 566n14, 565 (1981); *United States v. Wheeler,* 435 U.S. 313, 323, 325n22, 326 (1978). *Oliphant,* its holding, and its sources are discussed in chapter 7.

28. *In re Mayfield,* 141 U.S. 107 (1891). The case involved an effort by the United States to federally prosecute an Indian for adultery with a non-Indian under the Indian Country Crimes Act, a statute passed by Congress in 1817. The case merits one reference in the body of the more than nine hundred pages of *Felix S. Cohen's Handbook of Federal Indian Law,* ed. Rennard F. Strick-

land, Charles F. Wilkinson, et al. (Charlottesville, Va.: Michie, Bobbs-Merrill, 1982), 292, the leading treatise in the field. The case had been cited fewer than half a dozen times by the Supreme Court in the scores of Indian rights decisions issued by the justices during the twentieth century prior to *Oliphant*.

29. *Oliphant v. Suquamish Indian Tribe*, 204.

30. Ibid.

31. On the Indian Removal era in American history, see chapter 4. On the Removal-era Congress and its acts of "genocide-at-law," see Rennard Strickland, "Genocide-at-Law: An Historic and Contemporary View of the Native American Experience," *University of Kansas Law Review* 34 (1986): 713–55.

32. *Oliphant v. Suquamish Indian Tribe*, 210.

33. In parts II–IV, this book analyzes a number of opinions by the justices, written both for the Court majority and in dissent, that use this language of racism in describing Indians and their rights under U.S. law. There are many others that are not analyzed or even cited in this book but that use a long-established judicial language of Indian savagery. See, e.g., *Bd. of County Comm'rs v. Seber*, 318 U.S. 705, 715 (1943) (describing Indians as "an uneducated, helpless and dependent people needing protection against . . . their own improvidence"); *United States v. Chavez*, 290 U.S. 357, 364 (1933) (describing "the nomadic and savage Indians then living in New Mexico," citing *Montoya v. United States*, 180 U.S. 261, 266 [1901]); *New Mexico v. Texas*, 275 U.S. 279, 287 (1927) ("There was much evidence in those years the country was wild and infested with hostile Indians"); *Winters v. United States*, 207 U.S. 564, 576 (1908) ("The reservation was a part of a very much larger tract which the Indians had the right to occupy and use, and which was adequate for the habits and wants of a nomadic and uncivilized people"); *Oregon v. Hitchcock*, 202 U.S. 60, 62 (1906) (describing Indians who "were all in a savage state, uncivilized, without a fixed place of abode, and roaming from place to place within the region"); *Sena v. United States*, 189 U.S. 233, 239 (1903) (describing a residence that "had become too dangerous by reason of the presence of hostile Indians"); *Montoya v. United States*, 269 (describing "the Chiricahua Apache Indians, who numbered from three to five hundred warriors of a particularly savage type"); *Atlantic and P. R. Co. v. Mingus*, 165 U.S. 413, 417 (1897) ("[T]he route of the road ran through numerous reservations occupied by hostile and warlike Indians"); *Stoneroad v. Stoneroad*, 158 U.S. 240, 242 (1895) (describing an individual who was "expelled by the hostilities of the savage Indian tribes"); *Boyd v. Nebraska*, 143 U.S. 135, 147 (1892) ("[W]hen the lives and property of settlers were destroyed or endangered, when many settlers were massacred, when hostile Indians killed cattle before the door of the home of his family, he volunteered his services as a soldier of the United States"); *Holladay v. Kennard*, 79 U.S. 254, 258 (1870) (describing a period "when

nothing but a mail-coach traversed the prairie, and roving bands of hostile Indians infested the route"); *Thomson v. Pac. R.R.,* 76 U.S. 579, 583 (1869) (discussing efforts of the government in sending "troops and munitions of war to protect the defenceless [*sic*] men, women, and children of the frontier against Indian barbarities"); *Silver v. Ladd,* 74 U.S. 219, 223 (1868) (describing an individual who "settled among tribes of Indians which were both hostile and treacherous"); *United States v. Repentigny,* 72 U.S. 211, 244 (1866) ("It is well known that the British government, desirous to bring the boundary of Canada down to the river Ohio . . . persisted in withholding from us the Western posts, and stirring up the savages against us"); *The Kansas Indians,* 72 U.S. 737, 738 (1866) (discussing the "fact" of the "primitive habits and customs of the tribe, when in a savage state"); *United States v. Teschmaker,* 63 U.S. 392, 401 (1859) (describing "a multitude of savage Indians, who have committed and are daily committing many depredations" and the efforts of the government "to domesticate the Indians, and convert them by gentle means, if possible, to a better system of life"); *Fremont v. United States,* 58 U.S. 542, 562 (1854) ("[I]n this state of things, the uncivilized Indians had become more turbulent, and were dangerous to the frontier settlements"); *United States v. Percheman,* 32 U.S. 51, 66 (1833) ("The colony of Georgia was founded as a barrier against the encroachments of the Spaniards; and the refuge and encouragement afforded the latter to absconding slaves, hostile Indians, and other incendiaries"); *Worcester v. Georgia,* 590 (McLean, J., dissenting) ("Are not those nations of Indians who have made some advances in civilization, better neighbors than those who are still in a savage state?"); *Cherokee Nation v. Georgia,* 27–28 (Johnson, J., dissenting) (discussing tribes of Indians "which the law of nations would regard as nothing more than wandering hordes, held together only by ties of blood and habit, and having neither laws or government beyond what is required in a savage state"). See also *Trustees of Dartmouth College v. Woodward,* 17 U.S. 518, 524 (1819) ("Know ye, therefore, that [w]e, considering the premises, and being willing to encourage the laudable and charitable design of spreading Christian knowledge among the savages of our American wilderness . . . ," quoting Dartmouth College Charter).

34. See Getches, "Conquering the Cultural Frontier," 1575 (describing an internal memo written by Justice Antonin Scalia that states that the Court's opinions in Indian law reflect the "congressional 'expectations'" embodied in "all legislation" passed by Congress, historically from the eighteenth and nineteenth centuries "down to the present day").

35. The European colonial-era doctrine of discovery and conquest applied to North America under the European Law of Nations and its incorporation into U.S. law by the early-nineteenth-century Supreme Court are discussed in chapter 4.

36. This book is part of a two-volume research project that examines the history of the language of Indian savagery in the Western colonial imagination. In this book I am primarily interested in exploring the continuing force of the racial imagery generated by this language of Indian savagery in the Supreme Court's Indian law decisions. A second book, complementary to this volume, entitled *"The Savage as the Wolf": Indian Rights, the Western Colonial Imagination, and the Founders' First Indian Policy,* will explore the genealogy and organizing force of the idea of the savage in the Western colonial imagination and its use as an instrument of governmentality by the Founders and their will to empire in debating and deciding upon the first U.S. Indian policy.

37. *Dred Scott v. Sanford,* 60 U.S. 393, 403 (1856). As Chief Justice Roger Taney's opinion for the Court in *Dred Scott* explained, tribal Indians had "formed no part of the colonial communities, and never amalgamated with them in social communities or in government." On *Dred Scott* and Taney's role in the legal history of racism directed against blacks in America, see chapter 2. On Taney's contributions to the legal history of racism directed against Indians in America, see chapter 5.

38. On the idea of racial beliefs held "deep down" by individuals described in social science literature as aversive racists, see chapter 9. On unconscious forms of racism and the role of stereotypes and racial imagery in their construction, also see chapter 9.

39. On the role of the justices in giving legal sanction to a language of racism organized around racial stereotypes and images of Indian savagery, see chapter 2.

40. See Jim Adams, "Protecting Tribes from the Supreme Court," *Indian Country Today,* June 18, 2003. This article identifies law professors from "Harvard to the University of Washington" as believing that my "ideas" on protecting Indian rights "don't translate into a winning courtroom strategy." "'You can be so interested in being pure that you don't get anything done,' said Joseph Singer, professor at Harvard Law School." Singer is quoted in the article as saying, "The question is whether ignoring the Supreme Court is likely to be successful for a tribe as a practical matter. It probably won't be." Robert Anderson, a professor at the University of Washington School of Law, is quoted in the article as being in agreement with my basic "critique of the racist European doctrine of conquest" but then asks rhetorically, "do you think the Supreme Court is going to abandon the Marshall trilogy because of its racial origin and make its decision based on some independent standards?" See also Robert Laurence, "Learning to Live with the Plenary Power of Congress over Indian Nations," *Arizona Law Review* 30 (1988): 422: "Professor Williams, in the *Algebra,* finds that the plenary power is an unprincipled embodiment of the Discovery Doctrine and urges the uncontradicted recognition of tribal

sovereignty. . . . I am not sure that such a system is achievable in today's legal and political world. . . . Even if it is, I am not sure it is the wisest system."

41. Adams, "Protecting Tribes from the Supreme Court."

42. For example, I was cocounsel (along with counsel of record, S. James Anaya) for Respondent Floyd Hicks in *Nevada v. Hicks.* See chapter 10. I served as counsel of record for the Carrier Sekani Tribal Council in its human rights complaint petition filed before the Organization of American States Inter-American Commission on Human Rights, Case 12.279 (Canada). I also represented the council before the commission on its Admissibility Hearing on the Complaint, Amended Petition and Response to Inter-American Commission submitted by the Chiefs of the Member Nations of the Carrier Sekani Tribal Council against Canada (available from author). Also, I served as counsel of record for the National Congress of American Indians on its amicus curiae brief filed in *Mayagna (Sumo) Awas Tingni Community v. Nicaragua,* Case 11.555, Inter-American Court of Human Rights (Ser. C) no. 79 (August 31, 2001), http:/www.corteidh.or.cr/seriecing/mayagna_79_lng.html.

43. See, e.g., Thomas Buerganthal and Harold G. Maier, *Public International Law in a Nutshell* (St. Paul, Minn.: West, 1990), 149; Antônio Agusto Cançado Trindade, *The Application of the Rule of Exhaustion of Local Remedies in International Law* (Cambridge and New York: Cambridge University Press, 1983).

44. "The Ballot or the Bullet," in *Malcolm X Speaks: Selected Speeches and Statements,* ed. George Breitman (New York: Pathfinder, 1989), 35, 36. On Malcolm X, see the introduction to part I.

45. See, e.g., Robert A. Williams, Jr., "Encounters on the Frontiers of International Human Rights Law: Redefining the Terms of Indigenous Peoples' Survival in the World," *Duke Law Journal,* 1990: 667.

46. See "The Algebra," 222, which recounts Felix Cohen's story, told in his 1952 article, "Americanizing the White Man," *American Scholar* 21 (1952): 177, about the response of an unnamed Indian elder to Dillon S. Myer, the commissioner-designate of the BIA. On Myer's previous administrative experience as head of the War Relocation Authority, see "The Algebra," 220–23. BIA commissioner-designate Myer had been speaking of the benefits to be achieved by the Indian's "complete integration" into the mainstream of American public life when he asked the rhetorical question of the day: "What can we do to Americanize the Indian?" As Cohen tells the story, an Indian elder in the audience rose and answered Myer as follows with a bit of his own knowledge: "You will forgive me if I tell you that my people were Americans for thousands of years before your people were. The question is not how you can Americanize us but how we can Americanize you. We have been working at that for a long time. Sometimes we are discouraged at the results, but we will keep trying.

"And the first thing we want to teach you is that, in the American way of life, each man has respect for his brother's vision. Because each of us respected his brother's dream, we enjoyed freedom here in America while you people were busy killing and enslaving each other across the water.

"The relatives you left behind [in Europe] . . . are still trying to kill each other and enslave each other because they have not learned there that freedom is built on my respect for my brother's vision and his respect for mine. We have a hard trail ahead of us in trying to Americanize you and your white brothers. But we are not afraid of hard trails" (Cohen, "Americanizing the White Man," 177–78).

In his 1933 book *The Land of the Spotted Eagle* (1933; repr., Lincoln: University of Nebraska Press, 1978), the Lakota Sioux writer Luther Standing Bear discussed the sources of the white man's racism directed at the Indian: "[T]he man from Europe is still a foreigner and an alien. And he still hates the man who questioned his path across the continent" (248).

47. Sandra Day O'Connor, *The Majesty of the Law: Reflections of a Supreme Court Justice* (New York: Random House, 2003), 166.

48. See e.g., Gavin Clarkson, "Racial Imagery and Native Americans: A First Look at the Empirical Evidence behind the Indian Mascot Controversy," *Cardozo Journal of International and Comparative Law* 11 (2003): 393.

49. This closely watched and widely reported decision involves a legal challenge brought by American Indians to the trademark registration of the Washington "Redskins" of the National Football League. Under federal trademark law, section 2(a) of the Lanham Act, trademark registration may be denied or canceled if the mark "consists of or comprises immoral, deceptive or scandalous mater," or brings persons, living or dead, "into contempt or disrepute." 15 U.S.C.A. 1052(a). In *Pro-Football v. Harjo*, 284 F. Supp. 2d 96 (D.C. 2003), a federal district court judge reversed a U.S. Patent and Trademark Office Appeals Board decision to cancel the federal trademark registrations involving the "Redskins" football team. The board's decision against the team was based on its findings that the trademark "may disparage" American Indians or "bring them into contempt, or disrepute," thereby violating the Lanham Act. *Harjo v. Pro-Football, Inc.*, 50 U.S.P.Q. 2d. 1705, 1749 (T.T.A.B. 1999).

The board had cited dictionary definitions of the word "Redskins," sworn deposition testimony of "linguistic experts," "voluminous excerpts from newspapers, including cartoons, headlines, editorials, and articles from the 1940s to the present," a telephone survey "purporting to measure the views, at the time of the survey in 1996, of the general population and, separately, of Native Americans towards the word 'redskin' as a reference to Native Americans," and other evidence in making its findings (*Harjo v. Pro-Football, Inc.*, 1749). The federal district court, however, reversed the board on an appeal de novo, declining to rule on whether the word "Redskin" was insulting to American Indians (*Pro-Football v. Harjo,* 113, 145). Instead, the district court found that the board had improperly relied upon partial, dated, and irrelevant evidence and therefore restored the trademarks to the team (ibid., 144–45). The court also ruled that because of the substantial delay in bringing a challenge to the trademark (twenty-five years from the first trademark—1967—for "Redskins"), laches (undue delay), meaning that the Indian petitioners in the case had waited too long to bring an action seeking cancellation of the trademark, was available as a defense to the team (ibid., 144–45).

50. See, e.g., Arlene B. Hirschfelder, Paulette Fairbanks Molin, Yvonne Beamer, and Yvonne Wakim, eds., *American Indian Stereotypes in the World of Children: A Reader and Bibliography,* 2nd ed. (Lanham, Md.: Scarecrow Press, 1999); Sandra Cohen, "The Sign of the Beaver: The Problem and the Solution," in Hirschfelder, Molin, Beamer, and Wakim, *American Indian Stereotypes;* Floy C. Pepper, *Unbiased Teaching about American Indians and Alaska Natives in Elementary Schools,* ERIC *Digests,* ERIC/CRESS, ERIC Clearinghouse on Rural Education and Small Schools, Charleston, West Virginia, http://www.ericfacility.net/ericdigests/ed321968.html (1990). See also Council on Interracial Books for Children, Racism and Sexism Resource Center for Educators, *Stereotypes, Distortions, and Omissions in U.S. History Books* (New York: Council on Interracial Books for Children, Racism and Sexism Resource Center for Educators, 1977); Patricia Ramsey, "Beyond 'Ten Little Indians' and Turkeys: Alternative Approaches to Thanksgiving," *Young Children* 34 no. 6 (1979): 28–32, 49–52; Beverly Slapin and Doris Seale, eds., *Through Indian Eyes: The Native Experience in Books for Children* (Los Angeles: American Indian Studies Center, University of California, 1998).

51. I quote from the Web site (www.americangirl.com) link to "Meet Kaya": "Kaya™ (KY-yaah) is an adventurous Nez Perce girl growing up in 1764. She's happiest when she's riding her beloved horse Steps High, playing with her tiny pup Tatlo, or sharing stories with her blind sister as they work. Kaya dreams of becoming a courageous leader for her people who is ready to meet whatever the future brings. She draws strength from her family, the legends her elders tell, and the bold warrior woman who is her hero."

52. Patricia G. Devine, "Stereotypes and Prejudice, Their Automatic and Controlled Components," *Journal of Personality and Social Psychology* 56 (1989): 16. On the conscious use of a strategy of "intention, attention, and effort" in avoiding habitual responses to negative racial stereotypes, see chapter 9.

53. See, e.g., Kelsey Begaye, Tex Hall, John Echohawk, and Susan Williams, "Tribal Governance and Economic Enhancement Initiative," *Indian Country Today,* October 11, 2002, http://www.indiancountry.com/content .cfm?id=1034343948. On Congress's overturning of a major Rehnquist Court

Indian rights decision, *Duro v. Reina,* see chapter 11. The Court upheld the constitutionality of this congressional override of *Duro* in *United States v. Lara;* see chapter 10.

54. See Adams, "Protecting Tribes from the Supreme Court."

55. See Laurence, "Learning to Live with the Plenary Power of Congress over Indian Nations," 435.

56. *Plessy v. Ferguson,* 163 U.S. 537 (1896).

57. Marshall posed the following challenge to the justices at the 1953 oral argument in *Brown:* "[T]he only way that this Court can decide this case in opposition to our position . . . is to find that for some reason Negroes are inferior to all other human beings. . . . [W]hy of all the multitudinous groups of people in this country [d]o you have to single out Negroes and give them this separate treatment"? Leon Friedman, ed., *Argument: The Oral Argument before the Supreme Court in "Brown v. Board of Education of Topeka," 1952–1955* (New York: Chelsea House, 1969), 239. The Court responded directly to Marshall's confrontational challenge in finding that the segregation of black children under *Plessy*'s "separate but equal" doctrine, "from others of similar age and qualification solely because of their race generate[d] a feeling of inferiority as to their status in the community that may affect their hearts and minds in a way unlikely ever to be undone" (494). See A. Leon Higginbotham, Jr., "The Ten Precepts of American Slavery Jurisprudence: Chief Justice Roger Taney's Defense and Justice Thurgood Marshall's Condemnation of the Precept of Black Inferiority," *Cardozo Law Review* 17 (1996): 1695. On Thurgood Marshall's extraordinary life in the law, see Mark V. Tushnet, *Making Civil Rights Law: Thurgood Marshall and the Supreme Court, 1936–1961* (New York: Oxford University Press, 1994) and *Making Constitutional Law: Thurgood Marshall and the Supreme Court, 1961–1991* (New York: Oxford University Press, 1997).

58. In *Brown,* the justices were confronted by Thurgood Marshall and his fellow attorneys for the black plaintiffs in the case with the large body of contemporary social science research that showed the harmful effects of segregation and racial discrimination directed at blacks. See *Brown v. Board of Education,* 494–95. In accepting the trial court's finding that segregation of white and colored children in public schools has a detrimental effect upon the colored children, the *Brown* Court specifically cited this research in its opinion holding for the plaintiffs: "Whatever may have been the extent of psychological knowledge at the time of *Plessy v. Ferguson,* this finding is amply supported by modern authority. Any language in *Plessy v. Ferguson* contrary to this finding is rejected" (*Brown v. Board of Education,* 494–95 and 494n11, citing the following sources: K. B. Clark, "Effect of Prejudice and Discrimination on Personality Development," in Mid-Century White House Conference on Children

and Youth, *Personality in the Making,* ed. Helen Leland Witmer and Ruth Kotinsky [New York: Harper, 1952], c. VI; Deutscher and Chein, "The Psychological Effects of Enforced Segregation: A Survey of Social Science Opinion," *Journal of Psychology* 26 [1948]: 259; Chein, "What Are the Psychological Effects of Segregation under Conditions of Equal Facilities?" *International Journal of Opinion and Attitude Research* 3 [1949]: 229; Brameld, "Educational Costs," in *Discrimination and National Welfare,* ed. R. M. MacIver [New York: Institute for Religious and Social Studies; distributed by Harper, 1949], 44–48; Edward Franklin Frazier, *The Negro in the United States* [New York: Macmillan, 1949], 674–681. And see generally Gunnar Myrdal, *An American Dilemma* [New York: Harper, 1944]).

59. *Brown v. Board of Education,* 494.

60. Derrick Bell, "*Brown v. Board of Education* and the Interest Convergence Dilemma," *Harvard Law Review* 93 (1980): 518, 524–25. See also Mary Dudziak, *Cold War Civil Rights* (Princeton: Princeton University Press, 2000), 250–51. Summarizing the work of both Bell and Dudziak, Richard Delgado states that "*Brown v. Board of Education* and the softening of racial attitudes that it ushered in were attributable not so much to moral breakthroughs on the part of whites, but rather to changes in elite self-interest, which in turn were the result of Cold War competition." Richard Delgado, "Linking Arms: Recent Books on Interracial Coalition as an Avenue of Social Reform," *Cornell Law Review* 88 (2003): 855, 879.

61. *Brown v. Board of Education,* 494–95.

62. I was a student at Harvard Law School from 1977 to 1980, when I took Professor Bell's class on "Race, Racism and American Law," just at about the time he was writing his seminal 1980 Harvard Law Review article "*Brown v. Board of Education* and the Interest Convergence Dilemma." I was fortunate enough to be there, in other words, when he was testing his interest convergence theory on those of us who were in his class at the time. See also Derrick Bell, "Bakke, Minority Admissions, and the Usual Price of Racial Remedies," *California Law Review* 67 (1979): 3.

63. Derrick Bell, "Racial Realism," *Connecticut Law Review* 24 (1992): 363.

64. Delgado, "Linking Arms," 855. Malcolm X tried to teach us much the same lesson in his famous 1964 speech, "The Ballot or the Bullet": "Don't change the white man's mind—you can't change his mind, and that whole thing about appealing to the moral conscience of America—America's conscience is bankrupt. She lost all conscience a long time ago. Uncle Sam has no conscience. They don't know what morals are. They don't try and eliminate an evil because it's evil, or because it's illegal, or because it's immoral; they eliminate it only

when it threatens their existence. So you're wasting your time appealing to the moral conscience of a bankrupt man like Uncle Sam. If he had a conscience, he'd straighten this thing out with no more pressure being put upon him. So it is not necessary to change the white man's mind. We have to change our own mind" (53).

65. See, e.g., Felix S. Cohen, "The Erosion of Indian Rights, 1950–53," *Yale Law Journal* 62 (1953): 390. Cohen, one of the founders of the American legal realist movement, also authored the following proto-racial realist lesson on the interest convergence dilemma for the protection of Indian rights in America in this oft-cited 1953 article: "[T]he Indian plays much the same role in our American society that the Jews played in Germany. Like the Miner's canary, the Indian marks the shift from fresh air to poison gas in our political atmosphere; and our treatment of Indians, even more than our treatment of other minorities, reflects the rise and fall in our democratic faith" (390).

66. I elaborate upon this thesis on the singularly problematic nature of Indian rights claims to indigenous self-determination and cultural sovereignty under the Supreme Court's Indian law in the conclusion to this book.

67. Charles Wilkinson, "To Feel the Summer in Spring: The Treaty Fishing Rights of the Wisconsin Chippewa," *Wisconsin Law Review*, 1991: 378.

68. See Wilkinson, *American Indians, Time, and the Law*, 14–19 (noting that a central thrust of the treaties signed by tribes and the United States in the eighteenth and nineteenth centuries "was to create a measure of separatism. That is, the reservation system was intended to establish home lands for the tribes, islands of tribalism largely free from interference by non-Indians or future state governments. This separatism is measured, rather than absolute, because it contemplates supervision and support by the United States" [14]).

69. Wilkinson, *To Feel the Summer in the Spring*, 379.

70. My singularity thesis for protecting Indian rights is also in accord with the "differential racialization" hypothesis of Omi and Winant, *Racial Formation in the United States*, 55–61, positing that racial harms will differ from group to group and over time. See also Delgado, "Linking Arms," 857 ("It logically follows, therefore, that redress for those harms will take culturally specific forms").

71. See Getches, "Conquering the Cultural Frontier," 1575 (quoting Justice Scalia).

72. "The immobility to which the native is condemned can only be called in question if the native decides to put an end to the history of colonization—the history of pillage—and to bring into existence the history of the nation—the history of decolonization." Frantz Fanon, *The Wretched of the Earth* (New York: Grove Press, 1963), 51.

I. Discovering a Language of Racism in America

1. The incident at the airport is related by Alex Haley in the epilogue to
The Autobiography of Malcolm X (1965; repr., New York: Ballantine Books,
1999), 406. Haley went on from his autobiographical encounter with Malcolm X to author *Roots* (1976), a Pulitzer Prize–winning work that was turned
into the famous 1977 TV miniseries of the same name.

1. "Look, Mom, a Baby Maid!"

1. Besides his *Autobiography,* selected by *Time* magazine as one of the
ten most important nonfiction books of the twentieth century, other powerful
and illuminating examples of Malcolm X's "racial perspective" can be found
in *Malcolm X Speaks: Selected Speeches and Statements,* ed. George Breitman
(New York: Pathfinder, 1989).

2. They were "N's" with Attitude. N.W.A., *Straight outta Compton,* Pri-
ority Records, 1988.

3. See *Shady Records, Inc. v. Source Enterprises,* 2004 WL 1325795
(S.D.N.Y. 2004).

4. Ibid.

5. Ibid.

6. For a provocative discussion on the continuing significance of the "n"
word in American cultural life, see Randall Kennedy, *Nigger: The Strange Ca-
reer of a Troublesome Word* (New York: Pantheon Books, 2002).

7. See, e.g., Renee Graham, "Limbaugh's Attack of Kerry Is a Bad Rap,"
Boston Globe, Living Section, April 13, 2004: "On a segment of MTV's 'Choose
or Lose,' correspondent Gideon Yago asked [John] Kerry, 'Are there any trends
out there in music, or even in popular music in general, that have piqued your
interest?'

"'Oh sure, I follow and I'm interested,' Kerry replied. 'I don't always like,
but I'm interested. I mean, I never was into heavy metal. I didn't really like it.
I'm fascinated by rap and hip-hop. I think there's a lot of poetry in it. There's
a lot of anger, a lot of social energy in it. And I think you'd better listen to it
pretty carefully, 'cause it's important.'"

8. Jerry Kang, "Trojan Horses of Race," *Harvard Law Review* 118 (2005):
1506–14.

9. Charles R. Lawrence III, "The Id, the Ego, and Equal Protection: Reckoning with Unconscious Racism," *Stanford Law Review* 39 (1987): 322.

10. Jody David Armour, *Negrophobia and Reasonable Racism: The Hidden
Costs of Being Black in America* (New York: New York University Press, 1997).

11. Ibid., 2.

12. Ibid., 126.

13. See generally Winthrop D. Jordan, *White over Black: American Attitudes toward the Negro, 1550–1812* (Chapel Hill: Published for the Institute of Early American History and Culture at Williamsburg, Va., by the University of North Carolina Press, 1968); Samuel Stanhope Smith, *An Essay on the Causes of the Variety of Complexion and Figure in the Human Species,* ed. Winthrop D. Jordan (Cambridge, Mass.: Belknap Press, 1965); Winthrop D. Jordan, ed., *The Negro versus Equality, 1762–1826* (Chicago: Rand McNally, 1969); Eugene Genovese, *Roll, Jordan, Roll: The World Slaves Made* (New York: Pantheon Books, 1974), *From Rebellion to Revolution: Afro-American Slave Revolts in the Making of the Modern World* (Baton Rouge: Louisiana State University Press, 1979), *In Red and Black: Marxian Explorations in Southern and Afro-American History* (New York: Pantheon Books, 1971), and *The Political Economy of Slavery: Studies in the Economy and Society of the Slave South,* 2nd ed. (Middletown, Conn.: Wesleyan University Press, 1989); Elizabeth Fox-Genovese and Eugene Genovese, *Fruits of Merchant Capital: Slavery and Bourgeois Property in the Rise and Expansion of Capitalism* (New York: Oxford University Press, 1983); Eugene Genovese et al., eds., *Race and Slavery in the Western Hemisphere: Quantitative Studies* (Princeton: Princeton University Press, 1975); Robert M. Cover, *Justice Accused: Antislavery and the Judicial Process* (New Haven: Yale University Press, 1975) and *Narrative, Violence and the Law: Essays of Robert Cover,* ed. Martha Minnow et al. (Ann Arbor: University of Michigan Press, 1992).

14. *Brown v. Board of Education,* 347 U.S. 483 (1954). See the introduction to this book for a discussion of *Brown* and the social science research cited by the Supreme Court in that landmark civil rights case.

15. See, e.g., Charlotte Steel and Howard Schuman, "Young White Adults: Did Racial Attitudes Change in the 1980s?" *American Journal of Sociology* 98 (1992): 340–67; Charles E. Case and Andrew M. Greeley, "Attitudes toward Racial Equality," *Humboldt Journal of Social Relations* 16 (1990): 67–94; Harold Sigall and Richard Page, "Current Stereotypes: A Little Fading, a Little Faking," *Journal of Personality and Social Psychology* 18 (1971): 247–55; Patricia G. Devine, "Stereotypes and Prejudice: Their Automatic and Controlled Components," *Journal of Personality and Social Psychology* 56 (1989): 5–18; Mary Ellen Goodman, *Race Awareness in Young Children,* rev. ed. (New York: Collier Books, 1964); Harold M. Proshansky, "The Development of Intergroup Attitudes," in *Review of Child Development Research,* ed. Luis Wladis Hoffman and Martin L. Hoffman, vol. 2, 311–71 (Chicago: University of Chicago Press, 1966); David L. Ronis et al., "Attitudes, Decisions, and Habits as Determinants of Repeated Behavior," in *Attitude, Structure, and Function,* ed. Anthony R. Pratkanis et al., 213–39 (Hillsdale, N.J.: Erlbaum, 1989), 218.

16. See, e.g., Rebecca S. Bigler and Lynn S. Liben, "A Cognitive-Developmental Approach to Racial Stereotyping and Reconstructive Memory in Euro-American Children," *Child Development*, 1993: 1507–18; Paul E. McGhee and Nelda S. Duffey, "Children's Appreciation of Humor Victimizing Different Racial-Ethnic Groups," *Journal of Cross-Cultural Psychology* 14 (1983): 29–40; Mary A. Newman et al., "Ethnic Awareness in Children: Not a Unitary Concept," *Journal of Genetic Psychology* 144 (1983): 103–12. See also David Benjamin Oppenheimer, "Understanding Affirmative Action," *Hastings Constitutional Law Quarterly* 23 (1996): 956–57, for a succinct survey of the literature on racial stereotyping behavior of children.

17. Phyllis A. Katz, "The Acquisition of Racial Attitudes in Children," in *Towards the Elimination of Racism*, ed. Phyllis A. Katz (New York: Pergamon Press, 1976), 147.

18. Patricia Williams, "Spirit-Murdering the Messenger: The Discourse of Fingerpointing as the Law's Response to Racism," *University of Miami Law Review* 42 (1987): 127–57.

19. See Armour, *Negrophobia and Reasonable Racism*, 121–25; Patricia G. Devine, "The Acquisition of Racial Attitudes in Children," in Katz, *Towards the Elimination of Racism*, 147.

20. See generally George P. Fletcher, *A Crime of Self-Defense: Bernard Goetz and the Law on Trial* (Chicago: University of Chicago Press, 1990).

21. Goetz was acquitted of all charges at his trial except that of unlawfully carrying a firearm. See *People v. Goetz*, 68 N.Y. 2d 96, 497 N.E. 2d 41, 506 N.Y.S. 2d 18 (1986). In other words, the only thing he did wrong was to carry a gun onto the subway. But everything he did after that, according to the jury's verdict, was fine as far as they were concerned. See Aaron Goldstein, "Race, Reasonableness, and the Rule of Law," *Southern California Law Review* 76 (2003): 1191–94.

22. On the Goetz case, see Fletcher, *A Crime of Self-Defense;* Patricia Williams, *The Alchemy of Race and Rights* (Cambridge, Mass.: Harvard University Press, 1991), 58–59; Derrick Bell, *Race, Racism and American Law*, 4th ed. (Gaithersburg, Md.: Aspen Law and Business, 2000): 520–25; Stephen Carter, "When Victims Happen to Be Black," *Yale Law Journal* 97 (1988): 424, 426.

23. Armour, *Negrophobia and Reasonable Racism*, 122; Devine, "Stereotypes and Prejudice," 6.

24. Ronis et al., "Attitudes, Decisions, and Habits as Determinants of Repeated Behavior," 218.

25. Peggy C. Davis, "Law as Micro-Aggression," *Yale Law Journal* 98 (1989): 1565. See also Samuel L. Gaertner and John F. Dovidio, "The Aversive Form of Racism," in *Prejudice, Discrimination, and Racism*, ed. John F. Dovidio and Samuel L. Gaertner (Orlando, Fla.: Academic Press, 1986), 61, 84.

26. See Armour, *Negrophobia and Reasonable Racism,* 19: "The 'Reasonable Racist' asserts that even if his belief that Blacks are 'prone to violence' stems primarily from racism—that is, from a belief in the genetic predisposition of Blacks toward greater violence, from uncritical acceptance of the Black cultural stereotype, or from personal racial animus—he should be excused for considering the victim's race before using force because most similarly situated Americans would have done so as well."

27. "There is nothing more painful to me at this stage in my life than to walk down the street and hear footsteps and start thinking about robbery—then look around and see somebody white and feel relieved"(quoted in Armour, *Negrophobia and Reasonable Racism,* 35). Jackson made this remark nearly a decade ago, in a speech to a black congregation in Chicago, while discussing the tragedy of black-on-black crime. It was reported and commented upon widely in the media, including *U.S. News and World Report* and the *Washington Post.* The quote and some of the commentary and controversy it stirred in the national media are related in Armour, *Negrophobia and Reasonable Racism.*

28. See, e.g., Williams, "Spirit-Murdering the Messenger."

29. In the famous eighteenth-century case of *Campbell v. Hall,* 1 Cowp. 204 (1774), Lord Mansfield cited "the mad enthusiasm of the *Croisades*" as the reason for the "absurd exception as to pagans" recognized in Lord Coke's equally famous 1608 opinion in *Calvin's Case,* 77 Eng. Rep. 377 (1608) 1 Cowp. 204, 208–11. In *Calvin's Case,* Lord Coke had stated that the king's conquest of an infidel nation abrogated its laws ipso facto, "but the laws of a conquered country continue in force until they are altered by the conqueror" (*Calvin's Case,* 210, 211). See Robert A. Williams, Jr., *The American Indian in Western Legal Thought: The Discourses of Conquest* (New York: Oxford University Press, 1990), 301.

30. Much of this ground on the Crusades is gone over in Williams, *The American Indian in Western Legal Thought.*

31. Edward Said, *Orientalism* (New York: Pantheon Books, 1978).

32. On the October 6, 2002, CBS news program *60 Minutes,* Falwell said in an interview with Bob Simon, "I think Mohammed was a terrorist. He—I read enough of the history of his life written by both Muslims and—and—non-Muslims, that he was a—a violent man, a man of war." See "Falwell Brands Mohammed a 'Terrorist,'" *CBSNews.com,* October 6, 2002, http://www.cbsnews.com/stories/2003/06/05/60minutes/main557187.shtml. Falwell later apologized for calling the Prophet Muhammad a "terrorist," but only after his remarks had sparked outrage among many Muslims around the world and set off sectarian riots in India that left at least eight people dead. "I sincerely apologize that certain statements of mine made during an interview for CBS's 60 Minutes were hurtful to the feelings of many Muslims," Mr. Falwell said in a

statement. "I intended no disrespect to any sincere, law-abiding Muslim." "Falwell 'Sorry' for Mohammed Remark," *BBC New World Edition,* October 13, 2002, http://news.bbc.co.uk/2/hi/americas/2323897.stm.

33. "[L]ike a virus that mutates into new forms, old-fashioned prejudice seems to have evolved into a new type that is, at least temporarily, resistant to traditional . . . remedies" (Gaertner and Dovidio, "The Aversive Form of Racism," 85–86).

2. The Supreme Court and the Legal History of Racism in America

1. Many of these opinions are collected in Juan F. Perea, Richard Delgado, Angela Harris, and Stephanie M. Wildman, *Race and Races: Cases and Resources for a Diverse America* (hereinafter *Race and Races*) (St. Paul, Minn.: West Group, 2000).

2. See, e.g., A. Leon Higginbotham, Jr., "The Ten Precepts of American Slavery Jurisprudence: Chief Justice Roger Taney's Defense and Justice Thurgood Marshall's Condemnation of the Precept of Black Inferiority," *Cardozo Law Review* 17 (1996): 1695–1710.

3. That, at least, was Frederick Douglass's view of this landmark case that struck down the Missouri Compromise: "The infamous decision of the Slaveholding wing of the Supreme Court maintains that slaves are within the contemplation of the Constitution of the United States, property; that slaves are property in the same sense that horses, sheep, and swine are property; that the old doctrine that slavery is a creature of local law is false; that the right of the slaveholder to his slave does not depend upon the local law, but is secured wherever the Constitution of the United States extends; that Congress has no right to prohibit slavery anywhere; that slavery may go in safety anywhere under the star-spangled banner; that colored persons of African descent have no rights that white men are bound to respect; that colored men of African descent are not and cannot be citizens of the United States.

"You will readily ask me how I am affected by this devilish decision—this judicial incarnation of wolfishness? My answer is, and no thanks to the slaveholding wing of the Supreme Court, my hopes were never brighter than now.

"I have no fear that the National Conscience will be put to sleep by such an open, glaring, and scandalous tissue of lies as that decision is, and has been, over and over, shown to be." Frederick Douglass, "The Dred Scott Decision: Speech Delivered before American Anti-Slavery Society, New York, May 11, 1857," in *The Life and Writings of Frederick Douglass,* vol. 2, *The Pre-Civil War Decade, 1850–1860,* ed. Philip S. Foner (New York: International, 1950), 410–12. Douglass's speech can also be found, in edited form, in *Race and Races,* 126–29.

4. *Dred Scott v. Sanford,* 60 U.S. 393, 403–5 (1856).

5. Ibid., 403.

6. There is an immense literature on the case and its impact on the abolitionist movement in the United States and the events leading up to the Civil War. See, e.g., Don E. Fehrenbacher, *The Dred Scott Case: Its Significance in American Law and Politics* (New York: Oxford University Press, 1978); Stanley I. Kutler, ed., *The Dred Scott Decision* (Boston: Houghton Mifflin, 1967). See also John Hope Franklin and Alfred A. Moss, Jr., *From Slavery to Freedom,* 7th ed. (New York: McGraw-Hill, 1994).

7. See, e.g., Justice David Souter's concurrence to the majority opinion in *Washington v. Glucksberg,* 521 U.S. 702, 752 (1997), which denied a substantive due process challenge brought against a Washington State statute banning assisted suicide. Writing of the Court's holding in *Dred Scott* that substantive due process protected "an owner's property in a slave," Souter said of this antebellum view of the Constitution, "The ensuing judgment of history needs no recounting here" (*Washington v. Glucksberg,* 759–60).

8. *Dred Scott v. Sanford,* 407, 405, 407.

9. Ibid., 407.

10. Although Chief Justice Taney's opinion in *Dred Scott,* as Judge A. Leon Higginbotham, Jr., notes, made "twenty-one references to blacks as inferior and to whites as dominant or superior," Taney was careful to limit his remarks by referring to the way blacks were viewed throughout the history of America up through the time of the Declaration of Independence and the Constitution (see Higginbotham, "The Ten Precepts of American Slavery Jurisprudence," 1702). As Higginbotham further notes, however, Taney himself held strongly negative, stereotyped views of blacks, as evidenced by his defense of his *Dred Scott* opinion voiced later in his life, in which he described blacks as a "weak and credulous race," who enjoyed a "usually cheerful and contented" life in slavery, and who would find "sudden emancipation" to be their "absolute ruin" (quoted in ibid., 1703).

11. Robert Cover, "*Nomos* and Narrative," *Harvard Law Review* 97 (1983): 4–5.

12. Ibid., 53.

13. Ibid.

14. See *Black's Law Dictionary,* 6th ed. (St. Paul, Minn.: West, 1991), 978 (stare decisis: "To abide by, or adhere to, decided cases").

15. See *Plessy v. Ferguson* (Harland, J., dissenting): "[I]n view of the Constitution, in the eyes of the law, there is in this country no superior, dominant, ruling class of citizens. There is no caste here. Our constitution is color-blind, and neither knows nor tolerates classes among citizens" (559). On the Rehnquist Court's approach to pursuing a color-blind view of the Constitution

in its minority rights decisions, see Frank R. Parker, "The Damaging Consequences of the Rehnquist Court's Commitment to Color-Blindness versus Racial Justice," *American University Law Review* 45 (1996): 763–73. See also Neil Gotanda, "A Critique of 'Our Constitution Is Color Blind,'" *Stanford Law Review* 44 (1991): 1–68.

16. *Korematsu v. United States,* 323 U.S. 214, 228 (1944). The six judges agreeing in the decision were Chief Justice Harlan Stone and Justices Hugo Black, Felix Frankfurter, John Rutledge, William Douglas, and Stanley Reed.

Like Taney's opinion in *Dred Scott,* Black's majority opinion was careful to distance the Court from any active embrace of the racial stereotypes, images, and apocryphal tales of Japanese disloyalty that the military authorities and Congress had relied on to justify the wartime detention of persons of Japanese ancestry. It is worthwhile noting Black's own views, stated later, on the group of people affected by his opinion for the Court. In a newspaper interview in 1967, he remarked, "They all look alike to a person not a J[——]." It is also interesting to note that prior to his tenure on the Court, Black had joined the Ku Klux Klan (KKK) in his home state of Alabama in 1923. He resigned in 1926, the year of his first Senate campaign. In defending his membership in the KKK, Black later stated that he had joined mostly because the majority of Alabama jurors were also members. Basically, his argument was that being part of the KKK made him better able to serve his clients' best interests. However, his ties to the KKK would continue to serve him well. He was elected to the Senate with KKK support and remained indebted to the Klan for several years afterward. His membership was the source of much controversy during his nomination to the bench, but he was approved nonetheless to a lifetime position as justice of the Supreme Court by his former colleagues in the Senate. See *The Oxford Companion to the Supreme Court of the United States,* ed. Kermit L. Hall et al. (New York: Oxford University Press, 1992), 72–75.

17. *Korematsu v. United States,* 218, quoting *Hirabayashi v. United States,* 320 U.S. 81, 99 (1943). See Eugene Rostow, "The Japanese-American Cases—A Disaster," *Yale Law Journal* 54 (1945): 489–533; Peter Irons, *Justice at War* (New York: Oxford University Press, 1983). An illuminating discussion of the historical relationships between the Japanese-American World War II cases and the Bush administration's currently declared "War on Terrorism" can be found in Jace Weaver, *Turtle Goes to War: Of Military Commissions, the Constitution, and American Indian Memory* (New Haven: Trylon and Perisphere Press, 2002).

18. *Korematsu v. United States,* 227.

19. *Hirabayashi v. United States,* 320 U.S. 81 (1943).

20. *Korematsu v. United States,* 218.

21. Ibid., 232.

22. Ibid.

23. Ibid.

24. Ibid., 242, 233.

25. Ibid., 235–36.

26. Ibid., 237.

27. Ibid., 236n2 (quoting part 3, 739–40, 78th Cong., 1st sess.). In newspaper interviews, DeWitt declaimed his belief that "a J—— is a J——," regardless of how "Americanized" a particular Japanese individual might have become. See U.S. Commission on Wartime Relocation and Internment of Civilians, *Personal Justice Denied: Report of the Commission on Wartime Relocation and Internment of Civilians* (Washington, D.C.: U.S. Commission on Wartime Relocation and Internment of Civilians, 1983), 222.

28. *Korematsu v. United States,* 239n4 (quoting Edward K. Strong, *The Second-Generation Japanese Problem* [Stanford: Stanford University Press; London: Oxford University Press, 1934]); William Carlson Smith, *Americans in Process* (Ann Arbor, Mich.: Edwards Brothers, 1937); Eliot G. Mears, *Resident Orientals on the American Pacific Coast* (Chicago: University of Chicago Press, 1928); Harry A. Millis, *The Japanese Problem in the United States: An Investigation for the Commission on Relations with Japan Appointed by the Federal Council of the Churches of Christ in America* (New York: Macmillan, 1915).

29. *Korematsu v. United States,* 238, 239n9.

30. Ibid. (quoting Carey McWilliams, *Prejudice* [Boston: Little, Brown, 1944], 119–21; H.R. Report No. 2124, 77th Cong., 2d sess., 59–93).

31. See, e.g., *Terrace v. Thompson,* 263 U.S. 197 (1923) (upholding the "Alien Land Laws" of some western states, including Washington and California, which were aimed directly at those of Japanese ancestry and were designed to make it illegal for them to own property in those states). See generally, *Race and Races,* 397–412.

32. *Korematsu v. United States,* 242n15. Justice Murphy provided a sampling of public attitudes toward the Japanese on the West Coast that went well beyond even the gross racial caricatures of General DeWitt, noting in his dissent the racial animus of special-interest groups, who were extremely active in applying pressure for mass evacuation: "Mr. Austin E. Anson, managing secretary of the Salinas Vegetable Grower-Shipper Association, has frankly admitted that 'We're charged with wanting to get rid of the J[——]s for selfish reasons. We do. It's a question of whether the white man lives on the Pacific Coast or the brown men. They came into this valley to work, and they stayed to take over. . . . They undersell the white man in the markets. . . . They work their women and children while the white farmer has to pay wages for his help.

If all the J[——]s were removed tomorrow, we'd never miss them in two weeks, because the white farmers can take over and produce everything the J[——] grows. And we don't want them back when the war ends, either" (*Korematsu v. United States,* 240n12, quoting from Frank J. Taylor, "The People Nobody Wants," *Saturday Evening Post,* May 9, 1942, 24, 66). See H.R. Report No. 2124, 77th Cong., 2nd sess., 154B6; McWilliams, *Prejudice,* 126–28).

33. *Korematsu v. United States,* 239–42.

34. Following his dissent in *Korematsu,* Justice Jackson would go on to further reinforce his reputation as being totally attuned to the legal consequences of exactly what was at stake when a government set up concentration camps for a minority group in a time of war. Immediately following the conclusion of World War II, he was asked to prosecute Nazi war criminals at the Nuremberg Trials. See Eugene C. Gerhart, *America's Advocate* (Indianapolis, Ind.: Bobbs-Merrill, 1958), 25–27, and James E. Leahy, *Supreme Court Justices Who Voted with the Government* (Jefferson, N.C.: McFarland, 1999), 81–82.

Jackson began his opening statement to the Nuremberg Tribunal on November 21, 1945, as follows: "The privilege of opening the first trial in history for crimes against the peace of the world imposes grave responsibility. The wrongs which we seek to condemn and punish have been so calculated, so malignant and so devastating, that civilization cannot tolerate their being ignored because it cannot survive their being repeated. . . . What makes this inquest significant is that these prisoners represent sinister influences that will lurk in the world long after their bodies have returned to dust. They are living symbols of racial hatreds, of terrorism and violence, and of the arrogance and cruelty of power. They are symbols of fierce nationalisms and of militarism, of intrigue and war-making which have embroiled Europe generation after generation, crushing its manhood, destroying its homes, and impoverishing its life." Robert H. Jackson, *The Nürnberg Case* (New York: Cooper Square Publishers, 1971), 30–31.

35. *Korematsu v. United States,* 246.

36. Ibid., citing Benjamin Cardozo, *The Nature of the Judicial Process* (New Haven: Yale University Press, 1921), 51.

37. *Korematsu v. United States,* 246.

38. Like *Dred Scott* (see, e.g., note 7), *Korematsu* is usually cited today as an example of a very bad precedent for the Court to follow. Justice Scalia cited both *Korematsu* and *Dred Scott* in his 2000 dissent to *Stenberg v. Carhart,* 530 U.S. 914 (2000), a case in which the majority struck down a Nebraska statute banning "partial birth abortion": "I am optimistic enough to believe that one day *Stenberg v. Carhart* will be assigned its rightful place in the history of this Court's jurisprudence beside *Korematsu* and *Dred Scott*" (953).

II. "Signs Taken for Wonders"

1. See Michael Omi and Howard Winant, *Racial Formation in the United States: From the 1960s to the 1990s,* 2nd ed. (New York: Routledge, 1994), 65–67.

3. "The Savage as the Wolf"

1. The literature on the racial stereotypes and imagery directed at American Indians is quite extensive. The seminal text remains Roy Arvey Pearce, *Savagism and Civilization: A Study of the Indian and the American Mind* (Berkeley and Los Angeles: University of California Press, 1988) (originally published in 1953 as *The Savages of America*). Other important works include Robert F. Berkhofer, Jr., *The White Man's Indian: Images of the American Indian from Columbus to the Present* (New York: Knopf, 1978); Richard Drinnon, *Facing West: The Metaphysics of Indian-Hating and Empire Building* (Minneapolis: University of Minnesota Press, 1980). See also Philip J. Deloria, *Playing Indian* (New Haven: Yale University Press, 1998); S. Elizabeth Bird, ed., *Dressing in Feathers: The Construction of the Indian in American Popular Culture* (Boulder, Colo.: Westview, 1996); Devon Mihesuah, *American Indians: Stereotypes and Realities* (Atlanta, Ga.: Clarity, 1996); Raymond William Stedman, *Shadows of the Indian: Stereotypes in American Culture* (Norman: University of Oklahoma Press, 1982).

2. Michael Omi and Howard Winant, *Racial Formation in the United States: From the 1960s to the 1990s,* 2nd ed. (New York: Routledge, 1994), 62.

3. See ibid.

4. The discursive transformations occurring throughout Discovery-era Europe are suggested by a report on the acceptance by Queen Isabella of Spain of Antonio de Nebriga's Spanish *Gramática.* Upon presentation of the first-ever grammar of any modern European language in the momentous year 1492, the queen reportedly asked the scholar, "What is it for?" Nebriga dutifully answered Her Majesty, modestly, but with profound prescience and insight respecting the demands of the new, expansion-minded age. "Language," he reportedly said, "is the perfect instrument of empire." See Robert A. Williams, Jr., *The American Indian in Western Legal Thought: The Discourses of Conquest* (New York: Oxford University Press, 1990), 74.

5. See, e.g., June Namias, *White Captives: Gender and Ethnicity on the American Frontier* (Chapel Hill: University of North Carolina Press, 1993).

6. See, e.g., Shari M. Huhndorf, *Going Native: Indians in the American Cultural Imagination* (Ithaca, N.Y.: Cornell University Press, 2001).

7. See, e.g., Richard Slotkin, *Regeneration through Violence: The Mythology*

of the American Frontier, 1600–1800 (Middletown, Conn.: Wesleyan University Press, 1973).

8. See, e.g., Gretchen Battille and Charles P. Silet, eds., *The Pretend Indians: Images of Native Americans in the Movies* (Ames: Iowa State University Press, 1980); Richard Slotkin, *Gunfighter Nation: The Myth of the Frontier in Twentieth Century America* (New York: Atheneum, 1992).

9. *Dances with Wolves,* directed by Kevin Costner (Orion Pictures, 1990). Ward Churchill's entertaining critique of the film, "Lawrence of South Dakota: Dances with Wolves and the Maintenance of American Empire," can be found in *Fantasies of the Master Race: Literature, Cinema, and the Colonization of American Indians* (Monroe, Maine: Common Courage Press, 1992), 243–47.

10. See the sources cited in the introduction, note 50, and in this chapter, notes 1 and 5–9.

11. I discuss in depth the Founders' first Indian policy and their concerns with removing Indian tribes from the lands within the United States intended for white agricultural settlement in the forthcoming companion volume to this book, *"The Savage as the Wolf": Indian Rights, the Western Colonial Imagination, and the Founders' First Indian Policy,* which will explore the genealogy of the idea of the savage in the Western colonial imagination, and its use by the Founders in debating and deciding upon the first U.S. Indian policy. Works that I have relied on in this discussion of the Founders' Revolutionary-era Indian policy include Walter Mohr, *Federal Indian Relations: 1774–1788* (Philadelphia: University of Pennsylvania Press, 1933); Reginald Horsman, *Expansion and American Indian Policy: 1783–1812* (Norman: University of Oklahoma Press, 1992); Francis Paul Prucha, *American Indian Treaties: The History of a Political Anomaly* (Berkeley and Los Angeles: University of California Press, 1994); David H. Getches, Charles F. Wilkinson, and Robert A. Williams, Jr., *Federal Indian Law: Cases and Materials,* 5th ed. (St. Paul, Minn.: West Group, 2004), 84–93.

12. Reprinted in "George Washington to James Duane, September 7, 1783," *Documents of United States Indian Policy,* ed. Francis Paul Prucha, 2nd ed. (Lincoln: University of Nebraska Press, 1990), 1–2 (hereinafter *Documents*). The signal importance of this founding text in the history of U.S. Indian policy is indicated by its treatment in modern studies of the federal-tribal relationship. Father Prucha's widely used collection of documents on U.S. Indian policy commences with Washington's 1783 recommendations to Congress, accompanied by the textual note that its principles "were to form the basis for the Indian policy of the Continental Congress" (1). Walter Mohr, in his classic and still oft-relied-upon study of Indian policy during the Revolutionary era, *Federal Indian Relations,* has concluded that Congress, in the period immediately

following the signing of the Treaty of Paris, followed "closely the advice of Washington" in formulating the first U.S. Indian policy (102). Reginald Horsman, in his leading study on Indian policy in the post-Revolutionary period, *Expansion and American Indian Policy,* notes that Congress relied heavily on Washington's recommendations, to the point of directly quoting him in its official report setting out the principles of the first U.S. Indian policy (7–12).

13. See Homi K. Bhabha, "Signs Taken for Wonders: Questions of Ambivalence and Authority under a Tree outside Delhi, May 1817," in *The Location of Culture* (London and New York: Routledge, 1994), 102.

14. See generally Henry Nash Smith, *Virgin Land: The American West as Symbol and Myth* (1950; repr., Cambridge, Mass.: Harvard University Press, 1970), 3–18.

15. See Smith, *Virgin Land,* 133–44. See also J. G. A. Pocock, *The Machiavellian Moment: Florentine Political Thought and the Atlantic Republican Tradition* (Princeton: Princeton University Press, 1975), 506–33.

16. See generally the sources cited in note 11.

17. See generally Prucha, *American Indian Policy in the Formative Years,* 24–66.

18. Michel Foucault, in his 1978 lecture "Governmentality," reprinted in *The Foucault Effect: Studies in Governmentality with Two Lectures and an Interview with Michel Foucault,* ed. G. Burchell, C. Gordin, and Peter Miller, 87–104 (Chicago: University of Chicago Press, 1991), describes a rupture in the literature of Western European political thought leading to the creation of works on the "art of government," or governmentality: "From the middle of the sixteenth century to the end of the eighteenth, there develops and flourishes a notable series of political treatises that are no longer exactly 'advice to the prince,' and not yet treatises of political science, but are instead presented as works on the 'art of government.' Government as a general problem seems to me to explode in the sixteenth century, posed by discussions of quite diverse questions. . . . How to govern oneself, how to be governed, how to govern others, by whom the people will accept being governed, how to become the best possible governor—all these problems, in their multiplicity and intensity, seem to me to be characteristic of the sixteenth century, which lies, to put it schematically, at the crossroads of two processes: the one which, shattering the structures of feudalism, leads to the establishment of the great territorial, administrative and colonial states; and that totally different movement which, with the Reformation and Counter-Reformation, raises the issue of how one must be spiritually ruled and led on this earth in order to achieve eternal salvation" (87–88). Homi Bhabha, in his essay "The Other Question: Stereotype, Discrimination, and the Discourse of Colonialism," in Bhabha, *The Location of Culture,* draws upon this Foucauldian concept of governmentality to describe

the function of "racist stereotypical discourse, in its colonial moment." According to Bhabha, the art of colonial governmentality "is informed by a productive splitting in its constitution of knowledge and exercise of power": "Some of its practices recognize the difference of race, culture and history as elaborated by stereotypical knowledges, racial theories, administrative colonial experiences, and on that basis institutionalize a range of political and cultural ideologies that are prejudicial, discriminatory, vestigial, archaic, 'mythical,' and crucially are recognized as being so. By 'knowing' the native population in these terms, discriminatory and authoritarian forms of political control are considered appropriate. The colonized population is then deemed to be both the cause and effect of the system, imprisoned in the circle of interpretation. What is visible is the *necessity* of such rule which is justified by those moralistic and normative ideologies of amelioration recognized as the Civilizing Mission or the White Man's Burden. However, there coexist within the same apparatus of colonial power, modern systems and sciences of government, progressive Western forms of social and economic organization which provide the manifest justification for the project of colonialism. . . . It is on the site of this coexistence that strategies of hierarchization and marginalization are employed in the management of colonial societies" (83).

19. *Documents,* 1–2.

20. James Thomas Flexner's four-volume biography remains as one of the definitive works on Washington's life as the first Great American Hero. Volume 1, *George Washington: The Forge of Experience: 1732–1775* (1965), and volume 2, *George Washington in the American Revolution, 1775–1783,* detail Washington's Indian-fighting days. In the campaign against the English-allied Iroquois tribes during the Revolutionary War, he ordered the destruction of all food supplies and the burning of entire villages occupied by Iroquois women, children, and elderly, whom he hoped to take as prisoners. Washington's military orders to General John Sullivan, assigned to lead the expedition against the Iroquois into the Finger Lakes region of New York, were quite direct and unambiguous: "The immediate objects are the total destruction and devastation of their settlements, and the capture of as many prisoners of every age and sex as possible" (quoted in Flexner, *George Washington in the American Revolution, 1775–1783,* 350). See also Mohr, *Federal Indian Relations,* 79–84, describing the bloody warfare and civilian casualties on both sides of the conflict.

21. *Documents,* 2.

22. Washington's boundary-line policy did have the practical effect of recognizing a theoretical form of Indian "sovereignty" over the lands surrendered by treaty by the tribes of the Western Country. But recognizing a limited degree of tribal sovereign authority to sell land had long been a part of colonizing

practice in North America. This convenient principle of colonial governmentality was a widely practiced means of validating European titles to land in the New World, and the Founders' will to empire in North America had no problem in accepting the practice of negotiating treaties with tribes in order to serve the colonizing interests of the United States. See Getches, Wilkinson, and Williams, *Federal Indian Law*, 40–93.

23. See Robert A. Williams, Jr., *The American Indian in Western Legal Thought: The Discourses of Conquest* (New York: Oxford University Press, 1990), 118–308 (discussing sixteenth- through eighteenth-century Anglo-American confrontations with tribes of eastern North America). President Washington's secretary of war, Henry Knox, was speaking a familiar language of savagery in his 1789 report to Congress, which essentially reprised Washington's policy paradigm of "the Savage as the Wolf" and the inevitability of Indian tribalism's disappearance from the lands then part of the United States: "As population shall increase and approach the Indian boundaries, game will be diminished and new purchases may be made for small considerations. This has been and probably will be the inevitable consequence of cultivation. It is, however, painful to consider that all the Indian tribes, once existing in those states now the best cultivated and most populous, have become extinct. If the same causes continue, the effects will happen and, in a short period the idea of an Indian this side of the Mississippi will be found only in the pages of the historian" (Mohr, *Federal Indian Relations*, 171).

24. See Prucha, *American Indian Treaties*, 42, 44.

25. Article I, section 8, clause 3 of the Constitution grants Congress the power "to regulate commerce with foreign nations, and among the several States, and with the Indian tribes."

4. Indian Rights and the Marshall Court

1. See generally Henry Nash Smith, *Virgin Land: The American West as Symbol and Myth* (1950; repr., Cambridge, Mass.: Harvard University Press, 1970), 3–12; J. G. A. Pocock, *The Machiavellian Moment: Florentine Political Thought and the Atlantic Republican Tradition* (Princeton: Princeton University Press, 1975), 506–33.

2. See e.g., Robert A. Williams, Jr., "Documents of Barbarism: The Contemporary Legacy of European Racism and Colonialism in the Narrative Traditions of Federal Indian Law," *Arizona Law Review* 31 (1989): 237–78.

3. The sources relied upon by the Founders in developing this language of racism are analyzed in the forthcoming companion volume to this present book, *"The Savage as the Wolf": Indian Rights, the Western Colonial Imagination, and the Founders First Indian Policy*. Sources that I found particularly

useful in understanding the genealogy of the Founders' language of Indian savagery include Ronald K. Meek, *Social Science and the Ignoble Savage* (Cambridge and New York: Cambridge University Press, 1976); Edward P. Dudley and Maximillian Novak, eds., *The Wild Man Within: An Image in Western Thought from the Renaissance to Romanticism* (Pittsburgh, Pa.: University of Pittsburgh Press, 1972); Arthur O. Lovejoy and George Boas, *Primitivism and Related Ideas in Antiquity* (Baltimore: The Johns Hopkins University Press, 1935); Richard Gummere, *The American Colonial Mind and the Classical Tradition* (Cambridge, Mass.: Harvard University Press, 1963); Harry Levin, *The Myth of the Golden Age in the Renaissance* (Bloomington: Indiana University Press, 1969); Arthur O. Lovejoy, *The Great Chain of Being: A Study in the History of an Idea* (Cambridge, Mass.: Harvard University Press, 1936); Peter Gay, *The Enlightenment: An Interpretation/The Rise of Modern Paganism* (New York: Knopf, 1966); Richard Slotkin, *Regeneration through Violence: The Mythology of the American Frontier, 1600–1860* (Middletown, Conn.: Wesleyan University Press, 1973); Ronald Sanders, *Lost Tribes and Promised Lands: The Origins of American Racism* (Boston: Little, Brown, 1978).

4. Roy Harvey Pearce, *The Savages of America: A Study in the Idea of Civilization,* rev. ed. (Baltimore: The Johns Hopkins University Press, 1965), 73.

5. Tzvetan Todorov, *The Conquest of America: The Question of the Other,* trans. Richard Howard (Norman: University of Oklahoma Press, 1999), 42.

6. The creation of the pro-slavery constitution of 1787, which followed hard upon the heels of the adoption of Washington's "Savage as the Wolf" Indian policy by Congress, was the next, formal step taken by the Founders in defining a white racial identity for the United States at its birth. See generally Juan F. Perea, Richard Delgado, Angela Harris, and Stephanie M. Wildman, *Race and Races: Cases and Resources for a Diverse America* (St. Paul, Minn.: West Group, 2000), 103–5.

7. *Johnson v. McIntosh,* 21 U.S. 543 (1823); *Cherokee Nation v. Georgia,* 30 U.S. 1 (1831); *Worcester v. Georgia,* 31 U.S. 515 (1832).

8. See Homi K. Bhabha, "Signs Taken for Wonders: Questions of Ambivalence and Authority under a Tree outside Delhi, May 1817," in *The Location of Culture* (London and New York: Routledge, 1994), 102. See also Robert A. Williams, Jr., "The White Man's Indian Law: What's the Problem?" *Ayaangwaamizin: The International Journal of Indigenous Philosophy* 2 (1998–1999): 3, 2–16.

9. Bhabha, "Signs Taken for Wonders," 102.

10. Ibid.

11. Marshall's response to an 1828 address made by his close friend and colleague on the Court, Justice Joseph Story, suggests that Marshall himself was keenly aware of the Indian's essential fate as perpetual colonial subject

under U.S. control. In his speech commemorating the first settlement of Salem, Massachusetts, Story had clearly laid out Indians' inability to assimilate within U.S. society, so long as "their race" maintained its essential savage identity. By "their very nature and character," Story pronounced, "they neither unite themselves with civil institutions, nor can [they] with safety be allowed to remain as distinct communities." Their "ferocious passions," "independent spirit," and "wandering life" confronted the United States with the challenge and question of "whether the country itself shall be abandoned by civilized man, or maintained by his sword as the right of the strongest." Quoted in G. Edward White, *The Marshall Court and Cultural Change: 1815–35,* The Oliver Wendell Holmes Devise History of the Supreme Court, vols. 3–4 (New York: Macmillan, 1988), 712–13.

When Story sent a copy of his address to Marshall, the chief justice read it carefully, then responded with his own personal views on the "Indian question": "I have been still more touched with your notice of the red man than of the white. The conduct of our forefathers in expelling the original occupants of the soil grew out of so many mixed motives that any censure which philanthropy may bestow upon it ought to be qualified. The Indians were a fierce and dangerous enemy whose love of war made them sometimes the aggressors, whose numbers and habits made them formidable, and whose cruel system of warfare seemed to justify every endeavor to remove them to a distance from civilized settlements. It was not until the adoption of our present government that respect for our own safety permitted us to give full indulgence to those principles of humanity and justice which ought always to govern our conduct towards the aborigines when this course can be pursued without exposing ourselves to the most afflicting calamities. That time, however, is unquestionably arrived, and every oppression now exercised on a helpless people depending on our magnanimity and justice for the preservation of character. I often think with indignation on our disreputable conduct (as I think) in the affairs of the Cherokees in Georgia" (quoted in ibid., 712–13).

12. Bhabha, "Signs Taken for Wonders," 102.

13. My Indian law casebook coauthors and I are as guilty of this sin of quasi deification of Marshall's three famous opinions as anyone. See, e.g., David H. Getches, Charles F. Wilkinson, and Robert A. Williams, Jr., *Federal Indian Law: Cases and Materials,* 5th ed. (St. Paul, Minn.: West Group, 2004) (hereinafter *Federal Indian Law*), 257 ("The Marshall trilogy of early Indian law decisions, *Johnson v. McIntosh, Cherokee Nation v. Georgia,* and *Worcester v. Georgia,* provide foundational principles for guiding the deliberations of Congress and the decisions of courts on the nature of federal powers over tribes, Indian self-government, issues of jurisdiction in Indian country, and the special rights of tribal Indians as groups"). See also Charles F. Wilkinson,

American Indians, Time, and the Law: Native Societies in a Modern Constitutional Democracy (New Haven: Yale University Press, 1987), 24 ("In the Marshall Trilogy, Chief Justice John Marshall conceived a model that can be described broadly as calling for largely autonomous tribal governments subject to an overriding federal authority but essentially free of federal control"). David Getches, Introduction, "Conquering the Cultural Frontier: The New Subjectivism of the Supreme Court in Indian Law," *California Law Review* 84 (1996): 1577 ("The foundation principles [of the Supreme Court's Indian Law] . . . trace back to three landmark opinions of Chief Justice John Marshall, *Johnson v. McIntosh, Cherokee Nation v. Georgia,* and *Worcester v. Georgia,* the 'Marshall Trilogy'"). Williams, "The White Man's Indian Law," 12 (referring to the "Marshall Trilogy"). But we're not alone. See Robert N. Clinton, Carole E. Goldberg, and Rebecca Tsosie, *American Indian Law: Native Nations and the Federal System, Cases and Materials,* 4th ed. (Newark, N.J.: LexisNexis, 2004), 99 (referring to the Marshall Trilogy).

14. On Marshall's incorporation of the doctrine into the Supreme Court's Indian law in *Johnson v. McIntosh* and its directing influence on indigenous peoples' rights throughout the regions of the world conquered and colonized by other English-speaking Western settler states, see Robert A. Williams, Jr., *The American Indian in Western Legal Thought: The Discourses of Conquest* (New York: Oxford University Press, 1990), 288–317.

15. *Johnson v. McIntosh,* 573.

16. Ibid., 572–73.

17. Ibid., 573.

18. Ibid., 587.

19. Emmerich de Vattel (1714–1769), whose 1758 treatise *Le droit des gens; ou Principes de la loi naturelle* (The Law of Nations; or, The Principles of Natural Law) exercised a profound influence on the Founders' thought on international law and relations, laid out the argument derived from "natural law" justifying Europeans' rights to conquest over tribally occupied lands in the New World by citing the American Indian's inferior and inefficient savage hunter-gatherer state: "The whole earth is destined to furnish sustenance for its inhabitants; but it can not do this unless it be cultivated. Every nation is therefore bound by natural law to cultivate the land which has fallen to its share, and it has no right to extend its boundaries or to obtain help from other nations except insofar as the land it inhabits can not supply its needs. . . . Those who still pursue this idle [i.e., hunting] mode of life occupy more land than they would have need of under a system of honest labor, and they may not complain if other more industrious nations, too confined at home, should come and occupy part of their lands. Thus, while the conquest of the civilized Empires of Peru and Mexico was a notorious usurpation, the establishment of various colonies upon

the continent of North America, might, if done within just limits, have been entirely lawful. The peoples of those vast tracts of land rather roamed over them than inhabited them." Emmerich de Vattel, *Le droit des gens; ou Principes de la loi naturelle, appliqués à la conduite et aux affaires des nations et des souverains,* with an introduction by Albert de Lapradelle, vol. 3, *The Law of Nations; or, The Principles of Natural Law Applied to the Conduct and to the Affairs of Nations and of Sovereigns,* trans. Charles G. Fenwick, with an introduction by Albert de Lapradelle (Washington, D.C.: Carnegie Institution of Washington, 1916), 37–38.

20. *Johnson v. McIntosh,* 587.

21. Ibid., 590.

22. Ibid., 589.

23. Ibid., 590.

24. Ibid., 590–91.

25. Ibid., 591.

26. Ibid., 592.

27. Ibid., 588.

28. See the conclusion for a discussion of the contemporary human rights standards applicable to indigenous tribal peoples.

29. See S. James Anaya and Robert A. Williams, Jr., "The Protection of Indigenous Peoples' Rights over Lands and Natural Resources under the Inter-American Human Rights System," *Harvard Human Rights Journal* 14 (2001): 33–86; Note, "International Law as an Interpretive Force in Federal Indian Law," *Harvard Law Review* 116 (2003): 1759–60; Siegfried Wiessner, "Rights and Status of Indigenous Peoples: A Global Comparative and International Legal Analysis," *Harvard Human Rights Journal* 12 (1999): 57–128.

30. *Johnson v. McIntosh,* 590.

31. That's what the Supreme Court's 1955 opinion in *Tee-Hit-Ton v. United States,* 348 U.S. 272, 279 (1955) called the case. See chapter 6.

32. A fifth element, the reliance by Marshall on the European Law of Nations—that is, the international law norms of his time, used by the West to define the rights and status of American Indian tribes—also plays an important role in Marshall's decision in *Johnson,* as it does in the other cases of the Marshall Trilogy. But this fifth element, as I identify it, becomes quickly neglected in its application as a part of the Marshall Model of Indian Rights by later nineteenth-century Supreme Court Indian law decisions. As tribes come under the total control and domination of the expanding U.S. system of colonial governmentality on the reservation in the latter half of the nineteenth century, the Court comes to view tribal assimilation as a matter of exclusive concern under the sovereign's positive domestic law, enforced by the plenary power of Congress in Indian affairs. Much as in other areas of the law, the Marshall

Court's use of the international law principles of its day to decide important questions of minority rights under the Constitution falls into desuetude. In the conclusion to this book I reintegrate this missing fifth element of the Marshall model into an analysis of Indian rights that seeks to harmonize today's Supreme Court's Indian law decisions with present-day international human rights norms respecting indigenous peoples.

33. See generally William G. McLoughlin, *Cherokees and Missionaries: 1789–1839* (Norman: University of Oklahoma Press, 1995), 186–91. Gerard N. Magliocca, "The Cherokee Removal and the Fourteenth Amendment," *Duke Law Journal* 53 (2003): 875, provides an excellent treatment of the *Cherokee* cases and their relation to the growth of the abolitionist movement and to the passage of the Constitution's Fourteenth Amendment following the Civil War.

34. See *Federal Indian Law,* 95–126.

35. See Magliocca, "The Cherokee Removal and the Fourteenth Amendment," 883. There are numerous sources on the *Cherokee* cases, but the best account focusing on Marshall's central judicial role in the controversy is White, *The Marshall Court and Cultural Change: 1815–35,* 711–40.

36. Ch. 148, 4 Stat. 411–12.

37. See *Federal Indian Law,* 99.

38. As every student in constitutional law learns, Marshall adopted the same deferential approach of deciding whether the Court had jurisdiction over the case under the Constitution's grant of judicial power in *Marbury v. Madison,* 1 Cranch 137 (1803).

39. *Cherokee Nation v. Georgia,* 17.

40. Ibid., 16, 18, 17.

41. See materials collected in *Federal Indian Law,* 340–76.

42. *Cherokee Nation v. Georgia,* 20, 15.

43. Rennard Strickland, "Genocide-at-Law: An Historic and Contemporary View of the Native American Experience," *University of Kansas Law Review* 34 (1986): 713–55.

44. *Cherokee Nation v. Georgia,* 17–18.

45. Ibid., 18.

46. Ibid., 20.

47. See, e.g., *United States v. White Mountain Apache Tribe,* 537 U.S. 465, 475n3 (2003); *Alaska v. Native Village of Venetie Tribal Government,* 522 U.S. 520, 531 (1998); *Oklahoma Tax Com'n v. Citizen Band Potawatomi Indian Tribe of Oklahoma,* 498 U.S. 525, 509 (1991); *Brendale v. Confederated Tribes and Bands of Yakima Indian Nation,* 492 U.S. 408, 451 (1989); *Merrion v. Jicarilla Apache Tribe,* 455 U.S. 130, 1370 (1982); *Oliphant v. Suquamish Indian Tribe,* 435 U.S. 191, 208 (1978).

48. *Johnson v. McIntosh,* 587. See *Federal Indian Law,* 111–23.

49. *Worcester v. Georgia,* 543.

50. Ibid., 543–44 (quoting *Johnson v. McIntosh,* 573).

51. *Worcester v. Georgia,* 543.

52. Michel Foucault, "Two Lectures," in *Power/Knowledge: Selected Interviews and Other Writings, 1972–1977,* ed. and trans. Colin Gordon (New York: Pantheon Books, 1980): "[P]ower is war, a war continued by other means. This reversal of Clausewitz's assertion that war is politics continued by other means . . . implies that relations of power that function in a society such as ours essentially rest upon a definite relation of forces that is established at a determinate, historically specifiable moment, in war and by war. Furthermore, if it is true that political power puts an end to war, that it installs, or tries to install, the reign of peace in civil society, this by no means implies that it suspends the effects of war or neutralizes the disequilibrium revealed in the final battle. The role of political power, on this hypothesis, is perpetually to reinscribe this relation through a form of unspoken warfare; to reinscribe it in social institutions, in economic inequalities, in language, in the bodies themselves of each and every one of us" (90).

53. "The Cherokee Nation then, is a distinct community occupying its own territory, with boundaries accurately described, in which the laws of Georgia can have no force" (*Worcester v. Georgia,* 561).

54. See *Federal Indian Law,* 121–24.

55. "It is the *Worcester* case of which President Jackson purportedly said, 'John Marshall has made his decision; now let him enforce it.' Though the historians seem to agree that Jackson probably held such thoughts, the statement itself may be apocryphal. The only first-hand report of such a statement is by Horace Greeley." *Federal Indian Law,* 122 (citing Horace Greeley, *The American Conflict* [Hartford, Conn.: O. D. Case, 1864], 106).

56. See Eric Kades, "The Dark Side of Efficiency: *Johnson v. McIntosh* and the Expropriation of American Indian Lands," *University of Pennsylvania Law Review* 148 (2000): 1065–1190.

57. Many of the advocates of forcible removal of tribes to the west beyond the Mississippi viewed *Johnson v. McIntosh* as upholding states' rights to unilaterally extinguish at will the Indians' mere right of occupancy under the doctrine of discovery. See Joseph C. Burke, "The *Cherokee* Cases: A Study in Law, Politics, and Morality," *Stanford Law Review* 21 (1969): 500–531. Marshall let his own strong feelings of "indignation" be known on the "disreputable conduct" of Georgia in a letter to his colleague on the Court, Justice Joseph Story, written prior to his opinions in the *Cherokee* cases. See White, *The Marshall Court and Cultural Change: 1815–35,* 712–13.

58. *Worcester v. Georgia,* 547.

59. Ibid., 547, 544–45.

60. As Marshall himself had conceded in *Johnson v. McIntosh*, 588, the often-conflicting European claims to territory in the New World asserted under the doctrine had to be resolved by "the sword." From a historical perspective, the doctrine oftentimes functioned quite poorly as a tool of colonial governmentality and the European Law of Nations. See Williams, *The American Indian Western Legal Thought*, 121–85.

61. *Worcester v. Georgia*, 546, 553.

62. Quoted in Williams, *The American Indian in Western Legal Thought*, 201.

63. *Worcester v. Georgia*, 546.

64. Ibid., 545.

65. Ibid., 546, 547.

66. Williams, *The American Indian in Western Legal Thought*, 193–221.

67. *Worcester v. Georgia*, 558.

68. Ibid., 557.

69. See *Federal Indian Law*, 123–24.

70. As the Supreme Court itself would note in *United States v. Kagama*, 118 U.S. 375 (1886): "Because of the local ill feeling, the people of the States where they are found are often their deadliest enemies" (384). See Robert A. Williams, Jr., "'The People of the States Where They Are Found Are Often Their Deadliest Enemies': The Indian Side of the Story of Indian Rights and Federalism," *Arizona Law Review* 38 (1996): 981–97. To the extent that *Worcester's* principles as part of the Marshall Model of Indian Rights can be used to protect Indian tribes from state jurisdictional encroachment, its precedent on this point is certainly worth preserving, developing, and extending as part of our Indian law. It is worth noting, for instance, that the protective fiduciary-type principles that Marshall developed in *Worcester* as part of his model are in basic accord with contemporary international human rights norms respecting state responsibility for the protection of indigenous peoples' human rights. See the conclusion. Significantly, Marshall relied directly on his era's version of international law, the European Law of Nations, in defining this protective role: "[T]he settled doctrine of the law of nations is, that a weaker power does not surrender its independence—its right to self-government, by associating with a stronger, and taking its protection. A weak state, in order to provide for its safety, may place itself under the protection of one more powerful, without stripping itself of the right of government, and ceasing to be a state" (*Worcester v. Georgia*, 561). Marshall went on to cite Emmerich de Vattel, regarded as one of the leading international law theorists of the period (see note 19 above) for support of this fifth element of his model of Indian rights. As I discuss at length in the conclusion, subsequent courts have neglected this fifth element in their application of the Marshall model.

71. The fifth element of the Marshall model, the judicial reliance on international law of the time in defining Indian rights and status, which subsequent Court decisions neglected to include in their adoption of Marshall's precedents, is discussed in the conclusion to this book.

5. The Rise of the Plenary Power Doctrine

1. See David H. Getches, Charles F. Wilkinson, and Robert A. Williams, Jr., *Federal Indian Law: Cases and Materials,* 5th ed. (St. Paul, Minn.: West Group, 2004), 153–65 (hereinafter *Federal Indian Law*).

2. *Dred Scott v. Sanford,* 60 U.S. 393, 403–4 (1856).

3. *United States v. Rogers,* 45 U.S. 567 (1846).

4. See *Federal Indian Law,* 153–65.

5. Rogers was prosecuted under section 25, Act Cong., June 30, 1834.

6. *United States v. Rogers,* 572.

7. Ibid.

8. Ibid. As was sometimes the convention in nineteenth-century Supreme Court opinions, Taney neglected to provide a formal citation to support his statement of legal principle. In this instance, he could only be referring to the precedents established by the Marshall Trilogy.

9. Ibid.

10. Significantly, Taney does not turn to the international law principles of his day for guidance in defining Indian rights according to his interpretation of the Marshall model, treating the case as one governed solely by the domestic laws of the United States. *Rogers* would be the first significant instance in a long line of subsequent Supreme Court decisions in which a justice ignored this fifth element of the Marshall Model of Indian Rights. See the conclusion.

11. *United States v. Rogers,* 572.

12. Ibid.

13. Ibid.

14. Indians were not made citizens by birth in the United States until the Citizenship Act of 1921, 8 U.S.C. sec. 1401(b).

15. *Ex parte Crow Dog,* 109 U.S. 556 (1883); *United States v. Kagama,* 118 U.S. 375 (1886).

16. See Sidney L. Harring, *Crow Dog's Case: American Indian Sovereignty, Tribal Law, and United States Law in the Nineteenth Century* (Cambridge and New York: Cambridge University Press, 1994): 101. Harring has called the case an important "bridge between the ambiguous and ineffective sovereignty language of *Worcester* and the complete subjugation of tribal sovereignty" (100–101) under the congressional plenary power doctrine developed by the Court during the late nineteenth century.

17. See ibid., 100–141.

18. On tribal common law, see *Federal Indian Law,* 449–51.

19. See Harring, *Crow Dog's Case,* 1.

20. *Ex parte Crow Dog,* 556, 566, 567.

21. Ibid., 557.

22. Ibid., 568–69.

23. Ibid., 569–70.

24. See, e.g., Charles Wilkinson, *American Indians, Time, and the Law: Native Societies in a Modern Constitutional Democracy* (New Haven: Yale University Press, 1987), 56.

25. *Ex parte Crow Dog,* 571.

26. See *Federal Indian Law,* 157–58.

27. See Harring, *Crow Dog's Case,* 134–74, 132–41.

28. *United States v. Kagama,* 378–79.

29. *Kagama* was written at the height of the Court's *Lochner* era, when the justices routinely applied substantive due process analysis to a broad array of legislative initiatives, including those that were enacted under Congress's commerce clause power. This form of judicial review was often fatal to such legislation. See Laurence Tribe, *American Constitutional Law,* 3rd ed. (New York: Foundation Press, 2000), 807–11.

30. On constitutional transformations achieved outside the normal amendment processes of the Constitution's Article V, see Bruce Ackerman, *We the People* (Cambridge, Mass.: Belknap Press of Harvard University Press, 1991).

31. Like *Rogers* and *Crow Dog, Kagama* does not draw on the fifth element of the Marshall model, the use of contemporary international law as guidance in defining Indian rights.

32. *United States v. Kagama,* 381.

33. Ibid., 380–82.

34. Ibid., 383–84.

35. Harring, *Crow Dog's Case,* 142. Indian law scholars typically point to the Supreme Court's landmark decision in *Lone Wolf v. Hitchcock,* 187 U.S. 553 (1903), as the final consummation of the development of the congressional plenary power doctrine. In that case involving the treaty rights of the confederated tribes of Kiowas, Comanches, and Apaches of Oklahoma, the Court, citing and quoting *Kagama* and other leading Marshall model cases, held that Congress could unilaterally abrogate an Indian treaty under U.S. law, and there was nothing the Supreme Court could do about it: "Plenary authority over the tribal relations of the Indians has been exercised by Congress from the beginning, and the power has always been deemed a political one, not subject to be controlled by the judicial department of the government. Until the year 1871 the policy was pursued of dealing with the Indian tribes by means of treaties,

and, of course, a moral obligation rested upon Congress to act in good faith in performing the stipulations entered into on its behalf. But as with treaties made with foreign nations (Chinese Exclusion Case, 130 U.S. 581, 600), the legislative power might pass laws in conflict with treaties made with Indians.

"The power exists to abrogate the provisions of an Indian treaty, though presumably such power will be exercised only when circumstances arise which not only justify the government in disregarding the stipulations of the treaty, but may demand, in the interest of the country and the Indians themselves, that it should do so. When, therefore, treaties were entered into between the United States and a tribe of Indians it was never doubted that the *power* to abrogate existed in Congress, and that in a contingency such power might be availed of from considerations of governmental policy" (*Lone Wolf v. Hitchcock,* 565–66).

III. The Twentieth-Century Post-*Brown* Supreme Court and Indian Rights

1. See, e.g., Derrick A. Bell, Jr., "*Brown v. Board of Education* and the Interest-Convergence Dilemma," *Harvard Law Review* 93 (1980): 518: "In 1954, the Supreme Court handed down the landmark decision *Brown v. Board of Education,* in which the Court ordered the end of state-mandated racial segregation of public schools. Now, more than twenty-five years after that dramatic decision, it is clear that *Brown* will not be forgotten. It has triggered a revolution in civil rights law and in the political leverage available to blacks in and out of court. As Judge Robert L. Carter put it, *Brown* transformed blacks from beggars pleading for decent treatment to citizens demanding equal treatment under the law as their constitutionally recognized right."

2. See Homi K. Bhabha, "The Other Question: Stereotype, Discrimination and the Discourse of Colonialism," in *The Location of Culture* (London and New York: Routledge, 1994), 70. According to Bhabha, the "difference of colonial discourse as an apparatus of power," at a minimum, "turns on the recognition and disavowal of racial/cultural/historical differences" (70).

6. What "Every American Schoolboy Knows"

1. *Tee-Hit-Ton v. United States,* 348 U.S. 272 (1955).

2. The United States, in other words, had never negotiated a treaty or passed legislation recognizing and acquiring the Tee-Hit-Tons' occupancy, or "aboriginal title," rights in their traditional lands. See David H. Getches, Charles F. Wilkinson, and Robert A. Williams, Jr., *Federal Indian Law: Cases and Materials,* 5th ed. (St. Paul, Minn.: West Group, 2004), 91–93 (hereinafter *Federal Indian Law*).

3. This was the Justice Department's own estimate of what it would cost the United States to compensate similar aboriginal property rights claims before the Indian Claims Commission, a 1950s-era congressionally established tribunal designed to extinguish and provide compensation for various forms of Indian rights claims. See *Tee-Hit-Ton v. United States*, 283n17.

4. *Tee-Hit-Ton v. United States*, 289, 279.

5. Ibid., 237.

6. See Donald Craig Mitchell, *Sold America: The Story of Alaska Natives and Their Land, 1867–1959* (Hanover, N.H.: University Press of New England, 2003), 26–28; *Federal Indian Law*, 894–95.

7. See *Federal Indian Law*, 894–95.

8. 61 Stat. 920 sec. 2(a).

9. *Tee-Hit-Ton v. United States*, 275, 272.

10. Ibid., 282–83, 283n17. See *Miller v. United States*, 159 F.2d 997 (9th Cir. 1947). The government's lawyers had challenged *Miller* in a brief filed in another Alaska case involving "unrecognized Indian title," *United States v. Alcea Band of Tillamooks*, 341 U.S. 48 (1951). It was this brief that formed the basis for the $9 billion figure cited by Reed in note 17 in *Tee-Hit-Ton*. The charge has been made, however, that the Justice Department attorneys "cooked the books" in the second *Tillamook* case. See, e.g., Mitchell, *Sold America*: "In an appendix to the brief it filed in *Alcea Band of Tillamooks*, the Department of Justice represented to the U.S. Supreme Court that if the Indian Claims Commission determined that all claims of Indian tribes pending before the Commission were valid, the United States would be obligated to pay $1 billion as compensation for the unlawful abrogation of the tribes' aboriginal titles. But if aboriginal title was Fifth Amendment 'private property,' the United States would be required to pay the tribes an additional $8 billion in interest. Brief for Petitioner at 55–56, *United States v. Alcea Band of Tillamooks*, 341 U.S. 48 (1951). In fact, the U.S. liability for Indians Claims Commission judgments was slightly less than $150 million. If the United States had been required to pay interest on the judgments, the total interest payment would have been slightly more than $1 billion" (403). See also Nell Jessup Newton, "At the Whim of the Sovereign: Aboriginal Title Reconsidered," *Hastings Law Journal* 31 (1990): 1215–85.

11. See, e.g., Newton, "At the Whim of the Sovereign."

12. Significantly, despite the Cold War imperatives of the Court's *Brown* decision (see the introduction, note 60), the neglected fifth element of the original Marshall model, the use of contemporary international law to define Indian rights and status, did not enter into the *Tee-Hit-Ton* Court's analysis.

13. Justice William O. Douglas, who dissented in *Tee-Hit-Ton*, would later describe the "socially conservative Kentuckian," Justice Stanley Reed, as "one of

the most reactionary judges to occupy the bench in my time." William O. Douglas, *The Court Years: 1939 to 1975* (New York: Vintage Books, 1980), 21.

14. *Tee-Hit-Ton v. United States,* 279.

15. Ibid., 279–80, quoting *Johnson v. McIntosh,* 543, 587 (1823).

16. *Tee-Hit-Ton v. United States,* 285.

17. Ibid., 287–88.

18. Ibid., 289–90.

19. Ibid., 290–91.

20. Derrick A. Bell, Jr., "*Brown v. Board of Education* and the Interest-Convergence Dilemma," *Harvard Law Review* 93 (1980): 518.

21. Robert Cover, "*Nomos* and Narrative," *Harvard Law Review* 97 (1983): 53. Cover goes on to say, "Confrontation, on the other hand, challenges the judge's implicit claim to authoritative interpretation" (53). On confrontation as a strategy in attacking the justices' use of negative stereotypes in their opinions on Indian rights, see the conclusion.

7. Rehnquist's Language of Racism in *Oliphant*

1. *Oliphant v. Suquamish Indian Tribe,* 435 U.S. 191 (1978).

2. Ibid., 195.

3. Ibid., 209.

4. Ibid.

5. Ibid. (ellipses and brackets supplied in the opinion).

6. Ibid., 209, 210, 212.

7. Ibid., 210.

8. Ibid.

9. Ibid., 206.

10. Ibid., 196–97.

11. Ibid., 197, quoting H.R. Report No. 474, 23rd Cong., 1st sess., 91 (1834). Herring served the Jackson administration as the first commissioner of Indian affairs under a reorganized BIA within the War Department from 1832 through 1836. In his first official report to his immediate supervisor, Jackson's secretary of war, Lewis Cass, Herring fully elaborated his views on the racial inferiority of Indians: "On the whole, it may be matter of serious doubt whether, even with the fostering care and assured protection of the United States, the preservation and perpetuity of the Indian race are at all attainable, under the form of government and rude civil regulations subsisting among them. These were perhaps well enough suited to their condition, when hunting was their only employment, and war gave birth to their strongest excitements. The unrestrained authority of their chiefs, and the irresponsible exercise of power, are of the simplest elements of despotic rule; while the absence of the *meum* and *tuum*

in the general community of possessions, which is the grand conservative principle of the social state, is a perpetual operating cause of the *vis inertiae* of savage life. The stimulus of physical exertion and intellectual exercise, contained in this powerful principle, of which the Indian is almost entirely void, may not unjustly be considered the parent of all improvements, not merely in the arts, but in the profitable direction of labor among civilized nations. Among them it is the source of plenty; with the Indians, the absence of it is the cause of want, and consequently of decrease of numbers. Nor can proper notions of the social system be successfully inculcated, nor its benefits be rightly appreciated, so as to overcome the habits and prejudices incident to savage birth, and consequent associations of maturer years, except by the institution of separate and secure rights in the relations of property and person. It is therefore suggested, whether the formation of a code of laws on this basis, to be submitted for their adoption, together with certain modifications of the existing political system among them, may not be of very salutary effect, especially as co-operating with the influences, derivable from the education of their youth, and the introduction of the doctrines of the Christian religion; all centering in one grand object—the substitution of the social for the savage state." Indian Commissioner Herring on the Indian Race, "Extract from the *Annual Report of the Commissioner of Indian Affairs,* November 22, 1832," in *Documents of United States Indian Policy,* ed. Frances Paul Prucha, 2nd ed. (Lincoln: University of Nebraska Press, 1990), 63.

12. *Oliphant v. Suquamish Indian Tribe,* 201, 202.

13. Ibid., 202.

14. Ibid., 210–11.

15. The fourteen cases Rehnquist cited that were issued by the Supreme Court from 1810 to 1916 include *United States v. Nice,* 36 S. Ct. 696 (1916); *United States v. Detroit Timber and Lumber Co.,* 26 S. Ct. 282 (1906); *Morris v. Hitchcock,* 24 S. Ct. 712 (1904); *Draper v. United States,* 17 S. Ct. 107 (1896); *Talton v. Mayes,* 16 S. Ct. 986 (1896); *Ex parte Mayfield,* 11 S. Ct. 939 (1891); *United States v. Kagama,* 118 U.S. 375 (1886); *Ex parte Kan-gi-shun-ca,* 3 S. Ct. 396 (1883); *In re Kansas Indians,* 72 U.S. 737 (1866); *United States v. Rogers,* 45 U.S. 567 (1846); *Worcester v. Georgia,* 31 U.S. 515 (1832); *Cherokee Nation v. Georgia,* 30 U.S. 1 (1831); *Johnson v. McIntosh,* 21 U.S. 543 (1823); *Fletcher v. Peck,* 6 Cranch 87 (U.S. 1810).

16. *DeCoteau v. District County Court,* 420 U.S. 425, 444 (1975); *Morton v. Mancari,* 417 U.S. 535, 554 (1974); *McClanahan v. Arizona State Tax Comm'n,* 411 U.S. 164, 174 (1973).

17. *Oliphant v. Suquamish Indian Tribe,* 204.

18. Ibid.

19. Ibid., 208–9.

20. See Pierre Schlag, "Clerks in the Maze," *Michigan Law Review* 91 (1993): 2053.

21. *Oliphant v. Suquamish Indian Tribe*, 209 (quoting *Johnson v. McIntosh*, 574) and 208–9 (quoting *Cherokee Nation v. Georgia*, 5 Pet. 1, 15, 17-18, 8 L.Ed. 25 [1831]).

22. *Oliphant v. Suquamish Indian Tribe*, 209. *Oliphant*'s curiously edited quote of *Johnson* represents an early and striking example of Rehnquist's frequently noted problematic uses of precedent generally as a justice of the Supreme Court. See, e.g., Jim Chen, "Come Back to the Nickel and Five: Tracing the Warren Court's Pursuit of Equal Justice under Law," *Washington and Lee Law Review* 59 (2002): 1203–1307 (noting that the Court, as led by Chief Justice Rehnquist, has adopted an "emerging strategy of paying homage to precedent before proceeding to ignore or eviscerate it," 1284); David H. Getches, "Beyond Indian Law: The Rehnquist Court's Pursuit of States' Rights, Color-Blind Justice, and Mainstream Values," *Minnesota Law Review* 86 (2001): 267–362 (examining how the Rehnquist Court "regularly forges new rules and rarely cites or is encumbered by established precedent" [301] in its Indian law cases). In *Johnson v. McIntosh*, 574, Marshall had originally stated that the tribes' "rights to complete sovereignty, as independent nations, *were* necessarily diminished" (emphasis added). Rehnquist's majority opinion in *Oliphant* changes Marshall's verb "were" to "[are]" (see *Oliphant v. Suquamish Indian Tribe*, 209) without any explanation or reason given for this substantive change of verb tense. Rehnquist's sly change of verb tense can be fairly said to represent a significant misquoting of Marshall's original language. Marshall was referring in this sentence only to the two specific tribal powers that "were necessarily diminished" as a result of the doctrine of discovery: the power of tribes to dispose of their lands to whomsoever the Indians pleased, and the power of tribes to enter into foreign alliances with any other European nation besides the first discoverer. See *Johnson v. McIntosh*, 574. All subsequent limitations on tribal rights and sovereignty, including the ultimate and exclusive right "to extinguish the Indian title of occupancy," as Marshall expressly stated in *Johnson*, were to be obtained by "purchase or by conquest" (ibid., 587). The doctrine's effects, in other words, operated only in the past, at the point of discovery, and those effects were quite limited. The doctrine, as Marshall's original language in *Johnson* clearly establishes, does not continue to affect the present rights and sovereignty of Indian tribes protected under U.S. law, beyond the rights necessarily divested under the doctrine. These "were" the rights to alienate their land without Congress's permission and the right to enter into alliances with foreign nations. All the other inherent tribal rights that survived operation of the doctrine at the point of discovery, as *Johnson* makes clear, can only be diminished or extinguished subsequent to discovery by purchase or conquest,

i.e., by the exercise of congressional plenary power, and not by the Court's use of brackets or other convenient devices used to edit prior precedents into saying something they never really said. *Johnson v. McIntosh*, 574.

23. *Oliphant v. Suquamish Indian Tribe*, 209, quoting *Cherokee Nation v. Georgia*, 17–18: "And in *Cherokee Nation v. Georgia*, the Chief Justice observed that since Indian tribes are 'completely under the sovereignty and dominion of the United States, . . . any attempt [by foreign nations] to acquire their lands, or to form a political connexion with them, would be considered by all as an act of hostility."

24. *Oliphant v. Suquamish Indian Tribe*, 206–7.

25. See Robert A. Laurence, "Learning to Live with the Plenary Power of Congress over the Indian Nations: An Essay in Reaction to Professor Williams' *Algebra*," *Arizona Law Review* 30 (1988): 413–37. But see Robert A. Williams, Jr., "Learning Not to Live with Eurocentric Myopia: A Reply to Professor Laurence's 'Learning to Live with the Plenary Power of Congress over the Indian Nations,'" *Arizona Law Review* 30 (1988): 439–57. See also Charles Wilkinson, *American Indians, Time, and the Law: Native Societies in a Modern Constitutional Democracy* (New Haven: Yale University Press, 1987), 54–63.

26. *Ex parte Crow Dog*, 109 U.S. 556 (1883).

27. *Oliphant v. Suquamish Indian Tribe*, 210.

28. Ibid.

29. Ibid., 210–11.

30. Ibid., 211.

31. Ibid., 210–11.

32. Ibid., 210–11 (quoting *Ex parte Crow Dog*, 571).

33. On "color-clueless" decision making and the Rehnquist Supreme Court's twenty-first-century Indian law decisions, see chapter 10, "Scalia's Judicial Acts of Sly Elision in *Hicks*."

34. *Oliphant v. Suquamish Indian Tribe*, 211 (quoting *United States v. Kagama*, 379).

35. *United States v. Kagama*, 383.

36. *Oliphant v. Suquamish Indian Tribe*, 211.

37. The scholarly literature criticizing *Oliphant* is immense. See, e.g., Wilkinson, *American Indians, Time, and the Law*, 61; David H. Getches, "Conquering the Cultural Frontier: The New Subjectivism of the Supreme Court in Indian Law," *California Law Review* 84 (1996): 1595–99; Peter C. Maxfield, "*Oliphant v. Suquamish Tribe*: The Whole Is Greater Than the Sum of the Parts," *Journal of Contemporary Law* 19 (1993): 396. See also Robert A. Williams, Jr., "The Algebra of Indian Law: The Hard Trail of Decolonizing and Americanizing the White Man's Indian Jurisprudence," *Wisconsin Law Review*, 1986: 220–23.

38. *Oliphant v. Suquamish Indian Tribe,* 210.

39. See, e.g., Philip P. Frickey, "Doctrine, Context, Institutional Relationships, and Commentary: The Malaise of Federal Indian Law through the Lens of *Lone Wolf,*" *Tulsa Law Review* 38 (2002): 23 (describing *Oliphant*'s understanding "that tribes universally lost" criminal jurisdiction over non-Indians when "the United States generally asserted supervening authority over them" as historically and contextually "absurd"); David Getches, "Beyond Indian Law: The Rehnquist Court's Pursuit of States' Rights, Color-Blind Justice, and Mainstream Values," *Minnesota Law Review* 86 (2001): 274 (citing *Oliphant* as the first in a line of Supreme Court decisions that "created aberrant special rules concerning non-Indians"). See also the sources cited in note 37 above.

40. See chapter 4. Significantly, Rehnquist does not draw upon what I have identified as the fifth element missing from all of the post-Marshall Supreme Court's Indian law decisions, the reliance on contemporary international law for guidance in defining Indian rights and status under U.S. law.

41. *Oliphant v. Suquamish Indian Tribe,* 211–12.

8. The Most Indianophobic Supreme Court Indian Law Opinion Ever

1. *Oliphant v. Suquamish Indian Tribe,* 435 U.S. 191 (1978); *Tee-Hit-Ton v. United States,* 348 U.S. 272 (1955).

2. *United States v. Sioux Nation of Indians,* 448 U.S. 371 (1980).

3. See, e.g., "The Algebra of Federal Indian Law: The Hard Trail of Decolonizing and Americanizing the White Man's Indian Jurisprudence," *Wisconsin Law Review,* 1986: 219–99; "Documents of Barbarism: The Contemporary Legacy of European Racism and Colonialism in the Narrative Traditions of Federal Indian Law," *Arizona Law Review* 31 (1989): 237–78; "Columbus's Legacy: Law as an Instrument of Racial Discrimination against Indigenous Peoples' Rights of Self-Determination," *Arizona Journal of International and Comparative Law* 8 (1991): 51–75; and "Columbus's Legacy: The Rehnquist Court's Perpetuation of European Cultural Racism against American Indian Tribes," *Federal Bar News and Journal* 39 (1992): 358–69.

4. Albert Memmi, *The Colonizer and the Colonized* (New York: Orion Press, 1965).

5. Albert Memmi, "Attempt at a Definition," in *Dominated Man: Notes toward a Portrait* (New York: Orion Press, 1968), 185.

6. Memmi, "Attempt at a Definition," 186.

7. Homi K. Bhabha, "The Other Question: Stereotype, Discrimination, and the Discourse of Colonialism," in *The Location of Culture* (London and New York: Routledge, 1994), 70.

8. Ibid.

9. *United States v. Sioux Nation of Indians,* 386–90. "A more ripe and rank case of dishonorable dealings will never, in all probability, be found in our history, 207 Ct. Cl., at 241, 518 F.2d, at 1302" (quoted in *United States v. Sioux Nation of Indians,* 388). A compelling historical, social, and legal account of the U.S. taking of Paha Sapa, the Sioux name for the sacred Black Hills, is related in John P. LaVelle, "Rescuing *Paha Sapa:* Achieving Environmental Justice by Restoring the Great Grasslands and Returning the Sacred Black Hills to the Great Sioux Nation," *Great Plains Natural Resources Journal* 5 (2001): 42–101.

10. See Nell Jessup Newton, "Indian Claims in the Courts of the Conqueror," *American University Law Review* 41 (1992): 764–65. The Sioux tribes have refused to accept the judgment award, believing that only the return of the sacred Black Hills, not money, would constitute just compensation. Newton noted in her article that the accumulated amount of the judgment award for this victory for Indian rights exceeded $300 million as of 1992 (765n2).

11. *United States v. Sioux Nation of Indians,* 424 (Rehnquist, J., dissenting).

12. Ibid., 435.

13. Ibid.

14. Ibid. Ray Billington, introduction to U.S. Park Service, *Soldier and Brave; Indian and Military Affairs in the Trans-Mississippi West, Including a Guide to Historic Sites and Landmarks* (New York: Harper and Row, 1963).

15. *United States v. Sioux Nation of Indians,* 436.

16. Ibid.

17. Morison is the foremost American historian on the life and nautical achievements of Christopher Columbus, whom he uncritically examines in his most famous work. See Samuel Eliot Morison, *Admiral of the Ocean Sea,* vols. 1 and 2 (Boston: Little, Brown, 1942).

18. *United States v. Sioux Nation of Indians,* 436–37, quoting S. Morison, *The Oxford History of the American People* (New York: Oxford University Press, 1965), 539–40.

19. *United States v. Sioux Nation of Indians,* 437.

20. Walter Benjamin, "Theses on the Philosophy of History," in *Illuminations,* ed. Hannah Arendt (New York: Schocken, 1969), 256–57. For a useful critique of Benjamin's thoughts on the philosophy of history, see Hannah Arendt, "Introduction, Walter Benjamin: 1892–1940," 1–51, in Benjamin, *Illuminations;* Jürgen Habermas, "Walter Benjamin: Consciousness-Raising Critique," in *Philosophical-Political Profiles* (Cambridge, Mass.: MIT Press, 1983), 129–63.

9. The Dangers of the Twentieth-Century Supreme Court's Indian Rights Decisions

1. See chapter 1 on stereotype-congruent responses.

2. Linda Hamilton Krieger, "The Content of Our Categories: A Cognitive Bias Approach to Discrimination and Equal Employment Opportunity," *Stanford Law Review* 47 (1995): 1187–88. See, e.g., W. Edgar Vinacke, "Stereotypes as Social Concepts," *Journal of Social Psychology* 46 (1957): 229–43; Joshua A. Fishman, "An Examination of the Process and Function of Social Stereotyping," *Journal of Social Psychology* 43 (1956): 27–64. As Krieger notes, prior to the 1970s, researchers who studied intergroup bias understood stereotypes of "outgroups" as arising out of prejudice and as functioning to rationalize it. Stereotyping behavior was therefore viewed as "special" in the sense that it was discontinuous with normal cognitive processes. Based on the work of such researchers as Vinacke ("Stereotypes as Social Concepts"), Henri Tajfel and A. L. Wilkes (see, e.g., "Classification and Quantitative Judgement," *British Journal of Psychology* 54 [1963]: 101–14), and Donald J. Campbell ("Enhancement of Contrast as Composite Habit," *Journal of Abnormal and Social Psychology* 53 [1956]: 350–55), the view that stereotypes should be understood as cognitive structures no different in kind from other categorization-related constructs became more widely studied and accepted. This social cognition approach to intergroup bias and discrimination holds that, in the words of Krieger, "cognitive structures and processes involved in categorization and information processing can in and of themselves result in stereotyping and other forms of biased intergroup judgement previously attributed to motivational processes" (Krieger, "The Content of Our Categories," 1186–87). See generally David L. Hamilton and Tina K. Trolier, "Stereotypes and Stereotyping: An Overview of the Cognitive Approach," in *Prejudice, Discrimination, and Racism,* ed. John F. Dovidio and Samuel L. Gaertner (Orlando, Fla.: Academic Press, 1986), 127 (defining stereotypes as cognitive structures that contain the perceiver's knowledge, beliefs, and expectancies about some social category). See generally Diane M. Mackie and David Hamilton, eds., *Affect, Cognition, and Stereotyping: Interactive Processes in Group Perception* (San Diego: Academic Press, 1993) (discussing the role of "affective processes," that is, an individual's feelings and attitudes toward members of a particular social group, and cognitive determinants).

3. Krieger, "The Content of Our Categories," 1188.

4. Ibid.

5. Ibid., 1211.

6. See David Benjamin Oppenheimer, "Understanding Affirmative Action," *Hastings Constitutional Law Quarterly* 23 (1996): 947–52.

7. Oppenheimer explains that "survey results generally may underestimate the true level of white racism because the respondents are concerned about appearing to be racist. If overt racism is socially unacceptable behavior, persons being surveyed, even anonymously, may be reluctant to reveal their true beliefs" (ibid., 953). See generally Patricia G. Devine et al., "Prejudice with and without Compunction," *Journal of Personality and Social Psychology* 60 (1991): 817–30 (discussing research on subjects who report nonprejudiced attitudes on surveys but who also manifest prejudice in non–consciously monitored measures).

8. Oppenheimer, "Understanding Affirmative Action," 953.

9. Ibid.

10. See ibid., 954–55 (summarizing results of several such experiments).

11. See ibid.

12. Ibid., 955–56.

13. Ibid.

14. See H. J. Ehrlich, *The Social Psychology of Prejudice* (New York: Wiley, 1973): "No person can grow up in a society without having learned the stereotypes assigned to the major ethnic groups" (35).

15. *Tee-Hit-Ton v. United States,* 348 U.S. 272, 279 (1955).

16. *United States v. Sioux Nation of Indians,* 448 U.S. 371, 437 (Rehnquist, J., dissenting) (1980).

17. See, e.g., Devine et al., "Prejudice with and without Compunction," 817–19.

18. See, e.g., ibid.

19. See Jody David Armour, *Negrophobia and Reasonable Racism: The Hidden Costs of Being Black in America* (New York: New York University Press, 1997), 121–23.

20. See Patricia G. Devine, "Stereotypes and Prejudice: Their Automatic and Controlled Components," *Journal of Personality and Social Development* 56 (1989): 5, 6.

21. See Armour, *Negrophobia and Reasonable Racism,* 122.

22. See Charles F. Wilkinson, "To Feel the Summer in the Spring: The Treaty Fishing Rights of the Wisconsin Chippewa," *Wisconsin Law Review,* 1991: 379. See also Charles F. Wilkinson, *American Indians, Time, and the Law: Native Societies in a Modern Constitutional Democracy* (New Haven: Yale University Press, 1987), 14–19. See also the introduction to the present book.

23. Wilkinson, *American Indians, Time, and the Law,* 14–19.

24. Samuel L. Gaertner and John F. Dovidio, "The Aversive Form of Racism," in Dovidio and Gaertner, *Prejudice, Discrimination, and Racism,* 61.

25. John F. Dovidio and Samuel L. Gaertner, "On the Nature of Contemporary Prejudice," in *Confronting Racism: The Problem and the Response,*

ed. Jennifer L. Eberhardt and Susan T. Fiske (Thousand Oaks, Calif.: Sage, 1998), 5.

26. Ibid.

27. Charles R. Lawrence III, "The Id, the Ego, and Equal Protection: Reckoning with Unconscious Racism," *Stanford Law Review* 39 (1987): 317, 322, 335.

28. Ibid., 335.

10. Expanding *Oliphant*'s Principle of Racial Discrimination

1. *Korematsu v. United States,* 323 U.S. 214, 246 (1944) (dissenting opinion).

2. *Nevada v. Hicks,* 533 U.S. 353 (2001).

3. Along with my colleague and faculty cochair of the University of Arizona Rogers College of Law Indigenous Peoples Law and Policy Program, James Anaya, who served as counsel of record, I represented Hicks as cocounsel before the Supreme Court in *Nevada v. Hicks*. Brief for Respondent Floyd Hicks, *Nevada v. Hicks,* 533 U.S. 353 (2001).

4. See *Nevada v. Hicks,* 355–56.

5. See Harry A. Blackmun, "Section 1983 and Federal Protection of Individual Rights—Will the Statute Remain Alive or Fade Away?" *New York University Law Review* 60 (1985): 1–29 (exploring the historical origins of section 1983, its judicial reach, and the debate over the proper scope of its protection of individual rights).

6. *Nevada v. Hicks,* 357.

7. *Nevada v. Hicks,* 196 F.3d 1020 (9th Cir. 1999). (Further citations to *Nevada v. Hicks* are to 533 U.S.)

8. Justice Sandra Day O'Connor wrote a separate opinion, joined in by Justices John Stevens and Stephen Breyer, concurring in part and concurring in the judgment.

9. *Nevada v. Hicks,* 374, 358–59.

10. *Montana v. United States,* 450 U.S. 544 (1981); *A-1 Contractors v. Strate,* 520 U.S. 438 (1997).

11. *Nevada v. Hicks,* 358, quoting *A-1 Contractors v. Strate,* 445.

12. *Montana v. United States,* 563. *Montana* had also recognized two minor "exceptions" to its general rule prohibiting tribes, in the absence of an express treaty or statutory provision, from exercising "power inconsistent with their diminished status as sovereigns" under the doctrine of discovery (565). Under the *Montana* rule's two sole exceptions, tribes can regulate "through taxation, licensing, or other means, the activities of non-members who enter consensual relationships with the tribe or its members, through commercial dealings, contracts, leases, or other arrangements" (566). A tribe may also

regulate non-Indians on the reservation "when that conduct has some direct effect on the political integrity, the economic severity, or the health or welfare of the tribe" (566). Neither of those exceptions were held to apply in *Nevada v. Hicks,* 359, 364–65.

13. *Nevada v. Hicks,* 358.

14. Ibid., 359, quoting *Montana v. United States,* 565 (emphasis supplied by Scalia).

15. *Montana v. United States,* 548–49; *A-1 Contractors v. Strate,* 442–43.

16. *A-1 Contractors v. Strate,* 456.

17. As in *Montana,* the two exceptions permitting tribal jurisdiction over nonmembers (see note 12 above) were held not to apply to the non-Indian conduct involved in the *A-1 Contractors* lawsuits.

18. *Nevada v. Hicks,* 359.

19. Ibid.

20. Ibid., 360, 364, 364, 359.

21. *United States v. Kagama,* 118 U.S. 375 (1886) (cited in *Nevada v. Hicks,* 363); *Worcester v. Georgia,* 31 U.S. 515 (1832) (cited in *Nevada v. Hicks,* 361); *Draper v. United States,* 164 U.S. 240 (1896) (cited in *Nevada v. Hicks,* 365).

22. Recognizing the Court's broad application of *Oliphant*'s principle in subsequent decisions, some Indian law advocates and scholars have urged tribes to avoid bringing their cases before the justices at all. See, e.g., Philip P. Frickey, "Doctrine, Context, Institutional Relationships, and Commentary: The Malaise of Federal Indian Law through the Lens of *Lone Wolf,*" *Tulsa Law Review* 38 (2001): 33 (noting that "experienced practitioners now advise tribes to avoid the Supreme Court at all costs"). See also Louis F. Claiborne, "The Trend of Supreme Court Decisions in Indian Cases," *American Indian Law Review* 22 (1998): 588 ("In my view, it is very dangerous to press on the Court propositions that are bound to stir hostile instincts in the general public and may produce a like reaction from a majority of the Justices"); David H. Getches, "Beyond Indian Law: The Rehnquist Court's Pursuit of States' Rights, Color-Blind Justice, and Mainstream Values," *Minnesota Law Review* 86 (2001): 267–362 (discussing the dismal future for tribal interests in the present Supreme Court's hands).

23. *Nevada v. Hicks,* 375 (Souter, J., concurring).

24. Robert Cover, "*Nomos* and Narrative," *Harvard Law Review* 97 (1983): 53. See chapter 2.

25. *Nevada v. Hicks,* 376–77.

26. Ibid., 358n2.

27. Ibid., 374.

28. Ibid., 376–77, 383–85, 375–76.

29. Justice Souter's presumption that tribes lack civil jurisdiction over all

nonmembers on the reservation would apply unless tribes could meet one of the two *Montana* "exceptions" (*Nevada v. Hicks*, 376; see note 12 above). Souter joined with Scalia's analysis for the Court that neither of the exceptions applied in *Hicks*.

30. *Nevada v. Hicks*, 383, 385 (internal quotations omitted).

31. See, e.g., *Williams v. Lee*, 358 U.S. 217 (1959) (holding that Arizona courts are not free to exercise jurisdiction over a civil suit by a non-Indian against an Indian where the cause of the action arises on Indian reservation); *McClanahan v. Arizona State Tax Comm'n.*, 411 U.S. 164 (1973) (holding that under the Marshall model, state income tax infringes on the sovereignty of the Navajo Nation); *Merrion v. Jicarilla Apache Tribe*, 455 U.S. 130 (1982) (holding that the tribe has authority to tax nonmember businesses operating in Indian country); *National Farmers Union Ins. Co. v. Crow Tribe of Indians*, 471 U.S. 845 (1985) (stating that the scope of a tribe's judicial jurisdiction is a federal question arising under section 1331); *Iowa Mutual Ins. Co. v. LaPlante*, 480 U.S. 9 (1985) (extending *National Farmers Union* to include federal diversity jurisdiction in actions arising in Indian country between an Indian and a non-Indian).

32. *Talton v. Mayes*, 163 U.S. 376 (1896).

33. 25 U.S.C. secs. 1301 et seq.

34. *Oliphant v. Suquamish Indian Tribe*, 435 U.S. 191 (1978).

35. *United States v. Ant*, 882 F.2d 1389 (9th Cir. 1989).

36. *Gideon v. Wainwright*, 372 U.S. 335 (1963). The Sixth Amendment provides that "[i]n all criminal prosecutions, the accused shall enjoy the right to a speedy and public trial, by an impartial jury of the State and district wherein the crime shall have been committed, which district shall have been previously ascertained by law, and to be informed of the nature and cause of the accusation; to be confronted with the witnesses against him; to have compulsory process for obtaining witnesses in his favor, and to have the assistance of counsel for his defense" (U.S.C.A. Const. Amend. 6). In *Gideon*, the Supreme Court reaffirmed that the assistance of counsel "is one of the safeguards of the Sixth Amendment deemed necessary to insure fundamental human rights of life and liberty" (*Gideon v. Wainwright*, 343, citing *Johnson v. Zerbst*, 304 U.S. 458 [1938]). Noting that counsel in American courts was a necessity, not a luxury, the Court stated what it deemed an "obvious truth": A poor man is denied a fair trial if he is not appointed counsel and he cannot afford to pay a lawyer (ibid.).

37. See Robert J. McCarthy, "Civil Rights in Tribal Courts: The Indian Bill of Rights at Thirty Years," *Idaho Law Review* 34 (1998): 465–515.

38. *Santa Clara Pueblo v. Martinez*, 436 U.S. 49 (1978).

39. See, e.g., Melissa L. Koehn, "Civil Jurisdiction: The Boundaries between

Federal and Tribal Courts," *Arizona State Law Journal* 29 (1997): 705–68; Robert Laurence, "*Martinez, Oliphant,* and Federal Court Review of Tribal Activity under the Indian Civil Rights Act," *Campbell Law Review* 10 (1988): 411–38; Theresa R. Wilson, "Nations within a Nation: The Evolution of Tribal Immunity," *American Indian Law Review* 24 (2000): 99–128.

40. O'Connor, in her concurring opinion, joined by Stevens and Breyer, was willing to ask these questions and therefore departed from this part of Scalia's analysis for the Court in his opinion. As she explained: "In this case, the state officials raised their immunity defenses in Tribal Court as they challenged that court's subject matter jurisdiction. Thus the Tribal Court and the Appellate Tribal Court had a full opportunity to address the immunity claims. These defendants, like other officials facing civil liability, were entitled to have their immunity defenses adjudicated at the earliest stage possible to avoid needless litigation. It requires no 'magic' to afford officials the same protection in tribal court that they would be afforded in state or federal court. I would therefore reverse the Court of Appeals in this case on the ground that it erred in failing to address the state officials' immunity defenses. It is possible that Hicks' lawsuits would have been easily disposed of on the basis of official and qualified immunity" (*Nevada v. Hicks,* 400–401, O'Connor, J., concurring in part and concurring in the Court's judgment).

41. *Nevada v. Hicks,* 376.

42. *Nevada v. Hicks,* 378 (concurring opinion, citing *Montana v. United States,* 565).

43. *Duro v. Reina,* 495 U.S. 676 (1990). The decision was overturned by Congress the following year as not conforming to its understanding of Indian rights to criminal jurisdiction over nonmember Indians under the Marshall model. See 25 U.S.C. sec. 1301(4). See generally David H. Getches, Charles F. Wilkinson, and Robert A. Williams, Jr., *Federal Indian Law: Cases and Materials,* 5th ed. (St. Paul, Minn.: West Group, 2004), 518–20 (hereafter *Federal Indian Law*). It is worth noting that the Supreme Court recently upheld the constitutionality of the "*Duro-*fix" passed by Congress in 1991. See *United States v. Lara,* 541 U.S. 193 (2004). See Chapter 11 for a discussion of *Lara.*

See also 25 U.S.C. sec. 1301(2) (1991) ("'[P]owers of self-government' means . . . the inherent power of Indian tribes, hereby recognized and affirmed, to exercise criminal jurisdiction over all Indians"). See, e.g., Alex Tallchief Skibine, "The Dialogic of Federalism in Federal Indian Law and the Rehnquist Court: The Need for Coherence and Integration," *Texas Forum on Civil Liberties and Civil Rights* 8 (2003): 1–49.

44. *Nevada v. Hicks,* 383 (concurring opinion, citing *Duro v. Reina,* 693).

45. *Nevada v. Hicks,* 383–84.

46. Ibid., 383.

47. *Nevada v. Hicks,* 384. On these significant differences, Souter quotes Ada Pecos Melton, "Indigenous Justice Systems and Tribal Society," *Judicature* 79 (1995): 130–31.

48. 25 U.S.C. sec. 1302.

49. *Nevada v. Hicks,* 384 (Souter, J., concurring) (citing *Oliphant v. Suquamish Indian Tribe,* 194).

50. *Nevada v. Hicks,* 384, quoting Nell Jessup Newton, "Tribal Courts Praxis: One Year in the Life of Twenty Indian Tribal Courts," *American Indian Law Review* 22 (1998): 344n238. Quoting from another contemporary law review article that generally looked with favor upon the growth and development of tribal justice systems in the present-day United States, Souter explained, "Tribal Courts also differ from other American courts (and often from one another) in their structure, in the substantive law they apply, and in the independence of their judges. Although some modern tribal courts 'mirror American courts' and 'are guided by written codes, rules, procedures, and guidelines,' tribal law is still frequently unwritten, being based instead 'on the values, mores, and norms of a tribe and expressed in its customs, traditions, and practices,' and is often 'handed down orally or by example from one generation to another'" (*Nevada v. Hicks,* 384, concurring opinion, citing Melton, "Indigenous Justice Systems and Tribal Society," 130–31).

51. *Nevada v. Hicks,* 384 (Souter, J., concurring, quoting *Oliphant v. Suquamish Indian Tribe,* 210), 383.

52. *Nevada v. Hicks,* 383.

53. Ibid., 383, 384–85 (citing National American Indian Court Judges Association, *Indian Courts and the Future* [Washington, D.C.: NAICJA, 1978], 43), 385.

54. Ibid., 385 (quoting *Duro v. Reina,* 693).

55. See *Oliphant v. Suquamish Indian Tribe* (reciting the legal history of this view). Cf. *Federal Indian Law,* 140–65.

56. Homi K. Bhabha, *The Location of Culture* (New York: Routledge, 1994), 2.

57. See, e.g., Sandra Day O'Connor, "Lessons from the Third Sovereign: Indian Tribal Courts," *Tulsa Law Journal* 33 (1997): 1–6; Frank Pommersheim, *Braid of Feathers: American Indian Law and Contemporary Tribal Life* (Berkeley and Los Angeles: University of California Press, 1995); Barbara Ann Atwood, "Tribal Jurisprudence and Cultural Meanings of the Family," *Nebraska Law Review* 79 (2000): 577–656; Mary Jo B. Hunter, "Tribal Court Opinions: Justice and Legitimacy," *Kansas Journal of Law and Public Policy* 8 (1999): 142–46; B. J. Jones, "Tribal Courts: Protectors of the Native Paradigm of Justice," *St. Thomas Law Review* 10 (1997): 87–93; Tom Tso, "The Process of Decision Making in Tribal Courts," *Arizona Law Review* 31 (1989):

225–35; Robert Yazzie, "'Life Comes From It': Navajo Justice Concepts," *New Mexico Law Review* 24 (1994): 175–90. On North American Indian visions of law and peace, see generally Robert A. Williams, Jr., *Linking Arms Together: American Indian Visions of Law and Peace, 1600–1800* (New York: Oxford University Press, 1997).

11. The Court's Schizophrenic Approach to Indian Rights

1. See, e.g., Robert Laurence, "Learning to Live with the Plenary Power of Congress over Indian Nations," *Arizona Law Review* 30 (1988): 413–37; Robert S. Pelcyger, "Justices and Indians: Back to Basics," *Oregon Law Review* 62 (1983): 29–47.

2. *Worcester v. Georgia,* 31 U.S. 515 (1832); *Ex parte Crow Dog,* 109 U.S. 556 (1883).

3. *Williams v. Lee,* 358 U.S. 217 (1959); *Morton v. Mancari,* 417 U.S. 535 (1974); *Santa Clara Pueblo v. Martinez,* 436 U.S. 49 (1978).

4. *United States v. Lara,* 541 U.S. 193, 202 (2004).

5. *Duro v. Reina,* 495 U.S. 676 (1990). See chapter 9. See also Alex Tallchief Skibine, "*Duro v. Reina* and the Legislation that Overturned It: A Powerplay of Constitutional Dimensions," *California Law Review* 66 (1993): 767–806; Nell Jessup Newton, "Permanent Legislation to Correct *Duro v. Reina,*" *American Indian Law Review* 17 (1992): 109–27.

6. See, e.g., Jim Adams, "Judges Tour in 2001 Helped in *Lara* Win," *Indian Country Today,* May 19, 2004 (calling the *Lara* decision "the Court's strongest affirmation of tribal sovereignty in many years").

7. Laurence, "Learning to Live with the Plenary Power over Indian Nations," 423.

8. Ibid., 435, citing Marshall in *Worcester v. Georgia,* 31 U.S. 515, 543 (1832).

9. Laurence, "Learning to Live with the Plenary Power over Indian Nations," 424.

10. See. e.g., *Talton v. Mayes,* 163 U.S. 376, 384–85 (1896).

11. *Nevada v. Hicks,* 533 U.S. 353 (2001); *Oliphant v. Suquamish Indian Tribe,* 435 U.S. 191 (1978). On criticism of Rehnquist's interpretation of the Marshall model in *Oliphant,* see, e.g., Robert N. Clinton, "There Is No Federal Supremacy Clause for Indian Tribes," *Arizona State Law Journal* 34 (2003): 214; David Getches, "Beyond Indian Law: The Rehnquist Court's Pursuit of States' Rights, Colorblind Justice, and Mainstream Values," *Minnesota Law Review* 86 (2001): 274; Ralph W. Johnson and Berrie Martinis, "Chief Justice Rehnquist and the Indian Cases," *Public Land Law Review* 16 (1995): 11–12;

Russell Lawrence Barsh and James Youngblood Henderson, "The Betrayal: *Oliphant v. Suquamish Indian Tribe* and the Hunting of the Snark," *Minnesota Law Review* 63 (1979): 609–37.

12. *United States v. Lara,* 205–6.

13. Ibid., 208, quoting 25 U.S.C. sec. 1301(2).

14. *Duro v. Reina,* 685 (Justice William Brennan filed a dissenting opinion joined in by Justice Thurgood Marshall).

15. U.S. Senate Report no. 102-168 (1991); Newton, "Permanent Legislation to Correct *Duro v. Reina,*" 109–10; Skibine, "*Duro v. Reina* and the Legislation that Overturned Dimensions," 798.

16. *United States v. Lara,* 197–98.

17. Ibid., 196–97.

18. Ibid., 197 (emphasis supplied). U.S. Const. Amend. V.

19. See *Heath v. Alabama,* 474 U.S. 82, 88 (1985).

20. *United States v. Wheeler,* 435 U.S. 313, 313, 318, 322–23 (1978). As quoted by Breyer in *Lara, Wheeler* held that a tribe's "*sovereign* power to punish *tribal* offenders," while subject to congressional "defeasance," remains among those "'inherent powers of a limited sovereignty which has never been extinguished'" (*United States v. Lara,* 197, emphasis added and deleted by Breyer).

21. *Duro v. Reina,* 687.

22. See Act of November 5, 1990, secs. 8077(b)–(d), 104 Stat. 1892–93 (temporary legislation until September 30, 1991); Act of October 9, 1991, 105 Stat. 646 (codified as amended at 25 U.S.C. sec. 1301 (2004)).

23. 25 U.S.C. sec. 1301(2) (emphasis added).

24. U.S. Senate Report no. 102-168 (1991); Newton, "Permanent Legislation to Correct *Duro v. Reina,*" 112–13; Skibine, "*Duro v. Reina* and the Legislation that Overturned It: A Powerplay of Constitutional Dimensions," 769–70.

25. See L. Scott Gould, "The Congressional Response to *Duro v. Reina:* Compromising Sovereignty and the Constitution," *University of California at Davis Law Review* 28 (1994): 158–60.

26. *United States v. Lara,* 200.

27. E.g., *United States v. Wheeler,* 323; *Morton v. Mancari,* 417 U.S. 535, 552, 94 S. Ct. 2474, 41 L.Ed.2d 290 (1974); *McClanahan v. Arizona State Tax Comm'n,* 411 U.S. 164, 172n7, 93 S. Ct. 1257, 36 L.Ed.2d 129 (1973).

28. U.S. Constitution, Article I, section 8, clause 3 ("The Congress shall have power to . . . regulate commerce with foreign nations, and among the several states, and with the Indian tribes"), and Article II, section 2, clause 2 ("[The President] shall have power, by and with the advice and consent of the Senate, to make treaties, provided two thirds of the senators present concur").

29. *United States v. Lara,* 201 (citing *Felix S. Cohen's Handbook of Federal Indian Law,* ed. Rennard F. Strickland, Charles F. Wilkinson, et al. [Charlottesville, Va.: Michie, Bobbs-Merrill, 1982], 208).

30. Citing *United States v. Curtiss-Wright Export Corp.,* 299 U.S. 304, 315–322, 57 S. Ct. 216, 81 L.Ed. 255 (1936).

31. *United States v. Lara,* 202.

32. Ibid. See *United States v. Holliday,* 3 Wall. 407, 419 (1866); *Menominee Tribe v. United States,* 391 U.S. 404 (1968).

33. *United States v. Lara,* 203, citing 25 U.S.C. secs. 903–903f, restoring the Menominee Tribe, and citing 8 U.S.C. sec. 1401(b).

34. Section 4217, 100 Stat. 3207-146, codified at 25 U.S.C. sec. 1302(7) (raising the maximum from "a term of six months and a fine of $500" to "a term of one year and a fine of $5,000").

35. *United States v. Lara,* 205.

36. Ibid. According to Justice Breyer, *Oliphant* and *Duro* "make clear that the Constitution does not dictate the metes and bounds of tribal autonomy, nor do they suggest that the Court should second-guess the political branches' own determinations" (ibid.): "[T]he Court in these cases based its descriptions of inherent tribal authority upon the sources as they existed at the time the Court issued its decisions. Congressional legislation constituted one such important source. And that source was subject to change. Indeed *Duro* itself anticipated change by inviting interested parties to 'address the problem [to] Congress.' 495 U.S., at 698. . . . Consequently we do not read any of these cases as holding that the Constitution forbids Congress to change 'judicially made' federal Indian law through this kind of legislation. *Oliphant, supra,* at 206" (*United States v. Lara,* 206–7).

37. Ibid., 205.

38. *United States v. Lara,* 214 (Thomas, J., concurring in the judgment).

39. Ibid., 219, 214.

40. *United States v. Lara,* 215 (Thomas, J., concurring in the judgment).

41. Ibid.

42. Ibid., 218–19 (quoting *Black's Law Dictionary,* 6th ed. [St. Paul, Minn.: West, 1990], 1395), and 218.

43. *Cherokee Nation v. Georgia,* 30 U.S. 1, 16–17 (1831).

44. *Worcester v. Georgia,* 6 Pet. 515, 559, 8 L.Ed. 483 (1832).

45. *United States v. Lara,* 219, 226 (Thomas, J., concurring in the judgment).

Conclusion

1. Philip Frickey has said, for example, that the Rehnquist Court's decisions have displaced "the primary congressional responsibility for Indian af-

fairs with a judicial attempt to address contemporary contextual dilemmas in federal Indian law on a case-by-case basis. . . . The Court has performed this role quite poorly in recent years. It has produced incoherent doctrinal compromises, jettisoned the longstanding institutional understandings in the field in favor of an ill-defined judicial role, and destroyed practical incentives for congressional and negotiated solutions to the myriad of invariably differentiated local problems of tribal relations with states, local governments, and nonmembers. Rather than moving the field toward sounder structural, normative, and practical moorings, the Court has left the law in a mess, done little to promote effective solutions to practical problems, and been more normatively concerned about undermining tribal authority to protect nonmembers than about promoting a viable framework for tribal flourishing in the twenty-first century." Philip P. Frickey, "Doctrine, Context, Institutional Relationships, and Commentary: The Malaise of Federal Indian Law through the Lens of *Lone Wolf*," *Tulsa Law Review* 38 (2002): 8.

Robert N. Clinton has charged the Court with "neo-colonialism," seeming concerned only with protecting the "right of non-Indian political processes to control the rights, destinies, and interests of Indian minorities, but not the right of Indian governments to affect the rights and interests of non-Indians or non-member Indians who reside within their reservation and affect the lives of tribal members." Clinton, "Peyote and Judicial Political Activism: Neo-Colonialism and the Supreme Court's New Indian Law Agenda," *Federal Bar News and Journal* 38 (1991): 98–100.

The late Ralph Johnson coauthored an article singling out Chief Justice Rehnquist as leading the Court's jurisprudential assault on tribal rights: "Rehnquist's ideas about Indian law," Johnson wrote, "coupled with his position as Chief Justice, have had grave implications for Indian sovereignty and welfare." Ralph Johnson and Berrie Martinis, "Chief Justice Rehnquist and the Indian Cases," *Public Land Law Review* 16 (1995): 24.

David Getches has labeled the Rehnquist Supreme Court's approach to Indian rights as "subjectivism," with the Court defining the rights of Indians, including the powers of tribal government, according to the preferences of a majority of the justices as to what the result ought to be. Rather than relying on foundational principles that go back to the Marshall Trilogy and requiring clear expressions by Congress setting Indian policy, members of the Court have started writing their own policy in some recent cases. "[I]n Indian law, the Court has been engaged in a search for meaning that involves it in a hands-on project of finding legislative purpose and doing what the justices believe to be the best under the circumstances. In that context, I find the most troubling aspect of the inquiry to be the importation of current social values, an essentially ethnocentric enterprise that challenges even the wisest judge. . . .

"The Justices must also understand that their recent decisions have begun to dismantle Indian policy, and that this inevitably will cause confusion among state, local, and tribal governments, heighten tensions among Indians and their non-Indian neighbors, undermine reservation economic development efforts, and frustrate lower federal and state courts." David H. Getches, "Beyond Indian Law: The Rehnquist Court's Pursuit of States' Rights, Color-Blind Justice, and Mainstream Values," *Minnesota Law Review* 86 (2001): 301, 360.

2. See, e.g., Frickey, "Doctrine, Context, Institutional Relationships, and Commentary," 33. See also Louis F. Claiborne, "The Trend of Supreme Court Decisions in Indian Cases," *American Indian Law Review* 22 (1998): 588 ("In my view, it is very dangerous to press on the Court propositions that are bound to stir hostile instincts in the general public and may produce a like reaction from a majority of the Justices"); Getches, "Beyond Indian Law" (discussing the dismal future for tribal interests in the present Supreme Court's hands).

3. See Timothy D. Wilson and Nancy Brekke, "Mental Contamination and Mental Correction: Unwanted Influences on Judgments and Evaluations," *Psychology Bulletin* 116 (1994): 117–42; Linda Hamilton Krieger, "The Content of Our Categories: A Cognitive Bias Approach to Discrimination and Equal Employment Opportunity," *Stanford Law Review* 47 (1995): 1216.

4. In the final chapter of his book *Negrophobia and Reasonable Racism*, Armour outlines a similar approach to protecting minority rights that draws upon a "dissociation model" of stereotypes and prejudice: To get the justices to change the way they habitually decide cases about certain minority groups, they must be convinced of the need to inhibit and replace their stereotype-congruent responses to individual members of those groups with "non-prejudiced responses derived from non-prejudiced personal beliefs." In other words, applying this type of approach to Indian law, the justices need to dissociate their negative racial stereotypes about Indians from the way they decide Indian rights cases. They need to break what has become a "bad habit." See Jody David Armour, *Negrophobia and Reasonable Racism: The Hidden Costs of Being Black in America* (New York: New York University Press, 1997), 124.

5. Krieger, "The Content of Our Categories," 1217.

6. See, e.g., Neil Gotanda, "A Critique of 'Our Constitution is Colorblind,'" *Stanford Law Review* 44 (1991): 1–68. See chapter 10.

7. Krieger, "The Content of Our Categories," 17.

8. So that I am clear on this point, let me state that I am not advocating an entire abandonment of the Marshall model as a means of protecting Indian rights before the twenty-first-century Supreme Court. As previously discussed, the model has generated precedents and principles that have, in fact, secured important victories for Indian rights, and that also can be reconciled and made

consistent with contemporary international human rights norms respecting state obligations toward the protection of indigenous peoples' basic human rights. See chapter 4. In fact, the Marshall model as interpreted by the Supreme Court has generated principles and precedents that have contributed significantly to the progressive development of customary international law around the world respecting indigenous peoples' rights. See David H. Getches, Charles F. Wilkinson, and Robert A. Williams, Jr., *Federal Indian Law,* 5th ed. (St. Paul, Minn.: West Publishing, 2004), ch. 14. What I am arguing for in this book is a postcolonial approach to protecting Indian rights that closely scrutinizes the Court's Marshall model precedents and the racist judicial language they perpetuate, in order to assure that the model itself, in combination with the doctrine of stare decisis and judicial acts of editorial omission, does not work to promote unconscious racism in the way the justices think, talk, and write about Indian rights under U.S. law.

9. S. James Anaya, "Indigenous Rights Norms in Contemporary International Law," *Arizona Journal of International and Comparative Law* 8, no. 2 (1991): 38. As Anaya notes, the U.S. Supreme Court has declared that "[i]nternational law is part of our law, and must be ascertained and administered by the courts of justice of appropriate jurisdiction, as often as questions of right[s] depending upon it are duly presented for their determination" (*The Paquete Habana,* 175 U.S. 677, 700 [1900]). See also *Filartiga v. Pena-Irala,* 630 F.2d 876 (2d Cir. 1980) (applying customary human rights norms against torture in an action under the Alien Tort Claims Act). Frank Newman and David Weissbrodt, *International Human Rights* (Cincinnati, Ohio: Anderson, 1990), 569–618, outline the jurisdictional and other technical impediments often faced in attempts to base a cause of action on an international rule. See also Richard Bilder, "Integrating International Human Rights Law into Domestic Law—U.S. Experience," *Houston Journal of International Law* 4 (1981): 1–12; Kathryn Burke, "Application of International Human Rights Law in State and Federal Courts," *Texas International Law Journal* 18 (1983): 291–328; Gordon A. Christenson, "The Uses of Human Rights Norms to Inform Constitutional Interpretation," *Houston Journal of International Law* 4 (1981): 39–57; Richard B. Lillich, "Invoking International Human Rights Law in Domestic Courts," *University of Cincinnati Law Review* 54 (1985): 367–415. See Anaya, "Indigenous Rights Norms in Contemporary International Law," 38.

10. Philip P. Frickey, "Domesticating Federal Indian Law," *Minnesota Law Review* 81 (1996): 74. For over a decade, Frickey has produced an important and penetrating body of work on federal Indian law, particularly focusing on the Marshall model as applied by the Rehnquist Court; see also, e.g., Frickey, "Congressional Intent, Practical Reasoning, and the Dynamic Nature of Federal

Indian Law," *California Law Review* 78 (1990): 1137–1239, 1178; "Marshalling Past and Present: Colonialism, Constitutionalism, and Interpretation in Federal Indian Law," *Harvard Law Review* 107 (1993): 381–440.

11. Armour, *Negrophobia and Reasonable Racism,* 133.

12. Ibid., 132–39. According to H. J. Ehrlich, "Stereotypes about ethnic groups appear as a part of the social heritage of society. They are transmitted across generations as a component of the accumulated knowledge of society. They are as true as tradition, and as pervasive as folklore. No person can grow up in a society without having learned the stereotypes assigned to the major ethnic groups" (H. J. Ehrlich, *The Social Psychology of Prejudice* [New York: Wiley, 1973], 35).

13. William James, *Principles of Psychology* (New York: H. Holt, 1890), 112 (quoting William B. Carpenter, *Principles of Mental Physiology* [London: H. S. King, 1875], 339–45).

14. E. Tory Higgins and Gillian King, "Accessibility of Social Constructs: Information-Processing Consequences of Individual and Contextual Variability," in *Personality, Cognition, and Social Interaction,* ed. Nancy Cantor and John F. Kihlstrom (Hillsdale, N.J.: L. Erlbaum, 1981), 69. See generally Armour, *Negrophobia and Reasonable Racism,* 133.

15. See, e.g., *Nevada v. Hicks,* 533 U.S. 353, 358, 359, 376; *Montana v. United States,* 450 U.S. 544, 549, 563n12, 566n14, 565 (1981).

16. Patricia G. Devine et al., "Prejudice with and without Compunction," *Journal of Personality and Social Psychology* 60 (1991): 817–19.

17. Charles F. Wilkinson, "To Feel the Summer in the Spring: The Treaty Fishing Rights of the Wisconsin Chippewa, *Wisconsin Law Review,* 1991: 375–414, 378.

18. Ibid., 379.

19. See *Oliphant v. Suquamish Indian Tribe,* 435 U.S. 191, 210 (1978).

20. Frickey, "Domesticating Federal Indian Law," 74.

21. Ibid., 57.

22. Ibid., 52–57, 74.

23. See S. James Anaya, *Indigenous Peoples in International Law,* 2nd ed. (Oxford and New York: Oxford University Press, 2004), 129–56, which masterfully summarizes and analyzes the rejection by numerous international human rights bodies and organizations of colonial-era legal doctrines and principles of racial discrimination as being contrary to contemporary international law.

24. See generally, S. James Anaya and Robert A. Williams, Jr., "The Protection of Indigenous Peoples' Rights over Lands and Natural Resources under the Inter-American Human Rights System," *Harvard Human Rights Journal* 14 (2001): 33, 33–35; Siegfried Wiessner, "The Rights and Status of Indigenous

Peoples: A Global Comparative and International Legal Analysis," *Harvard Human Rights Journal* 12 (1999): 57–128; Robert A. Williams, Jr., "Encounters on the Frontiers of International Human Rights Law: Redefining the Terms of Indigenous Peoples' Survival in the World," *Duke Law Journal,* 1990: 660–704; W. Michael Reisman, "Protecting Indigenous Rights in International Adjudication," *American Journal of International Law* 89 (1995): 350–62.

25. Convention concerning Indigenous and Tribal Peoples in Independent Countries, September 5, 1991, 169 I.L.O. 1989.

26. The U.N. Working Group is composed of five rotating members of the U.N. Sub-Commission on Prevention of Discrimination and Protection of Minorities, who act in the capacity of experts rather than as government representatives. Through its activities, however, the working group has engaged states, indigenous peoples, and others in an extended multilateral dialogue on indigenous rights. Virtually every state with a significant indigenous population has made regular oral or written submissions to the working group. On the U.N. Working Group, see generally, Robert A. Williams, Jr., "Encounters on the Frontiers of International Human Rights Law: Redefining the Terms of Indigenous Peoples' Survival in the World," *Duke Law Journal,* 1990: 668–72. See also Hurst Hannum, "New Developments in Indigenous Rights," *Virginia Journal of International Law* 28 (1988): 649–78; Curtis G. Berkey, "International Law and Domestic Courts: Enhancing Self-Determination for Indigenous Peoples," *Harvard Human Rights Journal* 5 (1992): 65–94.

In 1995, the U.N. Commission on Human Rights began its review process of the Working Group's Draft Declaration on the Rights of Indigenous Peoples. The member-states of the U.N. Human Rights Commission must finalize the Declaration before the text can go before the U.N. General Assembly for approval. It may, therefore, be several more years until a Declaration on the Rights of Indigenous Peoples is formally presented for adoption by the United Nations.

27. Draft U.N. Declaration on the Rights of Indigenous Peoples, Report of the Sub-Commission on Prevention of Discrimination and Protection of Minorities, U.N. ESCOR, 46th Sess., Art. 26, para. 105, U.N. Doc. E/CN.4/Sub.2/1994/45 (1994).

28. See Anaya, *Indigenous Peoples in International Law,* at 134–37, 230–32.

29. *Indigenous Peoples,* Operational Directive 4.20, para. 13, World Bank (September 17, 1991) (requiring respect for indigenous peoples' land rights in connection with World Bank–financed projects); *Indigenous Issues and the Inter-American Development Bank: A Summary Report,* U.N. Doc. E/C.19/2003/CRP.4 (2003); Council of Ministers of the European Union, *Resolution on Indigenous People within the Framework of the Development*

Cooperation of the Community and Member States, 214 Mtg. (November 30, 1998); Resolution on Action Required Internationally to Provide Effective Protection for Indigenous Peoples, Eur. Parc. Doc. PV 58 (II) (1994). See generally Anaya and Williams, "The Protection of Indigenous Peoples' Rights over Lands and Natural Resources under the Inter-American Human Rights System," 34–35.

30. See Robert A. Williams, Jr., "Sovereignty, Racism, Human Rights: Indian Self-Determination and the Postmodern World Legal System," *Review of Constitutional Studies/Revue d'études constitutionnelles* 2 (1995): 146–202.

31. *Charter of the Organization of American States,* 119 U.N.T.S. 3 (entered into force December 13, 1951), reprinted in *Basic Documents Pertaining to Human Rights in the Inter-American System,* OEA/Ser.L.V/I.4 rev. 1 (January 31, 2003); American Declaration on the Rights and Duties of Man, adopted by the Ninth International Conference of American States (March 30–May 2, 1948), O.A.S. Res. 30, O.A.S. Doc. OEN/Ser.UVI/4, rev. (1965).

32. See Anaya, *Indigenous Peoples in International Law,* at 232–34, 258–71, 278n70.

33. See generally David Harris and Stephen Livingstone, eds., *The Inter-American System of Human Rights* (Oxford: Clarendon Press; New York: Oxford University Press, 1998); David Padilla, "The Inter-American System for the Promotion and Protection of Human Rights," *Georgia Journal of International and Comparative Law* 20 (1990): 395–405; Anaya and Williams, "The Protection of Indigenous Peoples' Rights over Lands and Natural Resources under the Inter-American Human Rights System," 35–42. The Inter-American Court on Human Rights has declared that the rights affirmed in the American Declaration are the minimum human rights that OAS member states are bound to uphold. See *Interpretation of the American Declaration of the Rights and Duties of Man in the Framework of Article 64 of the American Opinion,* OC-10/90 (Ser.A) no. 10 (1989), paras. 42–43.

34. Anaya, *Indigenous Peoples in International Law,* 68–69.

35. See Jack L. Goldsmith and Eric Posner, *The Limits of International Law* (New York: Oxford University Press, 2005): "International law has long been burdened with the charge that it is not really law. This misleading claim is premised on some undeniable but misunderstood facts about international law: that it lacks a centralized or effective legislature, executive, or judiciary; that it favors powerful over weak states; that it often simply mirrors extant international behavior; and that it is sometimes violated with impunity" (3).

36. See the introduction. Robert Laurence, "Learning to Live with the Plenary Power of Congress over Indian Nations," *Arizona Law Review* 30 (1988): "I am not optimistic that international forums hold any real promise of protection of American Indian rights. Perhaps I should be more hopeful; surely

I do not hope the opposite. But the active involvement of the international community in a restructuring of the legal and political relationship between the United States and the Indian nations that lie within its borders would be a change from the 1988 world as I know it, a change so profound as to be breathtaking in its implications, and I do not expect to see it soon. I am convinced, in fact, that a recognition of tribal sovereignty under domestic law—for which the contradictory recognition of the plenary power of Congress is, in my view, the price—is the best hope of improving the lot of Indian peoples in the United States. To the extent that advocating a place for the Indian nations among the states of the world distracts tribal advocates from the vigilance that this balance of contradictory forces at work in the domestic law requires, I think it to be folly" (429–30).

37. Lea Brilmayer, *American Hegemony: Political Morality in a One-Superpower World* (New Haven: Yale University Press, 1994).

38. Mark W. Janis, *An Introduction to International Law,* 4th ed. (New York: Aspen, 2003), 7.

39. Williams, "Sovereignty, Racism, Human Rights," 193–96.

40. In *Lawrence v. Texas,* 539 U.S. 558 (2003), the Supreme Court, for the first time ever, relied on an international tribunal decision to interpret individual liberties embodied in the U.S. Constitution (573, discussing *Dudgeon v. United Kingdom,* 45 Eur. Ct. H. R. [ser. A] [1981]). The Court's decision in *Lawrence* invalidated a Texas statute banning consensual sodomy between adults of the same sex.

In *Atkins v. Virginia,* 536 U.S. 304 (2002), the Supreme Court held that executing a mentally handicapped criminal defendant violated the Eighth Amendment's prohibition of "cruel and unusual punishments" (U.S. Const. Amend. VIII); see *Atkins v. Virginia,* 306. In a footnote to the opinion, the Court noted: "Moreover, within the world community, the imposition of the death penalty for crimes committed by mentally retarded offenders is overwhelmingly disapproved" (*Atkins v. Virginia,* 316n21).

The cases, and the Court's methodology of "constitutional comparativism," that is, the use of international and foreign material to interpret the U.S. Constitution, has been the focus of intense academic commentary. See, e.g., Roger P. Alford, "In Search of a Theory for Constitutional Comparativism," *UCLA Law Review* 52 (2005): 639–714; Harold Hongju Koh, "International Law as Part of Our Law," *American Journal of International Law* 98 (2004): 43–57. On the increasing use of foreign and international law by a "global community of courts," see Anne Marie Slaughter, "A Global Community of Courts," *Harvard International Law Journal* 44 (2003): 191, 193: "[U]nlike past legal borrowings across borders, judges are now engaged not in passive reception of foreign decisions, but in active and ongoing dialogue. They cite each other not as precedent, but as persuasive authority. They may also distinguish their views from the views of other courts that have considered similar problems. The result, at least in some areas such as the death penalty and privacy rights, is an emerging global jurisprudence" (193).

41. Thomas Buergenthal, "The Human Rights Revolution," in *International Law Anthology,* ed. Anthony D'Amato (Cincinnati, Ohio: Anderson, 1994), 205.

42. S. James Anaya, "The Rights of Indigenous Peoples and International Law in Historical and Contemporary Perspective," in *Harvard Indian Law Symposium* 191 (1989–90): 211–12.

43. Anaya, *Indigenous Peoples in International Law,* 50–51.

44. See Goldsmith and Posner, *The Limits of International Law,* 3, 107–34.

45. Buergenthal, "The Human Rights Revolution," 205.

46. Ibid., 205–6.

47. See generally Anaya and Williams, "The Protection of Indigenous Peoples' Rights over Lands and Natural Resources under the Inter-American Human Rights System"; Anaya, *Indigenous Peoples in International Law,* 258–66. See also the sources cited in note 33.

48. *Mary and Carrie Dann v. United States* (see note 65), quotation at para. 96.

49. See Anaya and Williams, "The Protection of Indigenous Peoples' Rights over Lands and Natural Resources under the Inter-American Human Rights System," 41–48.

50. The Universal Declaration of Human Rights, for instance, states that "[e]veryone has the right to own property alone as well as in association with others" and that "[n]o one shall be arbitrarily deprived of his property." Universal Declaration of Human Rights, G.A. Res. 217 A (III), Dec. 10, 1948, reprinted in *Human Rights: A Compilation of International Instruments,* U.N. Doc /ST/HR/1/rev. 4 (vol. 1, pt. 1), Sales No. E93.XIV.1 (1993). Besides the American Declaration and the American Convention on Human Rights (November 22, 1969, OAS Treaty Ser. no. 36, 1144 U.N.T.S. 123; entered into force July 18, 1978), the European Convention on Human Rights also recognizes the right to property. See Protocol (no. 1) to the European Convention for the Protection of Human Rights and Fundamental Freedoms, art. 1, March 20, 1952, Europ. T.S. No. 9 (entered into force May 18, 1954).

51. The American Declaration, however, unlike the later American Convention, includes social, cultural, and economic rights among its human rights provisions.

52. Inter-American Commission on Human Rights, *Report on the Situation of Human Rights of Asylum Seekers within the Canadian Refugee Determination System* (February 28, 2000), OEA/Ser.L./V/II.106/doc.40, rev., para. 169.

53. *Mayagna (Sumo) Awas Tingni Community v. Nicaragua,* Inter-Am. C.H.R. (Ser.C.) no. 79 (judgment on the merits and reparations of August 31, 2001).

54. See the *Western Shoshone* case (see note 65) and *Maya Indigenous Communities of the Toledo District v. Belize* (see note 66).

55. OAS Inter-American Human Rights, *Report on the Situation of Human Rights of a Segment of the Nicaraguan Population of Miskito Origin and Resolution on the Friendly Settlement Procedure Regarding the Human Rights Situation of a Segment of the Nicaraguan Population of Miskito Origin,* OEA/Ser.L/V/II.62 doc. 10 rev. 3 (1983), OEA/Ser.L/V/II.62, doc. 26 (1984), 81–82, para. 5.

56. See S. James Anaya, "The Awas Tingni Petition to the Inter-American Commission on Human Rights: Indigenous Lands, Loggers, and Government Neglect in Nicaragua," *St. Thomas Law Review* 9 (1996): 157–207; S. James Anaya and Claudio Grossman, "The Case of *Awas Tingni v. Nicaragua*: A New Step in the International Law of Indigenous Peoples," *Arizona Journal of International and Comparative Law* 19 (2002): 1–15.

57. See sources cited in note 56.

58. *Mayagna (Sumo) Awas Tingni Community v. Nicaragua* (1998), no. 27/98, at para. 142. The commission also specifically found Nicaragua in violation of Article 25 of the American Convention, affirming the right to judicial protection in failing to guarantee an effective remedy to respond to the claims of the Awas Tingni community regarding their rights to land and natural resources; see para. 143.

59. Ibid., paras. 141–42.

60. See the sources cited in note 56.

61. *Mayagna (Sumo) Awas Tingni Community v. Nicaragua.* The case was the first ever heard by the Inter-American Court in which the central issue involved the question of indigenous collective rights to traditional lands and natural resources. See Anaya, *Indigenous Peoples in International Law,* at 266–67.

62. *Mayagna (Sumo) Awas Tingni Community v. Nicaragua,* paras. 167 and 173 (6) and (7); para. 173 (3); and para. 173 (4).

63. See generally the sources cited in note 56.

64. Unlike Nicaragua, the OAS member states in these two cases, the United States (see note 65) and Belize (see note 66), are not parties to the American Convention on Human Rights. However, under the Inter-American Commission's statutes and regulations, human rights petitions may be adjudicated against OAS member states that are not parties to the convention by reference to the American Declaration. Thus, the petitions in each of these cases allege violations of the American Declaration, as opposed to the American Convention.

65. *Mary and Carrie Dann v. United States* (December 27, 2002), Inter-American Commission on Human Rights, case 11.140, Report no. 75/02, *An-*

nual Report of the Inter-American Commission on Human Rights: 2002, OAS Doc. OEA/Ser.L/V/II.117/doc.1, rev. 1, para. 167 (hereinafter the *Western Shoshone* case). In this case, the commission found the United States in violation of the human rights of the Dann sisters, two traditional Western Shoshone indigenous women ranchers who, for nearly two decades, have asserted aboriginal title rights to Western Shoshone ancestral lands as a defense to efforts by the United States to deprive them of the use and enjoyment of those lands. The commission recognized that the special connection of indigenous peoples to their lands and resources is crucial to the free and full enjoyment of their other human rights and their indigenous culture. The commission also found that under well-recognized principles of international human rights law, indigenous peoples have the right to state recognition of their permanent and inalienable title to their traditional lands and that this right to state recognition of their collective traditional land rights implies the right to state provision of an effective procedure for delimiting, demarcating, and securing indigenous title to those lands.

66. *Maya Indigenous Communities of the Toledo District v. Belize* (October 24, 2003), case 12.053, report no. 96/03. In 2004, following and relying closely upon the decisions in the *Awas Tingni* case and the *Western Shoshone* case, the Inter-American Commission found that Belize, an OAS member state, had violated the human rights of certain Mayan Indian indigenous communities "by granting logging and oil concessions to third parties to utilize the property and resources that could fall within the lands that must be delimited, demarcated and titled or otherwise clarified and protected, in the absence of effective consultations and the informed consent of the Maya people."

67. See, e.g., the *Western Shoshone* case, paras. 127, 130.

68. Proposed American Declaration on the Rights of Indigenous Peoples, approved by the Inter-American Commission on Human Rights on February 26, 1997, at its 133rd session, 95th regular session. O.A.S. Doc. OEA/Ser. L/v/II/95/doc.7, rev. (1996), para. 18.

69. See, e.g., Anaya, *Indigenous Peoples in International Law,* 146–47.

70. See Anaya and Williams, "The Protection of Indigenous Peoples' Rights over Lands and Natural Resources under the Inter-American Human Rights System," 54–55.

71. See generally Anaya, *Indigenous Peoples in International Law.*

72. Ibid., 54–55.

73. See the sources cited in note 47.

74. See, e.g., *Indigenous Peoples, Operational Directive* 4.20, para. 13, World Bank (September 17, 1991) (requiring respect for indigenous peoples' land rights in connection with World Bank–financed projects); *Resolution on Indigenous Peoples within the Framework of the Development Cooperation*

of the Community and Member States, Council of Ministers of the European Union, 214th Mtg. (November 30, 1998); *Resolution on Action Required Internationally to Provide Effective Protection for Indigenous Peoples,* EUR. PARL. DOC. PV 58(II) (1994).

75. See generally Williams, "Sovereignty, Racism, Human Rights."

76. See generally the sources cited in note 47.

77. Frickey, "Domesticating Federal Indian Law," 37.

78. Ibid., 36.

79. Ibid.

80. *Worcester v. Georgia,* 31 U.S. 515 (1832): "America, separated from Europe by a wide ocean, was inhabited by a distinct people, divided into separate nations, independent of each other and of the rest of the world, having institutions of their own, and governing themselves by their own laws. It is difficult to comprehend the proposition, that the inhabitants of either quarter of the globe could have rightful original claims of dominion over the inhabitants of the other, or over the lands they occupied; or that the discovery of either by the other should give the discoverer rights in the country discovered, which annulled the pre-existing rights of its ancient possessors" (542–43).

81. *Worcester v. Georgia,* 543–44 (quoting *Johnson v. McIntosh,* 573).

82. *Worcester v. Georgia,* 544.

83. Ibid., 545.

84. Ibid., 544–45.

85. See Charles G. Fenwick's introduction to Emmerich de Vattel, *The Law of Nations; or, The Principles of Natural Law Applied to the Conduct and to the Affairs of Nations and of Sovereigns,* trans. Charles G. Fenwick (Washington, D.C.: Carnegie Institution of Washington, 1916), viii–xii (examining Vattel's importance for American political legal thought).

86. *Worcester v. Georgia,* 561.

87. Quoted in Francis Paul Prucha, *The Great Father: The United States Government and the American Indians* (Lincoln: University of Nebraska Press 1984), 1:59.

88. See ibid., 52–60.

89. *City of Sherrill v. Oneida Indian Nation,* 125 S. Ct. 1478, 1483–84 (2005).

90. *Western Shoshone* case, para. 130.

91. Frickey, "Domesticating Federal Indian Law," 37. See also Note, "International Law as an Interpretive Force in Federal Indian Law," *Harvard Law Review* 116 (2003): 1751.

Index

Robert A. Williams, Jr. (Lumbee) is the E. Thomas Sullivan Professor of Law and American Indian Studies and faculty cochair of the Indigenous Peoples Law and Policy Program at the University of Arizona James E. Rogers College of Law in Tucson. He is author of *The American Indian in Western Legal Thought: The Discourses of Conquest* and *Linking Arms Together: American Indian Treaty Visions of Law and Peace, 1600–1800* and coauthor of the leading casebook in the field, *Federal Indian Law: Cases and Materials*. He has represented Indian clients, tribes, and indigenous groups before the U.S. Supreme Court, U.N. human rights organizations, and the Inter-American Human Rights system. He serves as chief justice of the Yavapai-Prescott Apache Tribe Court of Appeals and Pascua Yaqui Tribe Court of Appeals.